"In a world that craves instant answers has discovered that taking time with C slowing down; learning to 'chew it over minds in order that the Holy Spirit can a his work on Ephesians. This is not a sprint through Paul's letter. Part devotional, part commentary, Alan's work helps us engage with God through his word by allowing us to move slowly through Paul's letter, bringing us into God's plan for his Church, and ultimately for us whom he has graciously conjoined to this great historic caravan of faith as we journey heavenward! Enjoy every helping of this meal for the soul!"

Dr Johnny Markin, D.W.S.

Dr Johnny Markin has served in active ministry for more than 30 years as a worship pastor, musical artist, and university instructor in the theology and history of Christian worship. Based near Vancouver, Canada, he is the founder and director of Worship Leader Institute, a ministry for equipping and mentoring worship leaders for effective ministry.

"As an activist, I have always found the practice of slowing my pace and pausing over tiny chunks of truth one at a time, dwelling in them and pondering over them a challenging one. Alan's life embodies this essential habit of contemplation which infuses a beautiful compassion and sweet grace, making for a healing presence to the world around him. By applying this unhurried way of life to his mining of the book of Ephesians, Alan has produced a generous guide and a prophetic now word to the church. This meander into an ancient letter empowers us to stop and rest, to sip and taste and to drink in the rich and profound truths for the benefit of our souls and for the hope of our communities. This letter is as valuable for us now as for the ancient people of Ephesus and Alan dissects the words and rummages around the historic context to apply timely truths to our today. I am grateful for this miner and curator of hope and truth. His investment in my life has been precious."

– Joy

"Alan's combination of grounded, real life stories and deep biblical study is explosive! His writing will take you deeper into the word and into putting faith into practice. His love for God and for people is so evident through his writing and thinking." – **Paul**

Paul and Joy Blundell

Joy and Paul Blundell live in Lincoln with their two children. Together they lead the Lincoln North Location of Alive Church. Paul's background is in frontline psychiatric care in the community and he has a wise and gentle heart for people. Joy is passionate about the good news of Jesus bringing transformation to every area of society and is involved in various initiatives to mobilise the Body of Christ in that direction.

"Having served alongside Alan for many years I have always been impressed with his thorough approach to scripture. He has consistently encouraged the systematic daily reading of the Bible. I have watched as he has found joy in digging deeply into each verse to make sure he has squeezed out every shade of meaning from the text. His latest book on Ephesians is another example of this daily exercise. In fact, in this volume Alan brings together three of his greatest passions: love for scripture, love for daily devotion and love for the church. I stand with Alan in his desire to see a new generation of believers in Jesus both studying and loving God's word."

Stuart Bell

Stuart Bell is the Senior Pastor of Alive Church, a growing multi-site church with several locations in the UK. He also leads the Ground Level Network, a network of around 90 churches, and heads up 'Partners for Influence UK', a group of leaders representing influential churches and ministries across the UK. Stuart is actively involved in a number of national leadership forums and is an international speaker and teacher often working into both America and South Africa. Stuart has written four books.

"'Christ loved the church and gave himself up for her.' – Ephesians 5:25 This is the revelation that has shaped decades of service and ministry – Alan Hoare 'loves the Church'. Alan's book dives into the depths of wisdom and grace hidden and revealed in the book of Ephesians. Alan is a contemporary meditative. A modern-day mystic, he writes with the aptitude of a seasoned pastor and theologian. The book is more than academically 'sound' – he writes with the fine brush strokes of an artist and the blended harmonies of a composer. I am honoured to commend this latest outpouring of the pure heart of one of my most valued friends."

Rev. Canon Chris Bowater

Chris Bowater has for more than forty years been at the heart of the contemporary worship revolution that has taken place in the church, both in the UK and in many other countries across the world. He is constantly seeking to explore the cutting edge of music and his albums reflect the strong classical, hymnology and jazz influences of his roots as well as his desire to maintain the best of musical and lyricist traditions. Everything he does comes out of his deep love for Jesus, his long experience of local church life and his passion for 'oneness' in the church, particularly through worship.

"Living in a cross-cultural world; with the passion to see God's agenda for life transformation of the people we work with, it can all too easily bring us into a trap of distraction. Alan's deep desire to bring God's people to be enlightened with His word, in order to be more effective in serving the King of kings, has impacted our cross-cultural working lives. Through this latest daily devotional on Ephesians, Alan has led us to 'dig deeper' to get His living water that refreshes us, to follow God's design for His church in Cambodia."

Joko and Karen Kristiono

Joko hails from Indonesia, and was part of the leadership of a large church there, but has had a heart for Cambodia for many years. His English wife Karen, a trained cancer specialist nurse, shares the same missionary heart as he does, and together they have been working with World Horizons in Phnom Penh for a number of years. They have seen a good number of young people come to Christ. Together they demonstrate cross-cultural living to those around them.

"The first time I met Alan, I met a man whose every heartbeat showed pastoral love and care. He is a pastor's pastor and I learned so much working alongside him in Lincoln. His wisdom and biblical knowledge shine through every word he speaks and writes. This latest book is a gift from the throne room of God to every reader. His thoughts and insights on Paul's epistle to the Ephesians are so refreshing and encouraging. Just as the Ephesians must have looked forward to receiving Paul's writings, so I was just as excited waiting for this! It will bring many hours of reflection and insight for your encouragement and growth in your faith – enjoy and be blessed!" – **Malcolm**

"Any help with daily devotions is always welcome and I can think of no better person than our dear friend Alan. His years of biblical studies and bible school teaching enable him to unpack deep mysteries and make them easy to digest for challenged readers like myself. Highly recommended." – **Trish**

Malcolm and Trish Morgan

Malc and Trish have been involved in ministry for over 35 years. Trish has written well known worship songs and led worship from local to national events in the UK and in many nations around the world. Malcolm has an MA in theology and has been pastoring churches for over 20 years in the UK, Belfast, South Africa and they are currently pioneering faith communities in Greece. They have seen how church is expressed in many different cultures. Seeing men and women partner together in ministry and leadership has been a deeply held value in their lives and faith walk with Jesus.

"In a world that is too fast-moving, this book is like a restful, nourishing, challenging and comforting breath of fresh air. Alan peels back the layers of Ephesians to impart new revelation that not only gives understanding, but touches and changes hearts. His level of research and Bible knowledge is inspiring and it is a pleasure to begin our day with his writing. The format is easily accessible and quickly applicable. Having known Alan for over 20 years and often benefitted from his teaching, pastoring and friendship, we are thrilled that he has put his voice onto paper. We wholeheartedly recommend this book to you."

Dave and Helen Pennington

Dave works as the Head of Property Development at Lincolnshire County Council and was the Project Director for the Country's first emergency services £21.5m operational hub. The building comprises divisional HQ for Police and Fire, 24 cell custody suite, 22 Police departments and first line response for Police, Fire and Ambulances services. Helen has a teaching background and is chair of governors at a local school. She also works part time for the Joy Foundation, bringing the Christian message to junior schools right across the city.

"Reading Alan's books is like taking a long walk on a glorious day. Satisfying, life-affirming and filled with small beauties and great wonders. The path is always before you even if you don't know where you will end up. You could encounter beautiful waterfalls, deep, still pools and more than one mountain summit on your journey. Exploring these letters with Alan is such a privilege, for we have a guide who has walked these paths for years, knows the best views and the most refreshing springs. There is no pressure here, but peace, and wide, sun-lit spaces. It is as close as you can get to studying the letter with Jesus."

Andy and Gillian Fox

Andy and Gillian have been married for 16 years and live and work in Lincoln with their two fantastic children. Andy is a consultant in Public Health and honorary lecturer at the University of Sheffield medical school. Gillian works in a local primary school and writes whenever time allows. Together they love to worship God with music or by exploring his beautiful creation on foot, by bike or in the water.

EPHESIANS

The Church I See

A daily study of the letter of
Paul to the church at Ephesus

VOLUME 2

Alan Hoare

O&U
Onwards & Upwards

Onwards and Upwards Publishers

4 The Old Smithy, London Road, Rockbeare, EX5 2EA.

www.onwardsandupwards.org

First edition (2021) published in the UK by Onwards and Upwards Publishers Ltd.

ISBN: 978-1-78815-586-1
Typeface: Sabon LT
Graphic design: Ben Hoare

About the Author

 Alan was born in Rustington in West Sussex in 1948, and soon after the family moved to Littlehampton. This was followed by two younger brothers, Nigel and Simon. His first experience of church at the age of ten years old ended a few weeks later by him being banned from the local Sunday school for bad behaviour! Also during his final years at secondary school, he boycotted the RE lessons for two years, feeling that they were getting too personal! After leaving school he did an apprenticeship in precision engineering, gaining City and Guilds certificates at Worthing Technical College. It was the 'hippy' era of the 1960s, so weekends were spent with friends, often performing in their rock band, aptly named the 'St James' Infirmary'. A favourite pastime of his is still to pick up his guitar and play the music of that era.

Life changed dramatically for him in March 1969 when he became a Christian as the result of visiting a small Free Church in the little village of Fittleworth, near Petworth. Soon after that, the Baptist Church in Littlehampton became his home church, and also the place where he met Maureen (affectionately known as Mo), who was to become his wife in 1974. Before that, however, they parted company for two years – he to work on a church planting team with Operation Mobilisation in France for two years, and she to do teacher training in Portsmouth.

On returning to England in 1973, Alan studied theology at the Elim Bible College, which was then in Dorking in Surrey, graduating two years later with a Diploma in Theology. Marriage took place in the middle of the course – which was highly unusual in those days! This was followed by two years in London, during which time he was an assistant minister at two Elim Pentecostal churches, helped to pioneer two more churches and had two children: Ruth, who was born prematurely in August 1975, and Joseph, who was born in February 1977.

August 1977 saw a move to Lincoln, where he took up the pastorate of an Elim Pentecostal church for nearly ten years. The family meanwhile continued to grow with the added births of Simon in November 1980 and Sarah in March 1982.

In Lincoln, Alan quickly developed a strong connection with Stuart Bell, the leader of the large and growing New Life Church there (now 'Alive Church'), and was one of the founder members of the Ground Level network of churches which Stuart started and still leads. In 1987 he joined the New Life Church himself, serving as a member until 1991, when he joined the staff as part of the leadership team. His role was to head up the pastoral and teaching ministry of the church. Benjamin, his youngest son, was born in November that year, completing their family – a biblical quiver full!

In his work for Alive church, Alan has also, amongst other things, pastored a number of linked congregations around the area, written and delivered staff devotions, and led marriage preparation, baptismal and membership courses. From 2003, he wrote and delivered biblical courses, firstly at the New Life church, and then in a number of different church settings. These 'X-Plore' classes ran for 16 years, and topics covered included, amongst others, 'The Life and Times of Christ', 'The Life and Times of David', 'The Life of the Apostle Paul', 'Spiritual Theology', 'Systematic Theology' and 'Church History'. He has also delivered expositional lectures on the letters of Paul to the Philippians and Ephesians. For a number of years, he was also a contributor for Scripture Union's online WordLive daily devotions.

Alan had always dreamt of studying for a degree in theology, and was delighted when the church released him for one day a week in 2009 so that he could do this. He attended Mattersey Hall near Doncaster, and was accepted on to the Master's course, graduating three years later with a Master's in practical theology.

In January 2011, he reduced his time at Lincoln to three days a week, and took on a new role as the senior pastor of a thriving church in Kirton, near Boston, some forty miles east of Lincoln. After three years working for them two days a week, he helped them with the transition to a new senior pastor, and remained on their leadership team serving as their teaching pastor.

On reaching retirement age in August 2013, Alan retired from the staff at Lincoln, and was able to devote himself more to study, writing and teaching. Then, in January 2021, he retired completely from the New Life Community church in Kirton, but still visits the church once every three months on a Sunday to preach.

Over the years, he has ministered widely in the UK and also abroad in Mozambique, Vietnam, Cambodia, France, Spain, Poland and Greece.

Alan feels that his ministry is primarily about building strong and deep spiritual foundations. Strong and mature churches, in his view, are made up of strong and mature believers. He teaches about developing a close and mature walk with Christ, believing that spiritual roots are essential to growing a healthy Christian life. He is passionate about getting people to read the Bible for themselves!

Alan and Mo have now been married for forty-five years, and have seen their five children grow up into fine adults. They have, to date, eleven grandchildren!

Alan Hoare can be contacted by email:

alanerichoare@gmail.com

To see all the author's books published by
Onwards and Upwards, visit his author page:

www.onwardsandupwards.org/alan-hoare

Or scan the barcode below with your phone:

DAY ONE HUNDRED AND TWENTY-THREE

The Eternal Realm

1.Jn.5:11

And this is the testimony, that God gave us eternal life, and this life is in his Son.

In the previous two chapters Paul has been outlining the magnificent purpose of God that had been forged before time began. The name given to the dimension before, beyond and after time is eternity. I must confess that this is one of my favourite words. This dimension, if we may call it that, is the realm of God, where God is, and from where all of his wisdom and purposes emanate.

This eternal and invisible realm runs all the way through the sacred scriptures. I call it 'the blue line', and it can be traced from Genesis to Revelation. It is the realm that we are to seek, to gaze upon and to build our lives upon. Paul wrote to the church in Corinth concerning afflictions, calling them momentary, serving to prepare us for "an eternal weight of glory beyond all comparison". He goes on to say, "...as we look not to the things that are seen but to the things that are unseen. For the things that are seen are transient, but the things that are unseen are eternal." (2.Cor.4:17,18) He wrote to the believers in Rome of God's "invisible attributes, namely, his eternal power and divine nature" (Rom.1:20), clearly to be observed in creation. He also wrote to the Corinthians, concerning the temporary nature of our human bodies, "...we know that if the tent that is our earthly home is destroyed, we have a building from God, a house not made with hands, eternal in the heavens." (2.Cor.5:1) Are you getting the picture? This eternal realm, invisible to the natural eye, is the dimension and environment of God from which all that is true and solid emerges.

Moses wrote that "the eternal God is your dwelling place, and underneath are the everlasting arms" (Deut.33:27). Probably the most famous verse in the Bible says, "For God so loved the world, that he gave his only Son, that whoever believes in him should not perish but have eternal life." (Jn.3:16) Imagine this: the realm of the spiritual, where you and I now live, is not temporary. We have been created and designed for life in the eternal realm. This new life that comes through the gospel is of a far higher dimension than ordinary life and is a foretaste of what is to come.

It is a profound truth that we need to learn to live in the light of eternity. Everything we see and touch around us is temporary. It has a limited life span. Much of what is thought and taught is subject to political, legal, philosophical, medical and cultural changes. Not so the wisdom of God. He does not adapt to our world; we adapt to his. He does not accommodate himself to our way of thinking, feeling and even our choices. He does not follow us at all.

This eternal purpose of God had been hidden from Paul's eyes. There were hints and shadows in the Old Testament writings, but he, along with the religious leaders of Israel, hadn't seen them. Suddenly, this eternal purpose did come together in the person and work of Christ, and then it sprang into full view and action on the day of Pentecost. As the church became manifest, Paul found himself violently opposing it. But there came a day when, on the road to Damascus, he was literally wrestled to the floor by Jesus. Paul, the one in hot pursuit of Christians, found himself being hotly pursued and apprehended by Jesus. He then heard these words: "Saul, Saul, why are you persecuting me?" (Acts 9:4) It was at this point, I believe, that he received the embryonic revelation of the purpose of God – the church – the body of Christ. He saw that in touching and persecuting the believers, he had been touching and persecuting the Lord Jesus himself.

Thought

Only one book will teach us the principles of eternity, and that is the Bible.

Prayer

Dear Lord, help me to focus my gaze on the invisible and eternal things of heaven.

DAY ONE HUNDRED AND TWENTY-FOUR

The Desert

Gal.1:17

...nor did I go up to Jerusalem to those who were apostles before me, but I went away into Arabia...

Near Damascus, Jesus opened Paul's eyes, and in the realms of the eternal Spirit, he suddenly began to see what God had been planning before time began. F.F. Bruce wrote, "It did not come in its fullness all at once, of course, but, as Paul saw it, it was all implicit in the Damascus-road experience."[1]

After preaching in the streets of Damascus, stirring up a storm, he then left the city for a prolonged period in Arabia. We are not sure whereabouts in Arabia he was, but we do know that he was in conversation with the Lord Jesus himself. Paul wrote of this in his letter to the Galatians:

> *For I would have you know, brothers, that the gospel that was preached by me is not man's gospel. For I did not receive it from any man, nor was I taught it, but I received it through a revelation of Jesus Christ.*
>
> Galatians 1:11,12

He then added, "I did not immediately consult with flesh and blood." (Gal.1:16, NASB)

During these years in the desert, there came a strong divine impartation into his spirit. Still reeling inside from his first encounter with the risen Jesus, he then spent time walking, sitting and conversing with the Holy Spirit. The Scriptures began to shine with a heavenly light as they opened up before his eyes. The Holy Spirit was pointing things out to him, and suddenly he was seeing the plans and purpose of God as he had never seen them before. As he listened, this deep purpose of God began to flood his heart, mind and spirit, and it overwhelmed him. It was

---

[1] F.F. Bruce, *Paul, Apostle of the Free Spirit*, (Paternoster Press, Exeter, 1977), p.80

so profound that it actually took years for it all to settle into a deep and clear vision and conviction. This purpose was the church, and Paul saw it.

In fact, much of his theology comes from these times of lonely encounters with Christ and a renewed understanding of the Hebrew Scriptures. All the finest spiritual masters will tell us that the deepest spiritual formation takes place in the silence of solitude. The laying of authentic spiritual foundations is unseen and unheard for they are developed in these two disciplines of solitude and silence. Writing of Paul, Thomas Merton wrote, "He was qualified to be an apostle by the depths of his interior life."[1] Moses, Elijah, David and Jesus all knew the wilderness experience.

Some years later when, in his own words, he was "caught up into the third heaven ... into paradise" and there, in that eternal realm, he "heard things that cannot be told, which man may not utter" (2.Cor.12:2-4). Professor Philip Hughes wrote:

> ...this extraordinary revelation, though not communicable to other ears, must have exercised an incalculable influence on Paul's whole ministry and apostleship, providing, it may be, a key to his astonishing zeal and indefatigable labours through which untold blessing flowed not only to his own generation but to every subsequent generation in the history of the church. Though he was the sole recipient, its effects did not end in him.[2]

What Paul saw was far larger than him and his generation. It had eternity written into its foundations. It had started in the mind of God before time began, and it would go on to have no end. And it is exactly this that you and I have been brought into.

Thought

We are involved in something that goes well beyond time frames.

Prayer

Dear God, help me to see things from an eternal point of view.

---

[1]   Thomas Merton, *Merton on St Bernard*, (Michigan, Cistercian Publications, 1980), p.32

[2]   Philip E. Hughes, *The Second Epistle to the Corinthians*, (Eerdmans, Michigan, 1962), p.439

Day One Hundred and Twenty-Five

For This Reason

Eph.3:1

For this reason I, Paul, a prisoner for Christ Jesus on behalf of you Gentiles...

Chapter 3 starts with the words "for this reason". Paul has just outlined the magnificent eternal purpose of God, but now he realises that just writing it down is not going to be enough; he needs to pray for them. This is the second time that Paul has used these words in this letter and on both occasions they came out of him having just taught something of great importance. This is the essence of true ministry – praying for the recipients of what he is teaching. The word of God needs to be both spoken out of our mouths and prayed into the hearts of those listening.

Therefore, in the first verse of this chapter, Paul begins to pray again. As a result of all that he has previously written, and filled again with the wonder of what God has done and wants to do, he is drawn once more to prayer. This, too, is the end result of good theology – it draws us to prayer. Paul is never interested in theology that we can use, but rather in theology that inflames the heart. What he is describing is not the sort of truths that we can incorporate and adapt into our busy schedules, but truths that stun us a little, making us realise that we are simply part of something too immense for us at the time to take in. Eugene Peterson put it this way in one of his lectures: "This is not stuff that we can 'incorporate into our lives', but stuff that leaves us breathless, praying our way through."[1]

And so he makes a start and then, to our surprise, he goes off in typical Pauline fashion on another train of thought – another superb tangent – a holy parenthesis – and then, when that is done, he returns to the start of his prayer in verse 14 with his third use of the words "for this reason".

What has caught his attention this time? Maybe it's the fact that as he starts his prayer, he is not sitting in a beautiful synagogue or walking

---

[1]   Eugene Peterson, *Lectures on Ephesians*, Regents College, Vancouver

in the hills somewhere overlooking the sea, but rather, he has bent his knees in a prison cell somewhere in Rome. He says, "For this reason I, Paul, a prisoner for Christ Jesus on behalf of you Gentiles…"

This is the almost brutal reality of the spiritual life. Paul is filled with an immense vision of God and his purpose in the earth, and yet he is confined and shackled in a small room. We often think that a powerful vision will open great doors for us, whereas it's quite possible that we will find ourselves instead enclosed in situations not to our liking. If the vision is not being outworked somewhere, then it is probably being in-worked further into us.

His mission had got him arrested. The leadership of the nation of Israel had felt that he was a dangerous agitator who was ripping apart their national religion. And, if the truth be told, Paul had once shared those views himself! But now his God-given mission to the Gentiles had put him in direct opposition to the deeply held Jewish belief in the exclusivity of Israel from all the other nations of the world.

Paul was suffering for what he believed and practised. He began his letter saying that he was an apostle of Jesus Christ. Here he is saying that the apostle is also the prisoner for Jesus Christ. It is actually thought that he had been in prison at the time of writing this letter for well over three years.

Thought

Confinement can be the place where real growth occurs and vision is inwardly rooted.

Prayer

Dear Lord, may I find you in the confinements that come my way.

DAY ONE HUNDRED AND TWENTY-SIX

The Stewardship

Eph.3:2

...assuming that you have heard of the stewardship of God's grace that was given to me for you...

Paul was a prisoner for Jesus Christ, not a prisoner of Caesar. Humanly speaking he may have been in Caesar's prison but Paul never thought of life in that way. He was first and foremost a servant of Christ, and it was Christ who had led him here. As John Stott wrote, "Paul never did think or speak in purely human terms. He believed in the sovereignty of God over the affairs of men."[1]

Sitting in his cell in Rome, Paul had started to pray for the Ephesian believers but had quickly got sidetracked in his thoughts. Some might say that he got distracted, but at times distractions may be the interruptions of the Holy Spirit. It seems that he is being drawn into a new avenue of thoughts.

He writes, "...assuming that you have heard of the stewardship of God's grace that was given to me for you..." This is more accurately rendered "if, indeed, you have heard". He then goes on to mention "the stewardship of God's grace".

Paul uses this word "stewardship" in three other places (1.Cor.9:17; Col.1:25; 1.Tim.1:4). He uses the word "steward" in Titus 1:7. The Greek word is *oikonomian,* and means 'the management of household affairs'. The word is a compound word consisting of *oikos* – 'a house' and *nemo* – 'to arrange, to handle, to manage'. It really means therefore 'the handling and management of the house'. It is the word from which we derive our word 'economy' from. We often speak of 'the divine economy of things'.

Kenneth Wuest wrote:

> *The word speaks in general of the oversight, management, or administration one has over something. Paul was given the responsibility of having oversight or management over the*

---

[1] John Stott, *The Message of Ephesians*, (IVP, Leicester, 1979), p.114

grace of God in the sense that he was to administer it in its publicity. He was given the revelation of the grace of God and the responsibility of properly preaching and teaching it.[1]

Interestingly, the word *oikonomian* is found in Ephesians 1:10, where it has been translated "plan". Clinton Arnold wrote:

This term was common in the daily life of people living in the Graeco-Roman world because it related to the foundational social unit of society – the household. Every household, which included the extended family and the slaves, was overseen by a household manager.[2]

Adam Clark cites Dr Macknight, who wrote that the word described "the plan which the master of a family, or his steward, has established for the management of the family"[3].

There is an order in the household of God. There is a plan, and there are things to be handled rightly. In this context Paul found himself being given the stewardship and administration of the things of God. He was handling the plans and affairs of God in God's household and, as such, he was never to move out of that given sphere by implementing his own ideas and plans.

Thought

God is both a creative and a tidy thinker; both should be reflected in his house.

Prayer

Lord, when I am buzzing with ideas, help me to discern what you are up to.

---

[1] Kenneth Wuest, *Wuest's Word Studies,* Vol.1, 'Ephesians and Colossians', (Eerdmans, Michigan, 1953), p.81

[2] Clinton E. Arnold, *Ephesians,* (Zondervan, Michigan, 2010), pp.87,88

[3] Adam Clark, *Commentary on the Bible,* e-sword.net

DAY ONE HUNDRED AND TWENTY-SEVEN

The Stewardship of Grace

Eph.3:2

...assuming that you have heard of the stewardship of God's grace that was given to me for you...

Paul, writing to Titus, said, "...an overseer, as God's steward, must be above reproach." (Tit.1:7) He was describing the role of an overseer – an *episkopos*. He also wrote to the Corinthians, "This is how one should regard us, as servants of Christ and stewards of the mysteries of God. Moreover, it is required of stewards that they be found faithful." (1.Cor.4:1,2) Here, he describes the role of a servant as a *hupēretēs* – a word that Paul uses only here in his letters. It literally means 'an under-oarsman'. Vine describes the word as meaning "any subordinate acting under another's direction"[1].

The overall thrust of this is that whatever ministry we may have, we are all under orders. The church is God's household, not ours. His house is to run his way, according to his rules and in line with his long-term plan. This stewardship is held accountable.

In out text under consideration today, we are thinking about "the stewardship of God's grace". We must now ask the question, how do we adequately describe grace? In a nutshell, God's grace is both the demeanour and the ability of heaven. Grace is at the heart and activity of God. It restores and heals us; it does not break or damage us. It uplifts and builds us; it does not tear us down and destroy us. It releases us and brings a freedom into our environment; it does not imprison us. It enables and strengthens us; it does not weaken or debilitate us. Grace loves our unloveliness, makes beautiful our ugliness, is irrational (at least to our rational way of thinking) and is lavished upon us. It evokes, "I don't deserve this," and it has been properly understood when we simply say, "Thank you."

Paul had already written about "the riches of his grace" (1:7). The apostle Peter also wrote about God's "varied grace" (1.Pet.4:10), and the

---

[1]   W.E. Vine, *Expository Dictionary of Biblical Words,* (Thomas Nelson, New York, 1985), p.642

Greek word that he used was *poikilēs,* and literally meant 'variegated'. Grace, then, is like a spiritual warehouse, full of different spiritual resources, and the atmosphere there is the mercy and generosity of God.

Grace was firstly received and then modelled throughout Paul's life and ministry. Advanced as he had been in the Law of Moses and the traditions of Judaism, he had nevertheless come to realise that all of that could not provide salvation. He had seen that salvation cannot be earned in any way, but that it is a free gift of God that must be received simply by faith. Christ himself had fulfilled all of the Law, and therefore all Paul had to do was receive Christ.

And so, this grace was stewarded by Paul. He had charge of the management, the oversight, the administration of the grace of God. As we have already said, there is an order in the household of God. Grace is not lawless; rather, grace ushers in the graceful laws of heaven. It is to be gratefully received, worked in, walked in and then ministered to others. The grace that we receive is not only for our benefit. It must be handled well and given to others. What we receive from God, we must pass on. Paul writes, this grace was "given to me for you" (3:2). A good question to ask ourselves is, what do people receive from us? What do we leave in our wake? The true mark of the good and wise stewardship of grace is healthy and well-functioning people in the household of God. The goal of this stewardship is a healthy spiritual family life – a church that it is so refreshing to be part of, and who sing with David, "I was glad when they said to me, 'Let us go to the house of the LORD!'" (Ps.122:1)

Thought

People of grace are the most refreshing people in the earth.

Prayer

Lord, help me both to receive and give freely your life-giving grace.

DAY ONE HUNDRED AND TWENTY-EIGHT

The Mystery

Eph.3:3

...how the mystery was made known to me by revelation, as I have written briefly.

At times, Paul would use a word to describe the effect that certain people had on him. It was the word "refreshed". The word also means 'to cause someone to rest, to be relaxed, to be restored, to be reinvigorated, to be revitalised'. When we steward grace well, people are refreshed.

Now we come to another of Paul's important words. It is the word "mystery", and he uses it 21 times in his correspondence to churches and individuals.[1] The Greek word is *mustērion* which, according to Thayer, is "something hidden or secret"[2]. W.E. Vine puts it this way:

> *In the NT it denotes, not the mysterious (as with the English word), but that which, being outside the range of unassisted natural apprehension, can be made known only by divine revelation, and is made known in a manner and at a time appointed by God, and to those only who are illumined by His Spirit.[3]*

The first thing to say here is that God cannot be discovered. Neither can he be deduced. We can, by honestly looking at all that he has created, come to the conclusion that he exists (see Rom.1:18-20), but the experiential knowing of him comes only by revelation – where he reveals himself to us. Jesus himself said, "All things have been handed over to me by my Father, and no one knows the Son except the Father, and no one knows the Father except the Son and anyone to whom the Son chooses to reveal him." (Matt.11:27)

---

[1] S.S. Smalley, article on 'mystery', *The New Bible Dictionary,* (IVP, London, 1970), p.857

[2] *Thayer's Greek Definitions,* e-sword.net

[3] W.E. Vine, *Vine's Expository Dictionary of Biblical Words,* (Thomas Nelson, New York, 1985), p.424

The second thing to say is that the knowledge of God and his ways is far beyond our natural capacities to understand. Paul, in writing to the believers in Rome about the saving purposes of God, exclaimed, "Oh, the depth of the riches and wisdom and knowledge of God! How unsearchable are his judgments and how inscrutable his ways!" (Rom.11:33) Here he uses two words to try and express the futility of trying humanly to work these things out. The first Greek word is *anexeraunēta,* and it is only used here in the whole of the New Testament. It literally means 'that which cannot be searched out and is incapable of being investigated'.

Robert Haldane (1764-1842) spent 30 years pondering over the letter to the Romans. He eventually wrote a three-volumed commentary on it. On this verse above he wrote, "God's plan of redemption is so deep and peculiar to Himself, that man does not comprehend it, even when it is presented to his view, unless the eyes of his understanding are enlightened by the Holy Spirit."[1]

The second word is *anexichniastoi,* and means 'that which cannot be tracked'. Paul will use this word one other time, in Ephesians 3:8, where he will write about "the unsearchable riches of Christ".

God does not reveal everything, and often what little snippets he does reveal are, at times, enough to mentally, emotionally and spiritually floor us! Even when in heaven we will not stop learning and being astonished.

Thought

Where there is no room for mystery, faith is infantile.

Prayer

Lord, help me to see that all my majestic and brilliant thoughts "are but a breath" (Ps.94:11).

---

[1]   Robert Haldane, *The Epistle to the Romans,* (Banner of Truth Trust, London, 1958), p.550

DAY ONE HUNDRED AND TWENTY-NINE

The Mystery Revealed

Eph.3:3

...how the mystery was made known to me by revelation, as I have written briefly.

Concerning this mystery, Eugene Peterson wrote that it "refers to something more like the inside story of the way God does things that bring us into the story. This is a kind of knowledge that cannot be gained by gathering information or picking up clues. It has nothing to do with satisfying curiosity. It is a far cry from the inquisitive, clamouring questioning that wants 'answers'."[1] Kallistos Ware, a theologian of the Eastern Orthodox Church, wrote, "It is not the task of Christianity to provide easy answers to every question, but to make us progressively aware of a mystery. God is not so much the object of our knowledge as the cause of wonder."[2]

Paul seeks to explain in simple terms what the mystery actually is. Later in this letter he will write, "This mystery is that the Gentiles are fellow heirs, members of the same body, and partakers of the promise in Christ Jesus through the gospel." (Eph.3:6) To the Colossians he wrote of "the glory of this mystery, which is Christ in you, the hope of glory ... the knowledge of God's mystery, which is Christ..." (Col.1:27; 2:2) In Christ, both Jews and all other nations were to be forgiven, made holy by the Holy Spirit and reconstructed into one new nation – the church. William Hendriksen put it this way:

One can say that the mystery is, in a sense, Christ himself, that is Christ in all his glorious riches actually dwelling through his Spirit in the hearts and lives of both Jews and Gentiles, united in one body, the church.[3]

Although simple, the outworking of it is so profound.

---

[1] Eugene Peterson, *Practise Resurrection,* (Hodder & Stoughton, London, 2010), p.64

[2] *https://www.dailychristianquote.com/tag/mystery*

[3] William Hendriksen, *Ephesians,* (Banner of Truth, Edinburgh, 1976), p.153

In the text that we are looking at, Paul writes that "the mystery was made known to me by revelation". This word "revelation" comes from the Greek word *apokalupsin,* which means 'to uncover, to unveil'. It is, therefore, a revealing of something that is already there in place. The plan and purpose of God was up and ready to go, but was yet to be revealed.

This mystery is not so much a new thing, but an eternal thing that is being revealed at the right time. God is not locked into our timeframe. What is a new thing to us is something conceived in the spiritual realms of eternity. For him, there are no 'old things' and 'new things'. These things belong to us.

Clinton Arnold writes, "It is clearly not an insight or a plan that Paul himself has conceived. It has come to him directly by revelation from God."[1] We must heed this. Instead of coming up with myriads of new ideas, we must learn to wait in the presence of God and, like the prophets of old, we must also learn, in the Spirit, to frequent the boardroom of heaven to listen in and observe what God is up to. It is written in the book of Proverbs that, "Many are the plans in the mind of a man, but it is the purpose of the LORD that will stand.' (Prov.19:21) Many of our good ideas are actually stumbling blocks to the purposes of God.

Thought

It is the Holy Spirit who unveils the mysteries of God, not our finite minds.

Prayer

Dear Holy Spirit, open the eyes of my heart to see what you are always seeing.

---

[1]   Clinton E. Arnold, *Ephesians,* (Zondervan, Michigan, 2010), p.187

DAY ONE HUNDRED AND THIRTY

The Mystery Written

Eph.3:3

...how the mystery was made known to me by revelation, as I have written briefly.

Hans Urs von Balthasar was a profound Swiss Catholic theologian. He wrote, "There is much in Christianity which can be subjected to exact analysis. But the ultimate things are shrouded in the silent mysteries of God."[1] In September 2015, this was put on Eugene Peterson's Twitter page: "Mystery is not the absence of meaning, but the presence of more meaning than we can comprehend."[2]

Paul writes that the mystery "was made known to me by revelation", and then he writes, "...as I have written briefly." He continues, "When you read this, you can perceive my insight into the mystery of Christ..." We have here something written down, which is then read.

Firstly, let's mention Paul's style of writing. *Expositor's Bible Commentary* says this passage is...

> *...an extreme instance of St. Paul's amorphous style. His sentences are not composed; they are spun in a continuous thread, an endless chain of prepositional, participial, and relative adjuncts. They grow under our eyes like living things, putting forth new processes every moment, now in this and now in that direction.[3]*

The second thing to mention is that in Paul's day not many would have had access to these letters, written as they were on parchment, and not many either would be literate. This letter itself would have been read publicly in various church settings. Not many would have had personal access to the *Tanakh* – the Bible of the Hebrews – that which we call the

---

[1] *https://www.azquotes.com/quote/1446096?ref=mystery-of-god*
[2] *https://twitter.com/PetersonDaily* – originally written by Dennis Covington, *Salvation on Sand Mountain*
[3] *Expositor's Bible Commentary*, e-sword.net

Old Testament. In the main, a copy would be in each synagogue, portions of which would be read out in the various services.

There is much to be said about the hearing of the Scriptures. In our present day, we are totally spoiled by the amount of Bible versions, commentaries and books that are available to us, especially in the West. Eugene Peterson cites the English/American poet W.H. Auden, who made this shrewd comment:

> *This ease of access, when misused becomes a curse. When we read more books, look at more pictures, listen to more music, than we can possibly absorb, the result of such gluttony is not a cultured mind but a consuming one; what it reads, looks at, listens to, is immediately forgotten, leaving no more traces behind it than yesterday's newspaper.*[1]

Peterson himself wrote:

> *Listening and reading are not the same thing. They involve different senses. In listening we use our ears; in reading we use our eyes ... In listening, another initiates the process; when I read I initiate the process. In reading I open the book and attend to the words. I can read by myself; I cannot listen by myself. In listening, the speaker in in charge; in reading, the reader is in charge.*[2]

Ezra Pound's book *Hugh Selwyn Mauberly* has his subject saying, "Tell it to me, all of it, I guzzle with outstretched ears!"[3]

Thought

Faith comes by hearing. (Rom.10:17; Gal.3:2,5)

Prayer

Dear Lord, teach me again the value of my ears, and also what I listen to.

---

[1] Eugene Peterson, *Working the Angles,* (Eerdmans, Michigan, 1897), p.90
[2] Ibid, p.88
[3] Ibid, p.89

DAY ONE HUNDRED AND THIRTY-ONE

The Mystery Read

Eph.3:4

When you read this, you can perceive my insight into the mystery of Christ...

Yesterday we learned of the need to recover the art of listening well. One of my favourite scenarios in the New Testament is that of Lydia listening to Paul. Luke records, "The Lord opened her heart to pay attention to what was said by Paul." (Acts 16:14) As she listened to Paul, something happened in her heart. The Lord opened it. The word Paul uses here is *diēnoixen,* meaning 'to open thoroughly'. It is exactly the same word that Luke uses to describe what Jesus did, firstly with the two disciples on the road to Emmaus – they exclaimed, "Did not our hearts burn within us while he talked to us on the road, while he opened to us the Scriptures?" – and later with the gathered disciples – "Then he opened their minds to understand the Scriptures." (Lk.24:32,45) This work of grace opened Lydia's heart and she found herself transfixed by what was being said.

The phrase "to pay attention" is the one Greek word *prosechein.* It literally means 'to hold the mind'. One Greek commentator wrote, "She kept her mind centred on the things spoken by Paul whose words gripped her attention."[1] This is good listening! Compare this scenario with another one found in Acts 14:9, where Luke writes of a lame man, "He listened to Paul speaking. And Paul, looking intently at him and seeing that he had faith to be made well, said in a loud voice, 'Stand upright on your feet.' And he sprang up and began walking." (Acts 14:9,10) Again, faith comes by hearing.

There is also a learned art of reading well. Eugene Peterson, in his classic book *Working the Angles* has a whole chapter entitled 'Turning Eyes into Ears'. He wrote, "Every piece of writing was the record of a once-living voice and the means of bringing that voice to life again in the reader's ear."[2] He went on to write, "The genius of the book is that it

---

1   *Robertson's Word Pictures,* e-sword.net
2   Eugene Peterson, *Working the Angles,* (Eerdmans, Michigan, 1897), p.96

provides the means by which a speaker can be linked to a listener without being in the same room or in the same century."[1] When you read what Paul has written, can you hear his voice?

In essence, Paul is saying, "When you read (or hear) what I have written about this deep and strong mystery, can you not sense the movements of the Holy Spirit upon your hearts and minds, opening them up to see what I have seen?" We must not read to simply collect spiritual data; we must read to see something of the workings of heaven and to hear the voice of God from heaven.

Authentic and spiritual reading is primarily relational, rather than academic. I can do no better here than quote William of St Thierry, a twelfth century Cistercian monk. He wrote:

> *The scriptures need to be read and understood in the same spirit in which they were created. You will never enter into Paul's meaning until, by good intention in reading and diligent zeal in meditating, you drink of his spirit. You will never understand David, unless by experience you clothe yourself with the feelings expressed in the Psalms.*[2]

Let our reading not only inform our minds, but shape and warm our hearts.

Thought

Read to hear the voice of God, and be drawn into relationship with him.

Prayer

Dear Lord, dig out my spiritual ears so that I may hear your transforming voice.

---

[1] Ibid, p.99
[2] William of St Thierry, *The Golden Epistle,* #121; Schr 223, p.238, cited by Michael Casey, *Sacred Reading: the Ancient Art of Lectio Divina,* (Liguori/Triumph, Missouri, 1995), p.15

Day One Hundred and Thirty-Two

Paul's Insight

Eph.3:4

When you read this, you can perceive my insight into the mystery of Christ...

As Paul spent long days and long nights reflecting on and meditating in the Jewish Scriptures, and also trying to form into words and thoughts the things that he had seen in the realms of the Spirit, a beautiful and profound picture began to form in his mind. He began to see what God had been seeing all along.

Paul was gaining "insight" into the mystery of Christ. The word "insight" is from the Greek word *sunesin,* which basically means 'a running together, a flowing together with the understanding'. It is rooted in the word *suniēmi,* which means, in this context, 'to set or join together in the mind'. It is when things that were dispersed in our mind suddenly begin to fall into place. It is when, by the Holy Spirit, 'the penny drops' and we at last understand. For Paul, the picture was coming together. It was making sense.

The word *sunesis* has a long history. Deep insights into the realms and ways of God come from deep time spent with him, and deep thinking. Deep insight is deeply spiritual. The Psalmist wrote, "Deep calls to deep..." (Ps.47:2) As we give God time in meditating in the Scriptures, the Holy Spirit will take us there. Paul wrote to the Corinthians, "For the Spirit searches everything, even the depths of God." (1.Cor.2:10) This has very little to do with an intellectual grasp of the ways of God, but an understanding that takes place in the heart.

Charles Bridges (1794-1869) was one of the leaders of the Evangelical party in the Church of England in the nineteenth century. He wrote concerning the understanding of the ways of God through the diligent and deep reading of the Scriptures, "The book of God is indeed the living voice of the Spirit. To be intent therefore upon the study of it, must result in a clear apprehension of the mind of God."[1] Bridges also cited the Dutch theologian Hermann Witsius (1636-1708), who wrote:

> Let the Theologian ascend from the lower school of natural study, to the higher department of Scripture, and, sitting at the feet of God as his teacher, learn from his mouth the hidden mysteries of salvation, which "eye hath not seen, nor ear heard; which none of the princes of this world knew;" which the most accurate reason cannot search out; which the heavenly chorus of angels, though beholding the face of God, "desire to look into."[2]

Arnold Wayne Weckeman, a pastor in Arizona, wrote:

> Spiritual understanding is infinite (operating in the limitless, unseen, spiritual dimension of reality) and comes from God. Spiritual truth is intuitively revealed (without conscious reasoning; independent of the mind), taking place in the "inner man." God's Spirit illuminating man's spirit "...in thy light shall we see light" (Psalm 36:9). Spiritual understanding is not confined within the circumference of logic nor is it restricted to the realm of reason.[3]

Paul is in effect saying, "As you read what I have written, you will feel for yourselves the depths of the mystery of Christ, and will begin to see for yourselves what I have spent much time gazing upon." Such is the effect of this profound letter to the Ephesian believers.

Thought

Deep insight emerges from deep time with God.

Prayer

Lord, "open my eyes that I may behold wondrous things out of your law" (Ps.119:18).

---

[1] Charles Bridges, *The Christian Ministry*, (Banner of Truth, Edinburgh, 1976), p.58
[2] Ibid.
[3] *https://www.perfectingofthesaints.com/articles/articles-the-necessity-of-spiritual-understanding*

DAY ONE HUNDRED AND THIRTY-THREE

The Mystery of Christ

Eph.3:4

When you read this, you can perceive my insight into the mystery of Christ...

We need to pause a little around this subject. It has been a criticism of much of our preaching today that it is too full of anecdotes, quotes and stories. What seems to be missing is the kind of preaching that escorts you into the wonderful mysteries of God, and leaves you not a little breathless. Such preaching comes from one who has sat long in the presence of God and heard things and seen things.

John the Baptist spoke of Jesus to his disciples, after they had had a discussion with a Jew. At one point he said, "He bears witness to what he has seen and heard, yet no one receives his testimony." (Jn.3:32) Much later, the aged apostle John wrote, "...that which we have seen and heard we proclaim also to you..." (1.Jn.1:3) Obviously, he was speaking of his direct knowledge of Christ, but it is emblematic of true ministry. There are things to be seen and heard, and it is that which we must bring back into our preaching.

Revelation leads to insight. One of the greatest teachers on revelation from the Spirit in the Scriptures was Watchman Nee. He wrote:

God desires to have all things concerning Christ maintained livingly and nurtured through revelation. Only God's revelation can ever make an old thing new in us. Whatever is in Christ must always be kept in revelation; the absence of revelation will deaden everything.[1]

The Bloomsbury Dictionary describes insight as "the ability to see clearly and intuitively into the nature of a complex person, situation, or subject"[2]. Insight is seeing deeply inside something. It is far more than a

---

[1] Watchman Nee, *The Ministry of God's Word,* (Christian Fellowship Publishers, New York, 1971), p.134

[2] *The Bloomsbury Dictionary,* (Bloomsbury Publishing, London, 2004), p.962

cursory glance, or a 'sound bite' from a preacher. It comes as a gift of God, where God reveals something of such import that it seeks to grab and hold your attention. It wants to go on from there to inform and transform your spiritual walk. Insight happens when, instead of saying, "This is what I read somewhere," or, "This is what I heard someone say," we say instead, "This is what I have seen for myself."

As we saw earlier, the insight is into the mystery of Christ. C.S. Lewis caught sight of this when he wrote his famous second book in the Chronicles of Narnia – *The Lion, the Witch and the Wardrobe*. One of the main characters, Lucy, had been surprised and shocked by the appearance of the resurrected Aslan. "What does it all mean?" she had asked. "It means," said Aslan, "that though the witch knew the deep magic, there is a deeper magic still which she did not know. Her knowledge goes back only to the dawn of time. But if she could have looked a little further back, into the stillness and darkness before Time dawned, she would have read there a different incantation. She would have known that when a willing victim who had committed no treachery was killed in a traitor's stead, the Table would crack and Death itself would start working backwards."[1]

A lamb would come into the world of time from the eternal realm of the heavens. His sacrificial death would bring heart cleansing and deep forgiveness, the healing of broken hearts and relationships, reconciliation to the Father, and the restoration and renewing of the sons and daughters of Adam and Eve. What a wonderful mystery! Have you seen it for yourself?

Thought

Revelation comes not to the curious, but to humble and persistent seekers.

Prayer

Dear Lord, create in me an insatiable hunger to know you and your ways.

---

[1] C.S. Lewis, *The Complete Chronicles of Narnia,* (HarperCollins, London, 1998), p.125

DAY ONE HUNDRED AND THIRTY-FOUR

Not Made Known

Eph.3:5

...which was not made known to the sons of men in other generations as it has now been revealed to his holy apostles and prophets by the Spirit.

Timing is everything. In his second letter to Timothy, Paul wrote of the purpose and grace of God "which he gave us in Christ Jesus before the ages began, and which now has been manifested through the appearing of our Saviour Christ Jesus" (2.Tim.1:9,10). He also wrote to Titus, saying more or less the same thing. He put it this way in speaking of the hope of eternal life: "...promised before the ages began and at the proper time manifested in his word through the preaching..." (Tit.1:2,3)

After the fall of our first parents in the garden of Eden, God began to drop hints. The salvation of men and women was not a backup plan to be enacted just in case. Neither was it a reaction to something that had gone horribly wrong. He began to reveal something of that which he had purposed from all eternity.

The first hint was to the serpent who had deceived them. He said, "I will put enmity between you and the woman, and between your offspring and her offspring; he shall bruise your head, and you shall bruise his heel." (Gen.3:15) Satan would spawn the demonic forces of evil and the woman would spawn the fallen human race. In the natural, the result of the enmity is the difference between a major and a minor victory. Calvin wrote, "For in the terms 'head' and 'heel' there is a distinction between the superior and the inferior."[1] Keil and Delitzsch wrote, "The serpent can only seize the heel of the man, who walks upright; whereas the man can crush the head of the serpent, that crawls in the dust."[2]

The Preacher's Commentary says this text is...

---

[1] John Calvin, *Genesis,* (Banner of Truth, Edinburgh, 1965), p.168
[2] Keil and Delitzsch, *Commentary on the Old Testament,* e-sword.net

...[what] theologians call the "protevangelium" – literally, "a first gospel." The reason for this fine-sounding title for Genesis 3:15 is that it is seen to be the earliest promise of the coming Messiah, His suffering, and His ultimate triumph over the Evil One.[1]

This was the first hint, and according to H.C. Leupold:

...since it was intended to furnish light for the first believers and for centuries was the only light that their faith had, it certainly must have furnished, as God's providence no doubt intended that it should, sufficient light for these patriarchs to enable them to walk by that light.[2]

In other words, this little shaft of light was sufficiently strong and powerful enough to guide Abraham and those who followed him, and to light, and keep alight, a fire of hope.

Throughout the following centuries further hints were given. Scholars have found over 300 prophecies directly related to Christ. Tertullian wrote concerning the Old and New Testaments that "the new is in the old concealed; the old is in the new revealed". Sometimes the Old Testament writers would speak of things that were for a time to come – sometimes not knowing themselves the full meaning of their words. (1.Pet.1:10-12) Their words would contain both 'near' and 'far' aspects of the one who would come to save them, a Messiah, the Lamb of God, but they simply caught glimpses of him and the time of his appearance. They wrote prophetically, giving 'hints' and 'shadows' of the things that were to come.

Thought

God takes his time with his promises, and the timing of their manifestations is perfect.

Prayer

Dear Lord, please show me the new in the old concealed and the old in the new revealed.

---

[1] *The Preacher's Commentary*, e-sword.net
[2] H.C. Leupold, *Exposition of Genesis*, Vol.1, (Baker Book House, Michigan, 1980), p.164

DAY ONE HUNDRED AND THIRTY-FIVE

Now Revealed

Eph.3:5

...which was not made known to the sons of men in other generations as it has now been revealed to his holy apostles and prophets by the Spirit.

We have no idea how old Nicodemus was. All we know is that he was a ruler of the Jews. The Jewish *Talmud* mentions Nicodemus's full name, Nakdimon Ben Gurion. He was both an outstandingly wealthy man and a saintly Pharisee, and he was also a leading and well-respected member of the Sanhedrin. It seems also that he was from Galilee.

Jesus recognised him as "the teacher of Israel" (Jn.3:10). John Gill, the puritan theologian, wrote:

> *...the article before the word used will admit it to be rendered, "that master", doctor, or teacher; that famous, and most excellent one, who was talked of all over Jerusalem and Judea, as a surpassing one: and now, though he was not only an Israelite, with whom were the laws, statutes, judgments, and oracles of God, the writings of Moses, and the prophets, but a teacher of Israelites, and in the highest class of teachers, and of the greatest fame among them, yet was he ignorant of the first and most important things in religion...[1]*

What is my point here? Simply this: that Nicodemus, one of the finest and godliest of Jewish theologians, didn't see "this mystery of Christ". Jesus said to Nicodemus, "Truly, truly, I say to you, unless one is born again he cannot see the kingdom of God." He added, "Truly, truly, I say to you, unless one is born of water and the Spirit, he cannot enter the kingdom of God." (Jn.3:3,5) The lesson is clear: Christ is not learned by mere deduction, he is revealed to us by the Holy Spirit. Paul wrote to the church in Corinth, "...we impart a secret and hidden wisdom of God, which God decreed before the ages for our glory. None of the rulers of

---

[1] John Gill, *Exposition of the Entire Bible*, e-sword.net

this age understood this, for if they had, they would not have crucified the Lord of glory." (1.Cor.2:7,8)

The mystery of Christ had been revealed to the early apostles by the Holy Spirit. That which had been hidden was suddenly made known. Can you imagine their joy as they sat in the upper room, having their minds opened by the Lord? Luke records:

> *Then he said to them, "These are my words that I spoke to you while I was still with you, that everything written about me in the Law of Moses and the Prophets and the Psalms must be fulfilled." Then he opened their minds to understand the Scriptures, and said to them, "Thus it is written, that the Christ should suffer and on the third day rise from the dead, and that repentance and forgiveness of sins should be proclaimed in his name to all nations, beginning from Jerusalem."*

> Luke 22:44-47

Note: "he opened their minds". The word that Luke uses is *dianoigō*, and it means 'to open by dividing or drawing asunder, to open thoroughly'. In a nutshell, all that had been hidden under wraps was suddenly revealed and was becoming clear and falling into place.

Wayne Grudem writes, "If we are to know about God at all it is necessary that he reveal himself to us."[1] Jesus himself said, "All things have been handed over to me by my Father, and no one knows the Son except the Father, and no one knows the Father except the Son and anyone to whom the Son chooses to reveal him." (Matt.11:27) Revelation is not switched on at will. Revelation is given by God's Spirit, in his own time, mainly to those who are actively seeking, but also to those whom he catches unawares.

Thought

No one can receive anything unless God gives it from heaven. (Jn.3:27)

Prayer

Father, thank you for the revealing light you have already given to me. Help me to live in it.

---

[1] Wayne Grudem, *Systematic Theology,* (IVP, Leicester, 1994), p.149

DAY ONE HUNDRED AND THIRTY-SIX

Fellow Heirs

Eph.3:6

This mystery is that the Gentiles are fellow heirs, members of the same body, and partakers of the promise in Christ Jesus through the gospel.

The phrase "This mystery is" is not in the Greek text but is inferred from the context. Once again, we are drawn to this magnificent vision Paul has of the church – this new society, reflecting and demonstrating this one eternal kingdom. Clinton Arnold writes that "in a rhetorically powerful fashion, Paul reveals that at the heart of the mystery God has revealed is the fact that Gentiles now share equally with Jews in the blessings of the new covenant life with God"[1]. Williams Hendriksen clarified this perfectly when he wrote:

> *Paul makes it very clear that God's unveiled secret (mystery) has to do not merely with an alliance of Jew and Gentile, or perhaps a friendly agreement to live together in peace, or even an outward combination or partnership, but on the contrary, with a complete and permanent fusion, a perfect spiritual union of formerly clashing elements into one new organism, even a new humanity.*[2]

Three significant Greek words are used: *sunklēronoma, sunsōma* and *sunmetocha*. It literally reads that the Gentiles are joint-heirs, a joint-body and joint-sharers. He used the same preposition *sun* in Ephesians 2:5,6, and he did it for verbal effect. That passage literally reads, "...quickened with, raised with and seated with..."

Clinton Arnold writes again on our text for today:

> *This three-fold stress on 'together' emphasises the obliteration of any distinctions in God's way of bringing salvation to his*

---

[1]   Clinton E. Arnold, *Ephesians,* (Zondervan, Michigan, 2010), p.191
[2]   Willian Hendriksen, *Ephesians,* (Banner of Truth, Edinburgh, 1976), p.155

people. God's people will now be identified in a multi-ethnic group endowed by the Spirit of God...[1]

This new multi-ethnic group is the new society of heaven – the church – the body of Christ. The new society is in Christ. Paul wrote to the predominantly Gentile church in Galatia that "there is neither Jew nor Greek, there is neither slave nor free, there is no male and female, for you are all one in Christ Jesus. And if you are Christ's, then you are Abraham's offspring, heirs according to promise." (Gal.3:28,29)

Firstly then, Paul is saying that the Gentiles are now joint-heirs along with Jewish believers of God's kingdom. Now, in both ancient Roman and Jewish cultures, it was normally the children who were heirs, inheriting from their fathers, the firstborn getting a double portion. But, as F.F. Bruce points out, the Gentiles now had a claim on "an inheritance on which they had no claim by birth"[2]. Their natural ancestry was swallowed up by their new spiritual parentage. They had been born again, and God had become, in reality, their heavenly Father.

Paul wrote to the largely Gentile church in Rome, "The Spirit himself bears witness with our spirit that we are children of God, and if children, then heirs – heirs of God and fellow heirs with Christ..." (Rom.8:16,17) William Hendriksen also wrote, "In God's house there are no boarders; all are children."[3]

Thought

The culture of the house of God should supersede and overrule any national cultures.

Prayer

Dear Father, may the culture of your kingdom dictate my relationship with others today.

[1] Clinton E. Arnold, *Ephesians,* (Zondervan, Michigan, 2010), p.191
[2] F.F. Bruce, *The Epistle to the Ephesians,* (Pickering Paperbacks, Glasgow, 1983), p.62
[3] William Hendriksen, *Ephesians,* (Banner of Truth, Edinburgh, 1976), p.155

DAY ONE HUNDRED AND THIRTY-SEVEN

Members of the Same Body

Eph.3:6

This mystery is that the Gentiles are fellow heirs, members of the same body, and partakers of the promise in Christ Jesus through the gospel.

Yesterday I cited part of the text in Romans 8:16,17 – "The Spirit himself bears witness with our spirit that we are children of God, and if children, then heirs – heirs of God and fellow heirs with Christ..." The rest of the text says that all this happens "provided we suffer with him in order that we may also be glorified with him" (Rom.8:17). Suffering is included in the package. True and authentic Christianity will always find itself eventually on a collision course with the ways of the world.

Following on from yesterday, the second thing Paul says that the Gentiles are also a 'joint-body' with Jewish believers in the church. The word that Paul uses here is unique to him and has been coined by him.[1] It was later used by other Christian writers. It can be translated 'concorporate'. The idea is that they were "of the same body".

In the cultures of the day it was possible for slaves, whether bought or born in the house, to become heirs. Abram was faced with this dilemma. The book of Genesis records:

> *After these things the word of the LORD came to Abram in a vision: "Fear not, Abram, I am your shield; your reward shall be very great." But Abram said, "O Lord GOD, what will you give me, for I continue childless, and the heir of my house is Eliezer of Damascus?" And Abram said, "Behold, you have given me no offspring, and a member of my household will be my heir." And behold, the word of the LORD came to him:*

---

[1]   F.F. Bruce, *The Epistle to the Ephesians,* (Pickering Paperbacks, Glasgow, 1983), p.62

"This man shall not be your heir; your very own son shall be your heir."

Genesis 15:1-3

Paul begins to press the point home. The Gentiles are not adopted or bought slaves in the house; but children of the same Father, siblings of their elder brother Jesus. They are of the same body of Christ – the same "new man" (Eph.2:15). This is real family. These Gentiles could say with full confidence that they, with their Jewish brothers and sisters, are of equal standing in the true family of God.

Thirdly, he writes that the Gentiles are joint-sharers with Israel of all the promises of God in the church. The powerful word that he uses here is *summetocha,* and he only uses it once in all his writings. The word means 'joint participant, partner, sharer'. It can also mean a business partner, one who shares fully in the business and having an equal share of the profits. Clinton Arnold writes, "The promise that this new people share in goes beyond the gift of the Spirit to encompass all of what God promised in the OT in relationship to salvation."[1] They miss out on nothing.

Harold Hoehner, in his commentary on Ephesians, makes an important and significant point. He wrote that "Gentiles do not become Jews but rather Jews and Gentiles become 'one new person'. The church is not the new Israel, but a distinct body of believers comprised of believing Jews and Gentiles."[2] God has done a totally new thing.

Thought

National identities need to find a death, burial and resurrection into a new identity in Christ.

Prayer

Father, may this new nation in Christ, the glory of your kingdom, be my pride and joy.

---

[1]   Clinton E. Arnold, *Ephesians,* (Zondervan, Michigan, 2010), p.192

[2]   Harold Hoehner, *Ephesians: An Exegetical Commentary,* (Baker Academic, Michigan, 2002), p.447

Day One Hundred and Thirty-Eight

Made a Minister

Eph.3:7

Of this gospel I was made a minister according to the gift of God's grace...

Yesterday I quoted Harold Hoehner (1935-2009), who penned probably the most detailed commentary on Ephesians ever written. In it he strongly defends the apostle Paul's position concerning this mystery of God as he writes:

In conclusion, the mystery is not that Gentiles would be saved because the OT gives evidence for their salvation, but rather that believing Jews and Gentiles are together in Christ. This concept was revolutionary for Jews and Gentiles alike.

This is the good news that Paul is bringing.

There is an important connection between the "mystery" and the "gospel". John Stott wrote, "...this equation ... is significant, because the mystery was essentially truth revealed to Paul, while the gospel was essentially truth revealed by Paul."[1] What was revealed was now to be communicated, and he has been shaped to become the means of that communication. He says, "I was made a minister..."

The word "made" is from the Greek word *egenēthēn,* which literally means 'to cause to come into being'. The verb is passive which means that Paul engineered nothing; on the contrary, he was on the receiving end of God's activity. Paul shaped nothing; he was shaped by God. Behind all the circumstances of his life, God had been at work, crafting and moulding him into becoming the carrier of the message, fashioning him for what would become his life's vocation. As a raw bar of iron is thrust into the fire and then hammered on the anvil in order to be shaped into a sword; as a young branch is cut from a tree, stripped of its bark and split at both ends to receive the arrowhead and the feathers in order to become an arrow; so Paul has been through his Master's hand.

---

[1] John Stott, *The Message of Ephesians,* (IVP, Leicester, 1979), p.118

Kenneth Wuest feels that the word "minister" is an unfortunate translation of the Greek word *diakonos,* writing, "The word 'minister' is misleading, since it is the technical word used today to designate the pastor of a church."[1] Paul is not thinking so much of a title (what I am) but rather a function (what I do). In my experience of church life, once a title is given, the bearer of that title is subject to various temptations to power and prestige. Maybe that is why Paul later wrote to Timothy concerning the office of an overseer that, "He must not be a recent convert, or he may become puffed up with conceit and fall into the condemnation of the devil." (2.Tim.3:6) Titles can go to your head, whereas true ministry is primarily a heart issue.

The word basically means 'a servant', and it is to be differentiated from the word *doulos* which means 'a slave'. Commenting on this word *diakonos,* Hoehner wrote, "It is a synonym of *doulos,* which emphasises the servile relationship of a servant to a master, whereas *diakonos* emphasises the activity of a servant."[2] Nowhere is it a title. It is a function that in essence carries out the wishes of another, and therein is the key: the one with the title commands; the servant obeys. Humble obedience is at the heart of the matter. Servanthood is a learned function, and we want to learn it well, finding someone to obey. Servanthood in Christ is not commanded; it is consistently offered out of love for the Master. The way of the cross is when we allow Christ, and even others, to cross the 'I' of our will.

Thought

The continual surrender of the will is the primary way of real growth in Christ.

Prayer

Dear Lord, please help me to keep coming off the throne of my life, enthroning you instead.

---

[1] Kenneth Wuest, *Wuest's Word Studies,* Vol.1, 'Ephesians and Colossians', (Eerdmans, Michigan, 1953), p.83

[2] Harold Hoehner, *Ephesians: An Exegetical Commentary,* (Baker Academic, Michigan, 2002), p.449

Day One Hundred and Thirty-Nine

The Gift of God's Grace

Eph.3:7

Of this gospel I was made a minister according to the gift of God's grace...

One of the constants about Paul's life was this: he was always quick to acknowledge the grace of God that was at work within him. In his letter to the Corinthians, he writes concerning his ministry, "Who is sufficient for these things?" (2.Cor.2:16) Later in the letter, he writes, "Not that we are sufficient in ourselves to claim anything as coming from us, but our sufficiency is from God, who has made us sufficient to be ministers of a new covenant..." (2.Cor.3:5,6)

The word "sufficient" come from the Greek word *hikanos* which means 'competent'. It has been suggested that it carries the sense of 'having arrived' in it. This is something Paul would never feel in himself – that he had arrived. The opposite is true: he was always a learner. I often say to people that we must never take our 'L' plates off whilst walking through this life with the Lord. The moment we do, we have slipped! Further to that, when we get into heaven, they will exchange our red 'L' plates for green 'P' plates, because even there we will still be learning.

The ability to minister came from the workings of grace in his life. The word *kata* (which means 'according to, dominated by') is there again in the text, meaning that it was never by his own self-sufficiency or effort, but by a deep reliance upon the directing and empowering work of God's grace. His ardent endeavours were fuelled by divine energy, not human. In writing to the saints in Corinth about his ministry for the Lord, he put it this way:

> *Last of all, as to one untimely born, he appeared also to me. For I am the least of the apostles, unworthy to be called an apostle, because I persecuted the church of God. But by the grace of God I am what I am, and his grace toward me was not in vain. On the contrary, I worked harder than any of*

them, though it was not I, but the grace of God that is with me.

1 Corinthians 15:8-10

Here, the power came from divine resources, not human effort.

Philip Hughes, in his commentary on 2 Corinthians, wrote, "Only a man who, like the apostle, is humbly awake to his own utter weakness can know and prove the total sufficiency of God's grace."[1]

This grace was a gift. The word Paul uses for "gift" is *dōrean,* which means 'a gift graciously given without payment'. Howard Hoehner makes this insightful comment: "Certainly in this context grace is referring to God's enabling power to minister ... this passive participle further demonstrates that Paul is the recipient of the enabling power rather than the source of it."[2]

Paul leaned a lot upon the Lord. Grace was deeply operative within him. He had come to distrust his own efforts. Like Jacob of old, the natural was crippled within him to make way for the different dynamic of grace. No longer having to push or force anything, he learned to rest upon the gentle and enabling power of heaven. One of my favourite Bible teachers, Bob Mumford, used to say, "Never trust a man who doesn't walk with a limp." It is only through our natural brokenness that we can see the life-giving flow of grace emerge to touch the lives of those around us.

Thought

Only those who lean heavily upon God are truly strong.

Prayer

Father, today I lay aside my own efforts in order to receive your enabling grace.

---

[1]   Philip Hughes, *The Second Epistle to the Corinthians,* (Eerdmans, Michigan, 1977), p.92

[2]   Harold Hoehner, *Ephesians: An Exegetical Commentary,* (Baker Academic, Michigan, 2002), p.450

DAY ONE HUNDRED AND FORTY

The Working of his Power

Eph.3:7

Of this gospel I was made a minister according to the gift of God's grace, which was given me by the working of his power.

One sunny day, around 3.00pm, Peter and John were going up to the temple to pray. Just outside the building they encountered a crippled beggar seeking alms. Within minutes, the man was healed and dancing around with joy. All who saw him recognised him and were astounded at what had happened to him. Peter responded, "Men of Israel, why do you wonder at this, or why do you stare at us, as though by our own power or piety we have made him walk?" (Acts 3:12) In this case the power to heal came not from themselves but through the power of God, released through the invoking of the name of Jesus.

In our text for today, Paul is saying that this gift of grace was given to him "by the working of his power". We see something of that concept in 1:19 – "the working of his great might that he worked in Christ when he raised him from the dead" (cf. Phil.3:21). Behind every act of God is his incredible power. The ESV is weak here. It is better in the KJV: "...by the effectual working of his power..." Kenneth Wuest captures it more accurately: "...according to the operative energy of His power..."[1] There are two things to think about here. Firstly, God's power is effectual. It never fizzles out in failure, but it accomplishes each time his purpose. *Vincent's Word Studies* has it as "the active, efficient manifestation" of God's power.

Secondly, God is personally involved in every act of power. Behind every act of the power of God is his full attention. Paul used the word *energeia* to describe the working of the power of God. All God's personal energy goes into manifesting his power. Dr Martyn Lloyd-Jones wrote, "...the apostle used it in order to explain what it was that turned that persecuting, blaspheming hater of Christ into one of his foremost

---

[1]   Kenneth Wuest, *The New Testament, An Expanded Translation,* (Eerdmans, Michigan, 2004), p.452

preachers and apostles."[1] This power is what Paul was receiving in his life.

It was also that same power that energised Paul's ministry. Not only was he on the receiving end of God's power but it empowered and sustained him in all his trials and difficulties, and it also flowed through him to others. Churches and people were on the receiving end of the power of God cascading through him. His ministry was marked and saturated with the power of God. Paul wrote to the believers in Colossae that, "Him we proclaim, warning everyone and teaching everyone with all wisdom, that we may present everyone mature in Christ. For this I toil, struggling with all his energy that he powerfully works within me." (Col.1:28,29) The truth of the matter is that there is nothing we can muster up of ourselves that can achieve the works of God. It will always be by the power of God.

Paul had discovered a secret. It was never going to be his own energetics that produced the works of God; it was going to be his acknowledged weakness. In a time of extreme weakness, Jesus had said to him, "My grace is sufficient for you, for my power is made perfect in weakness." Paul then shared with those around him these words: "Therefore I will boast all the more gladly of my weaknesses, so that the power of Christ may rest upon me." (2.Cor.12:9)

Thought

Our present culture encourages us to 'big up' our abilities. Not so with God's kingdom.

Prayer

Father, deliver me from thinking too much of what I can do. Align me to your power.

---

[1] Martyn Lloyd-Jones, *The Unsearchable Riches of Christ,* (Banner of Truth, Edinburgh, 1979), p.54

46

DAY ONE HUNDRED AND FORTY-ONE

The Very Least of All the Saints

Eph.3:8

To me, though I am the very least of all the saints, this grace was given...

It is when we reach bottom that we begin to rise. God will often have to take us to the places where we 'bottom out', and having run out of our own resources, we realise that without him we can do nothing.

Here, Paul is being truly honest. This is no false humility, but a genuine surprise that God has touched his life and given him such a huge responsibility. Howard Hoehner puts it like this: "It is a sudden outburst of amazement that God would use him, giving him not only the responsibility but also the power to communicate this gospel to all people."[1]

Eugene Peterson wrote:

His self-deprecating reference as 'the very least of all the saints' catches our attention by creating a novel form of the adjective 'least' that doubles its comparative emphasis. Translated literally it comes out 'I am the leaster or smallester of all the saints.'[2]

In an earlier lecture on Ephesians given at Regents College, he said that the word *elachistoterō* meant "the very least" – "less than the least, lower than the lowest". The word, coined by Paul, is found nowhere else in the New Testament. Hoehner writes, "Paul wishes to convey that he considers himself to be less than the least of all believers who have been given this grace."[3]

It is instructive to see that Paul's value of himself changes as time goes on. In his first letter to the Corinthians, written around 52-55AD, he

---

[1] Harold Hoehner, *Ephesians: An Exegetical Commentary,* (Baker Academic, Michigan, 2002), p.452

[2] Eugene Peterson, *Practise Resurrection,* (Hodder & Stoughton, London, 2010), p.132

[3] Harold Hoehner, *Ephesians: An Exegetical Commentary,* (Baker Academic, Michigan, 2002), p.452

describes himself as "the least of the apostles" (1.Cor.15:9). Around 61-62AD he wrote to the Ephesians in the text that we are looking at today that he considers himself to be "the very least of all the saints". Sometime later he wrote to Timothy "that Christ Jesus came into the world to save sinners, of whom I am the foremost" (1.Tim.1:15).

It seems to me that the nearer Paul gets to Jesus, and the more he walks with him, the less he thinks of himself. I guess that in a similar vein, the nearer we get to the light, the more we see our imperfections. The lesson is clear: genuine maturity does not bring with it a growing self-image but rather a genuine humility. And to be sure, an image is just that – an image. It is not the real thing. The only image we are legitimately allowed to project is the image of Christ, not our own.

We need to stop worrying about our image, what people think about us and what we do. We need to cease from promoting our own image. Our goal, our only goal, should be that of reflecting the image of Christ. And the Holy Spirit is most desirous to help us in that.

Let me finish today with some thoughts from *The Imitation of Christ*, written by Thomas à Kempis:

> *He that knoweth himself well groweth ever more conscious of his own sinfulness, and findeth no delight in the praises of men ... If thou wouldst learn anything of lasting benefit, seek to be unknown and little esteemed of men.*[1]

Ponder these words. They cut right across the thinking of today.

Thought

A false humility gives off a stench, whereas a true humility is fragrant.

Prayer

Lord Jesus, deliver me from self-projection, and help me to promote you and your kingdom.

---

[1] Thomas à Kempis, *The Imitation of Christ*, translated by George F. Maine, (Collins, London, 1971), pp.34,35

DAY ONE HUNDRED AND FORTY-TWO

The Unsearchable Riches of Christ

Eph.3:8

...to preach to the Gentiles the unsearchable riches of Christ...

I remember hearing the story of a little girl who was at the beach with her family Once there, she took her little bucket down to the water's edge, filled it with seawater, and rushed back exclaiming, "Look! I've got the sea in my bucket!"

On a number of occasions, I have stood at the threshold of Scripture, and there has comes a deep ache into my heart because there is so much to see, yet my span of life is only long enough to take in a mere portion of what is there. On top of that I have a library full of great books and commentaries, collected over decades, and it would take more than a lifetime to thoroughly read and absorb them all.

Paul looked into the life of Christ – before the foundation of the world, his incarnation and his present ministry at the right hand of the Father – and he gasped. It took his breath away. It was all too much. And here he tries to describe it all as "the unsearchable riches of Christ".

The word "unsearchable" is the Greek word *anexichniaston,* meaning 'untraceable, inexhaustible, incomprehensible, unfathomable, bottomless, limitless'. The Good News Bible uses the word "infinite". To give you an idea of this immensity, Job, in talking about God, said that he "does great things and unsearchable, marvellous things without number" (Job 5:9). He repeats this again later, saying that he "does great things beyond searching out, and marvellous things beyond number" (Job 9:10). It is felt that Paul got this word from the Greek version of Job. He also used the word in his letter to the Romans, writing, "Oh, the depth of the riches and wisdom and knowledge of God! How unsearchable are his judgments and how inscrutable his ways!" (Rom.11:33)

Clinton Arnold says that the word is built on the word 'footprint', which in the Greek language is *ichnos.* He goes on to write that "the verbal form *ēxichneūs* or *ēxichniazo* was used literally in Greek literature for a tracker, that is, someone who pursues another by tracing their footprints"[1]. Asaph, the psalmist, wrote of God, "Your way was through the sea, your path through the great waters; yet your footprints were unseen." (Ps.77:19) Robertson wrote, "Paul undertook to track out the untrackable in Christ."[2]

We shall never exhaust the riches of Christ. We will explore them both in this life and the next, yet we will never come to the end of them. They are beyond measure. Before us lies an eternity of learning.

These riches are to be preached. It is as if Paul is saying, "You know what? You have drunk from dirty puddles all of your lives, but now let me introduce you to vast oceans of crystal clear, life-giving water." Any true preaching of the richness of Christ should leave the congregation both fully satisfied and gasping for air. Our congregations should exit our churches hungering and thirsting for more.

One last thought. The apostle Peter wrote that contained in this good news of the gospel are "things into which angels long to look". Things too beautiful, too astonishing and yet so appealing.

Thought

Uncontainable and immeasurable – this is the Lord Jesus we preach.

Prayer

Dear Lord of heaven and earth, please stop me in my tracks with your immensity.

---

[1]   Clinton E. Arnold, *Ephesians,* (Zondervan, Michigan, 2010), p.194
[2]   *Robertson's Word Pictures,* e-sword.net

DAY ONE HUNDRED AND FORTY-THREE

Bringing to Light the Plan

Eph.3:9

...and to bring to light for everyone what is the plan of the mystery hidden for ages in God who created all things...

Sometimes over the years I have watched people being led into a darkened room, and suddenly the lights have come on and they have found themselves surrounded by a host of family and close friends who have come together in secret to celebrate their birthday. Their surprise is always a highlight of the party!

Paul is, in effect, saying to the Ephesians, "You have walked blinded by the darkness all of your lives. Now, let me bring you into Christ." He has escorted them in, the light has come on and they are astonished by what they now see. He writes to them that his preaching was "to bring to light for everyone what is the plan of the mystery hidden for ages in God".

The phrase "to bring to light" is taken from the one Greek word *phōtisai,* which means 'to enlighten'. We came across a form of this word in Ephesians 1:18.[1] Colloquially speaking, Paul is saying, "I am going to turn the light on and let you see what God is up to in Christ." That is what authentic ministry does – it turns the light on. It's what I would call 'revelation ministry' – 'eye-opening ministry' – where the response is, "We have never seen that before!" The psalmist wrote, "The unfolding of your words gives light; it imparts understanding to the simple." (Ps.119:130)

From Ephesians 1:18 we also learned that the word *phōtisai* comes from the root *phōs,* which simply means 'light'. I wrote that some scholars say that *phos* and another Greek word, *phonē,* share the common root *phaō,* which means 'to shine'. The word *phonē* means 'a

---

[1]   Alan Hoare, *The Church I See,* Vol.1, (Onwards and Upwards, Exeter, 2021), 'Day Sixty-One', p.146

voice'.[1] If this be true, then in this kind of preaching, the light comes and the voice of God is heard.

Paul also used the phrase "the plan of the mystery". The word "plan" is taken from the Greek word *oikonomia* (used in 1:10 and 3:2), which in this context means the administration and unfolding of the great mystery and purpose of God. Harold Hoehner wrote, "Here it could have the idea of strategy. Paul's responsibility is to enlighten all as to what is the strategy or administration of the mystery."[2] This previously hidden mystery is now being unfolded and administered to both Jews and Gentiles – to all in fact. One can imagine the sequence: "This is what it is and this is how it works." Clinton Arnold wrote, "Jesus Christ is the apex of God's plan. Christ himself is the mystery. He is the basis, means, goal and incorporational centre of all that the one true God has set out to accomplish."[3]

Paul is bringing to light the one who said, "I am the light of the world," (Jn.8:12), and who would go on to say to those who followed him, "You are the light of the world." (Matt.5:14) The light of the world came to set a light into our hearts that we might bring that light into our darkened world. The sharing of the good news of Christ, and also the sharing of our lives in serving others, has that effect. This plan has now been revealed to the church, and from the church it must be spoken out loudly and clearly.

Thought

We have both an enormous eye-opening message and a life-changing mandate.

Prayer

Lord, help me to see to it that my plans get caught up in this huge plan of yours.

---

[1] *New American Exhaustive Concordance of the Bible,* Holman Bible Publishers, Nashville, 1981), p.1692
[2] Harold Hoehner, *Ephesians: An Exegetical Commentary,* (Baker Academic, Michigan, 2002), p.456
[3] Clinton E. Arnold, *Ephesians,* (Zondervan, Michigan, 2010), p.202

DAY ONE HUNDRED AND FORTY-FOUR

Through the Church

Eph.3:10

...so that through the church the manifold wisdom of God might now be made known to the rulers and authorities in the heavenly places.

Today, I want to remind us that the church is God's great idea. The first mention of the word in the New Testament is found in Matthew's Gospel where Jesus said to Peter, "I will build my church..." (Matt.16:18) The Greek word is *ekklēsia,* and literally means 'the called-out ones'. The thought is that we are all individually called out of something into a gathering together. We are called out of our personal worlds into the world of the kingdom of heaven. Jesus called this gathering the church, and so did Paul, several times. Each local church is an embassy of the kingdom of heaven.

God's intention is to have a local church everywhere. Eugene Peterson wrote:

> *God created church as a place on earth accessible and congenial for being present to us, listening to us and speaking to us on our home ground. Simultaneously it is his gift to us, a place in our neighbourhood within walking distance or driving distance for being present to God, listening to God and speaking to him.[1]*

Church, however, is not perfect, but it is what we have been called to be a part of, and it is where we grow both individually and together. Eugene Peterson also said in one of his lectures:

> *The church is not a pure place for spiritual formation but it is the only authentic and realistic place for spiritual formation. If we keep looking for some kind of spiritual 'utopia setting'*

---

[1]   Eugene Peterson, *Practise Resurrection,* (Hodder & Stoughton, London, 2010), p.167

*in which to grow up in Christ, we never will. If God's purpose
is to have church, then we had better accept it.[1]*

God designed the church with us in mind. But that's not the end of
the story. He also designed it with others in mind. The church was not
only to be a spiritual home, but a spiritual vehicle. God wants to use the
church to demonstrate his manifold wisdom. The word "manifold" is
taken from the Greek word *polupoikilos*, and it is used only here in the
New Testament. It means 'many-tinted, much variegated'. In the Greek
Old Testament, the word is used to describe Joseph's coat of many
colours.

Looking at the makeup of the church, and in particular the company
of the second-born people who were in it, John Stott wrote:

> *The church as a multi-racial, multi-cultural community is like
> a beautiful tapestry. Its members come from a wide range of
> colourful backgrounds. No other human community re-
> sembles it. Its diversity and harmony are unique. It is God's
> new society.[2]*

This profound 'many-tinted' wisdom also includes the different ways
in which God works, the different people whom he uses, the different
ways of ministry, teaching and discipling, and the different forms of
church government. With God, variety is always going to be here to stay.
It is within this very deliberate variety that we learn to wonder at and
appreciate the beautiful varied grace and wisdom of God at work in the
church.

Thought

Among the various imperfections, touched by various spiritual
means, God shines forth.

Prayer

Dear God, I love what you have created in the earth, and I love how
you are working.

---

[1]   Eugene Peterson, lectures on 'Soulcraft; The Formation of a Mature Life in
      Christ', Regents College, Vancouver
[2]   John Stott, *The Message of Ephesians,* (IVP, Leicester, 1979), p.123

DAY ONE HUNDRED AND FORTY-FIVE

The Audience

Eph.3:10

...so that through the church the manifold wisdom of God might now be made known to the rulers and authorities in the heavenly places.

As we noted yesterday, the church is God's great idea. It is not perfect because not one of us is perfect. But God is into 'perfecting' the saints – slowly and lovingly over long periods of time. He created spiritual homes where this might take place. He created the church also as a vehicle from which to display his incredible multi-faceted wisdom. And this is where it gets interesting. Paul writes that the 'many-tinted' wisdom of God was to be manifested through the church to "the rulers and authorities in the heavenly places".

We need to take note that it is not to the world, but to a heavenly audience, that this multi-coloured wisdom of God is manifested and made known. John Stott painted this beautiful picture when he wrote:

It is as if a great drama is being enacted. History is the theatre, the world is the stage, and church members in every land are the actors. God himself has written the play, and he directs and produces it. Act by act, scene by scene, the story continues to unfold. But who are the audience? They are the cosmic intelligence, the principalities and powers in the heavenly places. We are to think of them as spectators of the drama of redemption.[1]

The mission of the church is part of the drama, while heaven observes.

Dr W. Graham Scroggie was one of the finest expositors of the Bible of the last century. He wrote:

To celestial intelligences the wisdom of God is being made known 'through the Church'. This brings two worlds into

---

[1] John Stott, *The Message of Ephesians,* (IVP, Leicester, 1979), pp.123,124

relationship and intercourse. How great a mystery is this, and one of which we are profoundly ignorant![1]

Kenneth Wuest wrote:

The Church thus becomes a university for the angels, and each saint a professor. Only in the Church can the angels come to an adequate comprehension of the grace of God. They look at the Church to investigate the mysteries of redemption.[2]

William Hendriksen wrote:

The Church, therefore, does not exist for itself. It exists for God, for His glory. When the angels in heaven behold the works and the wisdom of God displayed in the Church, their knowledge of the God they adore is increased and they rejoice and glorify Him.[3]

This needs to grab our attention and fill us with wonder. Somewhere in the heavenlies, Gabriel and his angelic companions are sitting with clipboards, watching and learning as various individuals and people groups come together and the church grows. People from all persuasions and walks of life have been, and are being, called and brought together to live in graceful harmony with each other. One can only imagine some of the angelic comments.

Thought

Heaven is watching and learning from the life and witness of the church.

Prayer

Dear Lord, help me to play my part so well that the angels applaud.

---

[1] W. Graham Scroggie, *The Unfolding Drama of Redemption,* Vol.3, (Pickering & Inglis, London, 1970), p.188

[2] Kenneth Wuest, *Wuest's Word Studies,* Vol.1, 'Ephesians and Colossians', (Eerdmans, Michigan, 1953), p.85

[3] William Hendriksen, *Ephesians,* (Banner of Truth, Edinburgh, 1976), p.158

DAY ONE HUNDRED AND FORTY-SIX

The Eternal Purpose

Eph.3:11

This was according to the eternal purpose...

W e time dwellers, in our minds, live either in the past, the present or the future. Empirically, we live in the present, lapping up or suffering each moment, yearning for or regretting the past, and either dreading or anticipating the future. God, however, lives in an eternal dimension and is able to touch all three dimensions of human life. He can heal our past, touch our present and speak into our future.

Paul was absolutely filled up in his thinking with this eternal dimension of God. In fact, in his thinking, everything happened "according to" God's eternal purpose. The Greek word *kata* appears again, and Paul is saying that everything is happening under the direction of, and controlled by, this one eternal purpose which will not veer off course. Francis Foulkes wrote:

> *We are back again to this great, central theme of the letter. Behind all the events of this world's history there is an eternal purpose being worked out. God's is no ad hoc plan, but one conceived from eternity and eternal in its scope.[1]*

F.F. Bruce pointed out that the phrase "the eternal purpose" is more accurately translated "the purpose of the ages"[2]. Note that "purpose" is in the singular and "ages" is in the plural. We could rewrite this as "the one divine purpose that drives through all the undulating ages of the earth".

John Stott asked this rhetorical question about human history: "Is history just the random succession of events, each effect having its cause and each cause its effect, yet the whole betraying no overall pattern but

---

[1] Francis Foulkes, *Ephesians,* (IVP, Leicester, 1999), p.106
[2] F.F. Bruce, *The Epistle to the Ephesians*, (Pickering Paperbacks, Glasgow, 1983), p.65

appearing rather as the meaningless development of the human story?"[1] He answered by writing, "God is at work, moving from a plan conceived in eternity, through a historical outworking and disclosure, to a climax within history, and then on beyond it to another eternity of the future."[2]

This purpose, then, has its origins in eternity, and its implementation is neither governed nor influenced by any of the changing circumstances, politics and philosophies of life "under the sun". God is not modifying or modernising his purpose as time progresses. Here is a thought: much of animate creation adapts to circumstances, conditions and sur-roundings, but is the word 'adapt' in heaven's vocabulary?

We are all called to lift our sights above the changing face of life on the earth, to the unchanging God whose character and purposes reflect who he is. Like Paul, we are to be filled with a deep consciousness that there is an eternal strand woven into the tapestry of life. Have you seen it and does it affect the way you think?

Paul wrote, "Set your sights on the realities of heaven, where Christ sits in the place of honour at God's right hand. Think about the things of heaven, not the things of earth." (Col.3:1,2, NLT) Bishop Lightfoot wrote, "You must not only seek heaven, you must think heaven."[3] Seek to see what God sees.

Thought

If eternity fills your mind and heart, life takes on a settled divine perspective.

Prayer

Dear Father, drench my mind and heart with the perspectives of your eternal mind.

---

[1]   John Stott, *The Message of Ephesians,* (IVP, Leicester, 1979), p.127
[2]   Ibid.
[3]   Cited in *Vincent's Word Studies,* e-sword.net

DAY ONE HUNDRED AND FORTY-SEVEN

Realised in Christ Jesus Our Lord

Eph.3:11

...that he has realised in Christ Jesus our Lord...

Concerning the eternal purpose, Harold Hoehner wrote: "...this manifold wisdom of God was not the result of a last-minute idea which God had. Israel's rejection of their Messiah did not make it necessary for God to create hastily a new plan, namely the church."[1] Clinton Arnold put it this way: "The idea here is not that God thought up this plan, but that he had this plan in mind before he created humanity and is now bringing it into realisation. Jesus Christ is the central figure in the fulfilment of God's plan."[2]

The word "realised" is taken from the Greek word *epoiēsen,* which means 'to make, to carry into effect'. Other words would be 'achieved' or 'accomplished'. The word also carries the sense of something conceived, but in this context it has the sense of accomplishment. We can say that overall, it is both. It was conceived in heaven and it was accomplished on the earth.

Writing of this eternal purpose of God, realised in Christ, F.F. Bruce wrote, "And the one to whom we are thus united is Himself the centre and circumference of this purpose: it was conceived (literally 'made') in Him and it attains its fulfilment through him."[3]

Paul was not only filled with a massive vision of God's eternal purpose of the church, he was also carrying an immense vision and understanding of who Jesus is. In his sight, this eternal purpose was, and is, all about Jesus the Messiah, the Lord of all. For him, Jesus is the goal and the centre of everything. Read it from Paul's letter to the Colossians:

He is the image of the invisible God, the firstborn of all creation. For by him all things were created, in heaven and on

---

[1] Harold Hoehner, *Ephesians: An Exegetical Commentary,* (Baker Academic, Michigan, 2002), pp.462,463
[2] Clinton E. Arnold, *Ephesians,* (Zondervan, Michigan, 2010), p.198
[3] F.F. Bruce, *The Epistle to the Ephesians,* (Pickering Paperbacks, Glasgow, 1983), p.65

earth, visible and invisible, whether thrones or dominions or rulers or authorities – all things were created through him and for him. And he is before all things, and in him all things hold together. And he is the head of the body, the church. He is the beginning, the firstborn from the dead, that in everything he might be preeminent. For in him all the fullness of God was pleased to dwell, and through him to reconcile to himself all things, whether on earth or in heaven, making peace by the blood of his cross.

Colossians 1:15-20

The mysterious purpose realised by Jesus is enormous in its outworking. We are still feeling the effects. The Holy Spirit is still opening our eyes to see the wonder and the beauty of it all. Sing the words of Charles Wesley: "'Tis mystery all! The Immortal dies! Who can explore His strange design? In vain the firstborn seraph tries to sound the depths of love Divine! 'Tis mercy all! Let earth adore, let angel minds inquire no more."[1]

Jesus is the Head of the church, and the church is both his body and his bride – they are destined to be together forever. The Head is inseparable from the body and the Bridegroom is inseparable from the bride. Let no theological surgery, deceitful spirit or cultural agenda separate what God has joined together.

Thought

Jesus and we, his new family, are the plan.

Prayer

Lord, you did it! Now help me to keep talking up the wonder of you and your bride.

---

[1]   Charles Wesley, 'And can it be', *Songs of Fellowship,* no.21, (Kingsway music, Eastbourne, 2003)

Day One Hundred and Forty-Eight

Access Through Christ

Eph.3:12

...in whom we have boldness and access with confidence through our faith in him.

On the morning that I wrote this, I saw in my mind's eye a somewhat overweight, smartly dressed, fun-loving individual. What surprised me was the size of his head. It was tiny! The body seemed to dwarf it. Sometimes, the church can be like that. So much attention is on feeding the body image of the church that the Head seems hardly visible, having very little influence at all. Jesus, our Head, must always be the centre of our attention and thinking. The church must never take her cue from what the world expects or is looking for; she must look to him for direction in everything.

We must, therefore, ensure that our models of attractional church do not distract us from our Head. Jesus, and all he stands for, must never be discreetly hidden from view; he must ever be the main focus. His life and his ways must be evidenced among us and manifest in us. Like Paul, our vision needs to be full of the Lord Jesus. The Father and the Spirit both point to him, and so should the church. By all means we need have a vision for the church, but we need to have a much larger one for Jesus, the Head of the church.

Here, then, is the truly authentic attractional model: speaking of the cross, Jesus said, "And I, when I am lifted up from the earth, will draw all people to myself." (Jn.12:32) Paul, writing to the Corinthians, put it this way:

For Christ did not send me to baptise but to preach the gospel, and not with words of eloquent wisdom, lest the cross of Christ be emptied of its power. For the word of the cross is folly to those who are perishing, but to us who are being saved it is the power of God.

1 Corinthians 1:17,18

There is a strong and strangely attractional power in the message of the cross.

Everything is to be rooted in him, revolving around who he is, what he has done, and what he is doing. He only is the true sphere of operations. "In him" is one of Paul's favourite expressions. He now writes of Jesus, "in whom we have boldness and access with confidence through our faith in him". Note the "in whom".

In him, and through him, we have bold and confident access to the Father. The word "access" is from the Greek word *prosagōgēn,* which we encountered in Ephesians 2:18. The word is used only by Paul in the New Testament, twice in Ephesians and once in his letter to the church in Rome where he writes, "Through him we have also obtained access by faith into this grace in which we stand." (Rom.5:2) Lawrence Richards writes that the word has three main meanings: "entrance", "introduction", "access".[1] W.E. Vine writes that the word means "a leading or bringing into the presence of"[2]. Thayer describes it as "that relationship with God whereby we are acceptable to him and have assurance that he is favourably disposed towards us"[3].

Paul is anxious to emphasise again that the way to the Father is wide open to the child of God. The old methods of sacrificing animals and birds are gone forever. Jesus was the final and extraordinary sacrifice that tore the veil of the temple, ushering all who believe into the immediate presence of the Father.

Thought

The Father bids us welcome and the Spirit takes us by the hand, drawing us in.

Prayer

Jesus, thank you so much that you have made me so welcome in your Father presence.

---

[1] Lawrence O. Richards, *Expository Dictionary of Bible Words,* (Marshall Pickering, Basingstoke, 1988), p.10

[2] W.E. Vine, *Vine's Expository Dictionary of Biblical Words,* (Thomas Nelson, New York, 1985)

[3] *Thayer's Greek Definitions,* e-sword.net

DAY ONE HUNDRED AND FORTY-NINE

Bold and Confident Access

Eph.3:12

...in whom we have boldness and access with confidence through our faith in him.

When the enemy of our souls whispers in our ear that we are not worthy to enter the Father's presence, we must not retreat, feeling intimated by his words. Instead, we are to rise up within, brandishing the sword of the Spirit, the word of God, and see him off.

Paul uses the word "boldness". In the Greek language it is *parrēsian,* and, according to Thayer, it meant "freedom in speaking, unreservedness in speech"[1]. John Gill, the puritan theologian wrote that it meant that the children of God have "a liberty in their own souls to speak out their minds plainly and freely; and a holy courage and intrepidity of soul, being free from servile fear, or a spirit of bondage"[2].

Bear with me as I go on a little ramble here. In the book of Acts, there is the scenario where the apostles were badly treated by the ruling Sanhedrin. When they were released, they went back to their brothers and sisters in Christ and prayed. Hear their prayer: "And now, Lord, look upon their threats and grant to your servants to continue to speak your word with all boldness..." (Acts 4:29) The same Greek word is used. Luke further records, "And when they had prayed, the place in which they were gathered together was shaken, and they were all filled with the Holy Spirit and continued to speak the word of God with boldness." (Acts 4:31) The point that I want to make here is this: boldness is not only the infusion of God's power; it is also a choice. The apostles were filled with boldness and they then continued to speak.

We must learn to take this principle with us as we approach God. When the enemy comes with his withering attacks, we must become somewhat ruthless in our response to him. Let me add here that boldness is vastly different from an ignorant arrogance. Boldness shows respect,

---

[1]   *Thayer's Greek Definitions,* e-sword.net
[2]   John Gill, *Exposition of the Whole Bible,* e-sword.net

whereas arrogance shows none. Even the angels acknowledge and respect the existence of Satan. Jude wrote that when "the archangel Michael, contending with the devil, was disputing about the body of Moses, he did not presume to pronounce a blasphemous judgment, but said, 'The Lord rebuke you.'" (Jd.1:9) Adam Clark noted that "it was a Jewish maxim, as may be seen in Synopsis Sohar, page 92, note 6: 'It is not lawful for man to prefer ignominious reproaches, even against wicked spirits.'"[1] Be respectfully bold.

Be bold as you enter. The Father does not intimidate. Even the Jewish poets were unafraid to voice what they really felt before God. That is the beauty of the psalms of lament. They certainly honoured him but they also felt free to pour out their souls before him.

Be confident as you enter. The word Paul uses is *pepoithēsei,* and it means 'confidence, reliance, trust'. When we put the three words together, we get a composite picture that basically says, "Our trust is in what Jesus has done and in who the Father is. We rely on these truths and they inspire confidence in us as we enter." Trust breeds reliance, and reliance breeds confidence. Walk confidently, therefore, into the Father's presence today, carrying the sword with you, and feel at home there to speak freely.

Thought

Faith sometimes manifests itself as a fighting spirit.

Prayer

Father, today I choose to enter boldly and confidently into your presence.

---

[1] Adam Clark, *Commentary on the Bible,* e-sword.net

DAY ONE HUNDRED AND FIFTY

Our Faith in Him

Eph.3:12

...in whom we have boldness and access with confidence through our faith in him.

Dr Mark Roberts, Executive Director of the Max De Pree Centre for Leadership at Fuller Seminary, wrote, "The Greek more literally reads that in Christ and through faith in him we have 'freedom of speech' (*parrēsia*) and 'freedom of access' (*prosagōgē*)."[1] We can now walk freely into our Father's presence and speak freely with him with confidence. The Greek word translated "have" is *echomen,* and Harold Hoehner observes that it is "in the present tense indicating repeated action"[2]. In other words, we can keep confidently walking in, to be with him and talk with him, whenever we feel the need.

This has, however, nothing to do with self-confidence. The world around us will extol what they call 'the virtue of self-confidence'. On the surface it seems to have value, but underneath it actually erodes our spiritual life. Our culture will tell us that with a sure confidence in ourselves, we can go anywhere and do anything. The opposite is true in the life of the kingdom of heaven. Our confidence needs to be placed not in ourselves but in God.

The Scriptures are replete with stories and examples of those who had a misplaced confidence in themselves, or others, or in their own abilities, or their own wisdom, and failed. A verse in Proverbs springs to mind as I write: "Trust in the LORD with all your heart, and do not lean on your own understanding." (Prov.3:5) It is of great significance that the word "trust" had "originally the idea of lying helplessly face downwards"[3]. Charles Bridges, commenting on this verse, wrote, "This is the polar-star of a child of God – faith in his Father's providence, promises and grace."[4]

---

[1]   Mark D. Roberts, *Ephesians,* (Zondervan, Michigan, 2016), p.99
[2]   Harold Hoehner, *Ephesians: An Exegetical Commentary,* (Baker Academic, Michigan, 2002), p.467
[3]   Derek Kidner, citing G.R. Driver, *Proverbs,* (IVP, London, 1974), p.63
[4]   Charles Bridges, *Proverbs,* (Banner of Truth, Edinburgh, 1977), p.23

Paul, writing to the believers in Philippi, put it like this: "For we are the circumcision, who worship by the Spirit of God and glory in Christ Jesus and put no confidence in the flesh..." (Phil.3:3) Here, he writes that "we have boldness and access [to God] with confidence through our faith in him". The only valid confidence is the result of a faith issue.

No one can confidently walk into the presence of God without a sure faith in Jesus. Faith in who he is and what he has done. Faith in the one who said, "I am the way, and the truth, and the life. No one comes to the Father except through me." (Jn.14:6) Faith in the one of whom it is written, "Therefore, brothers, since we have confidence to enter the holy places by the blood of Jesus, by the new and living way that he opened for us through the curtain, that is, through his flesh..."

This was fabulous news to the Gentiles who were listening to this letter being read. Paul is saying that now, because of what Jesus has accomplished on the cross, there are no more barriers, no more religious walls, just an open invitation to those who put their faith in him. They are to come in and feel at home with God.

Thought

Faith in Christ is the door-opener to the presence and activity of God.

Prayer

Lord, may my faith in you remove any trepidation from my heart.

DAY ONE HUNDRED AND FIFTY-ONE

Don't Lose Heart

Eph.3:13

So I ask you not to lose heart over what I am suffering for you, which is your glory.

Paul began this chapter by describing himself as "a prisoner of Christ Jesus on behalf of you Gentiles" (3:1). The vision of Christ and the commission of God had brought him to a prison cell. Because he was convinced of the reality of this mystery of God – the bringing together of Jews and Gentiles into one new entity and identity in Christ – he had suffered much. And so, in this verse that we are looking at today, he wants them to know that his suffering is not in vain.

The main point of this is that, as Harold Hoehner puts it, "If Paul had never carried out his ministry of the mystery to the Ephesians, he would not have been in prison and the Ephesians would never had been introduced to Christ."[1]

He says two things to them. Firstly, "...don't lose heart..." He felt that as they saw what this ministry and message was costing him, it would dishearten them. Perhaps they did not want him to have so much pain on their behalf. Perhaps they saw a hint of what it might cost them. Adam Clark wrote, "In those primitive times, when there was much persecution, people were in continual danger of falling away from the faith who were not well grounded in it."[2]

The word that Paul uses here in the Greek language is *enkakein,* which literally means 'to behave badly in a difficult situation, to give in to evil'. Albert Barnes wrote that the phrase literally meant "to turn out 'a coward', or to lose one's courage; then to be fainthearted"[3]. Another way of putting it is 'to become dispirited' or 'to have the stuffing knocked out of you'.

---

[1]   Harold Hoehner, *Ephesians: An Exegetical Commentary,* (Baker Academic, Michigan, 2002), p.470

[2]   Adam Clark, *Commentary on the Bible,* e-sword.net

[3]   Albert Barnes, *Notes on the Bible,* e-sword.net

Paul was quite clear about the cost of preaching Jesus and following him. He wrote to Timothy that "all who desire to live a godly life in Christ Jesus will be persecuted" (2.Tim.3:12). Don't run from it; embrace it.

Secondly, he writes to them saying that his suffering was their glory. They shone because he suffered. Most certainly it was also his glory. The apostle Peter wrote concerning suffering that "if you are insulted for the name of Christ, you are blessed, because the Spirit of glory and of God rests upon you" (1.Pet.4:14). John Stott noted that suffering and glory are constantly coupled in the New Testament.[1] Paul's suffering was a jewel in their crown.

To sum up, Clinton Arnold wrote:

> *Suffering can make God feel far away from us. The suffering of those we know, love, and respect can cause deep discouragement. It is important for us to realise that suffering is encompassed within the plan of God. This is apparent in the life of Jesus and the life of Paul.*[2]

Thought

The tough call of following Christ must not be allowed to discourage us. Bite the bullet!

Prayer

Lord Jesus, walking with you will at times hurt. Help me to find the courage to be faithful.

---

[1]   John Stott, *The Message of Ephesians,* (IVP, Leicester, 1979), p.129
[2]   Clinton E. Arnold, *Ephesians,* (Zondervan, Michigan, 2010), p.203

DAY ONE HUNDRED AND FIFTY-TWO

For This Reason I Bow My Knees

Eph.3:14

For this reason I bow my knees before the Father…

The 'holy parenthesis' – the twelve verses packed with in-depth and powerful theology – has come to an end. Paul now writes for the third time, "For this reason…" (cf. 1:15; 3:1) The reason is simply that he is so overwhelmed by the truths of the gift of grace, the mystery of Christ and the fabulous purpose of God, that he finds himself dropping to his knees in prayer. The truths of God ought to do that to us.

Perhaps the reason that it does not happen to us is because we are not gripped enough by truth, or because we are simply living off spiritual 'soundbites and snippets' of truth. Paul had been, and still was, totally absorbed by what he had experienced of the grace of God and seen of the purpose of God in Christ. I can only imagine that each time he spoke of these things one would feel the passion trembling within him.

Both George Müller and George Whitfield read the Bible on their knees. For them it was a posture of deep respect for the Scriptures, and also for the God who spoke to them out of the Scriptures.

The normal posture for a Jew at prayer was standing, but there were examples of people on their knees. Solomon knelt at the dedication of the temple, Jesus knelt in the garden of Gethsemane, and Paul himself knelt on the beach with the elders of the Ephesian church. Mark Roberts wrote:

> *The use of 'I bow my knees', a more literal translation of the Greek, might indicate a sense of reverent urgency, or perhaps it underscores the sovereignty of God. It is also profoundly worshipful, part of what it means to live for the praise of God's glory.[1]*

---

[11] Mark D. Roberts, *Ephesians,* (Zondervan, Michigan, 2016), p.105

Francis Foulkes wrote that it was "an expression of deep emotion or earnestness, and on that basis we must understand Paul's words here"[1]. John Stott called it "an exceptional degree of earnestness"[2].

Strong words were written by William Hendriksen, who put it like this: "Posture in prayer is never a matter of indifference. The slouching position of the body while one is supposed to be praying is an abomination to the Lord."[3] In this strong rebuke, can we not hear some truth about how we should be approaching prayer with a deep respect for the one to whom we are praying?

Hendriksen went on to qualify his words: "On the other hand, it is also true that Scripture nowhere prescribes one, and only one, correct posture. Different positions of head, arms, hands, knees, and of the body as a whole, are indicated. All of these are permissible as long as they symbolise different aspects of the worshipper's reverent attitude, and as long as they truly interpret the sentiments of his heart."[4]

Paul dropped to his knees, his spirit and heart charged with vision, passion and a deep sense of urgency. All this truth now had to be deeply inserted into the hearts and souls of those to whom he was writing. And it was only Father God in heaven who could make that happen.

Thought

When was the last time a truth from heaven gripped and transfixed you?

Prayer

Dear Lord, may my deep respect for you and your words grow some more today.

---

[1] Francis Foulkes, *Ephesians,* (IVP, Leicester, 1999), pp.108,109
[2] John Stott, *The Message of Ephesians,* (IVP, Leicester, 1979), p.132
[3] William Hendriksen, *Ephesians,* (Banner of Truth, Edinburgh, 1976), p.166
[4] Ibid.

DAY ONE HUNDRED AND FIFTY-THREE

Before the Father

Eph.3:14,15

...before the Father, from whom every family in heaven and on earth is named...

'Father' is the familiar name that Jesus used when he was addressing God and, thanks to his incredible work on the cross, all who trust him are now able to use the same name in their own prayers. According to Paul, the cultural and social barriers that divided Jews and Gentiles are now demolished. Their national identities do not matter anymore. They have become brothers and sisters, part of the same spiritual family, all sharing the same Father in heaven. The same goes for us today. Irrespective of culture or race, we who have trusted in Christ have been brought into the new family of God. 'Nationalism' is a word not found in heaven's dictionary.

In this text before us today, Paul uses a little wordplay on the two words *patēr* (father) and *patria* (family). The words sound similar in the Greek language. The word *patria* describes more properly "a group of families" all who claim a common *patēr* – "father"[1].

The first thing to think about here is that the whole concept of fatherhood is derived from God. Francis Foulkes wrote, "God is not only Father, but he is the one from whom alone all the fatherhood that there is derives its meaning and inspiration."[2] F.F. Bruce wrote:

That is to say, every species of fatherhood in the universe is derived from the original, archetypal Fatherhood of God: His is the only underived fatherhood. And the more nearly any fatherhood, natural or spiritual, approaches in character to God's perfect Fatherhood, the more truly does it manifest fatherhood as God intended it to be.[3]

---

[1] *Vincent's Word Studies,* e-sword.net
[2] Francis Foulkes, *Ephesians,* (IVP, Leicester, 1999), p.109
[3] F.F. Bruce, *The Epistle to the Ephesians,* (Pickering Paperbacks, Glasgow, 1983), p.67

The second thing to think about is that God names us, and he does it early. Isaiah the prophet said, 'The LORD called me from the womb, from the body of my mother he named my name.' (Is.49:1) Zechariah, the father of John the Baptist, was told by the angel, "Do not be afraid, Zechariah, for your prayer has been heard, and your wife Elizabeth will bear you a son, and you shall call his name John." (Lk.1:13) Mary, the mother of Jesus, was told by the same angel, "And behold, you will conceive in your womb and bear a son, and you shall call his name Jesus." (Lk.1:31) In all cases, God chose the name. You and I were known to him by our name before anyone else did. He chose also the family name, and often behind the naming is a prophetic purpose.

The third thing to consider is that in naming us, God is exerting his sovereignty over our lives. Mark Roberts put it quite powerfully when he wrote, "In the ancient world, the one who named something claimed authority over it. So if every grouping of created beings acquires its name from God the Father, then he is implicitly sovereign over all beings."[1] Before we belong to our parents, our family or our tribe, we belong firstly and foremostly to our Father in heaven. He is sovereign over the whole of our lives, and to him belongs our primary allegiance.

Thought

Our names were written in heaven before the foundation of the world. Yours and mine.

Prayer

Father, you have known me much longer than my parents and family. I feel safe with you.

---

[1] Mark D. Roberts, *Ephesians,* (Zondervan, Michigan, 2016), p.106

DAY ONE HUNDRED AND FIFTY-FOUR

Every Family

Eph.3:14,15

...before the Father, from whom every family in heaven and on earth is named...

T he Father is still naming every family because he is still creating them. The Greek tense is the present tense, indicating a continuous action.[1] It reads literally, "...from whom every family in heaven and on earth is being named..." God created the heavens and the earth, he created Adam and Eve, and he is still and always creating, personally involved every time. He was involved in your coming into being, he is involved now, and he will be involved in the whole of your life, not just during your earthly lifespan, but for eternity.

Before we move into the content of Paul's prayer, I also want to linger a little on this phrase "every family". It can also mean 'from whom the whole family'. In the Greek language it is *pāsa patria,* which, according to Bishop Westcott's commentary on the Greek text, means "every group of beings united by a common descent or origin"[2]. Francis Foulkes feels that the word *patria* strictly means 'lineage' or 'pedigree' (on the father's side) or more often a 'tribe' or even a 'nation'.[3]

At this point, it is important to insert an important qualifier. Kenneth Wuest correctly points out:

> *...we must be careful here to note that the fatherhood of God over all created intelligences is in the sense of Creator, as in Paul's word to the Athenians, "We are the offspring of God," not at all in the sense of salvation where only saved individuals are children of God.[4]*

[1] Harold Hoehner, *Ephesians: An Exegetical Commentary,* (Baker Academic, Michigan, 2002), p.474
[2] B. F. Westcott, *St Paul's Epistle to the Ephesians,* (Macmillan & Co, London, 1906), pp.50,51
[3] Francis Foulkes, *Ephesians,* (IVP, Leicester, 1999), p.109
[4] Kenneth Wuest, *Wuest's Word Studies,* Vol.1, 'Ephesians and Colossians', (Eerdmans, Michigan, 1953), p.87

The whole theme of the letter to the Ephesians is that God is gathering to himself, through and in Christ, a new family. The end time vision was seen by the aged apostle John on the island of Patmos. He wrote it down in these words:

> After this I looked, and behold, a great multitude that no one could number, from every nation, from all tribes and peoples and languages, standing before the throne and before the Lamb, clothed in white robes, with palm branches in their hands, and crying out with a loud voice, "Salvation belongs to our God who sits on the throne, and to the Lamb!"
>
> Revelation 7:9,10

All of creation originates from God. All of mankind can claim God as their Originator and Creator, but not as Father in the truly filial sense. In this new covenantal family, our second birth is from God. Entrance into this family is initiated by God the Father, through the death and resurrection of Christ, and enabled and facilitated by the Holy Spirit. Paul wrote to the believers in Rome, "The Spirit himself bears witness with our spirit that we are children of God..." (Rom.8:16)

This family of God is immense, without number, and spans time and eternity. It includes all the twice-born children of God, living and departed, and also angelic and heavenly beings. Mark Roberts wrote:

> The one who created all things seeks to unite all things in Christ. Everything in the cosmos, including all groupings of people and heavenly powers, comes from God, exists under his authority, and figures in his plan for the fulness of time.[1]

Thought

The sphere of this uniting is "in Christ" alone, and in no one, or nowhere, else.

Prayer

Father, your family is immense! Thank you for bringing me into it!

---

[1] Mark D. Roberts, *Ephesians,* (Zondervan, Michigan, 2016), p.106

DAY ONE HUNDRED AND FIFTY-FIVE

According to the Riches of His Glory

Eph.3:16

...that according to the riches of his glory he may grant you to be strengthened with power through his Spirit in your inner being...

Of this whole prayer section that we are going to explore over the next few days, A.T. Robertson wrote, "Nowhere does Paul sound such depths of spiritual emotion or rise to such heights of spiritual passion as here. The whole seems to be coloured with 'the riches of His glory.'"[1] John Stott referred to it as a staircase "with which he climbs higher and higher in his aspiration for his readers"[2]. Eugene Peterson wrote:

Paul's prayer for his congregation is nothing if not exuberant. There is nothing cautious or restrained in his prayer ... his prayers of intercession flow out of the plenitude of God. The plenitude of God, not the penury of the human condition, undergirds the intercession.[3]

He added:

Paul dives. He goes deep and explores the conditions that keep us afloat ... in his intercessions he dives, listens for and names what God is and is always doing beneath us – and as he comes up from the depths, he prays...[4]

We often hear the phrase, 'learn to live within, or according to, your means', and the conversation usually concerns the wise usage of limited resources. It is pretty good advice. So many have spent, to their dismay, beyond their means. Now imagine applying that comment to the

---

[1] *Robertson's Word Pictures,* e-sword.net
[2] John Stott, *The Message of Ephesians,* (IVP, Leicester, 1979), p.134
[3] Eugene Peterson, *Practise Resurrection,* (Hodder & Stoughton, London, 2010), pp. 157,158
[4] Ibid, p.158

Almighty. There is no measuring of God's means. His resources are limitless.

We have come across the word "riches" before in this letter. We have already thought about "the riches of his grace" (1:7); "the riches of his glorious inheritance in the saints" (1:18); "the immeasurable riches of his grace" (2:7) and "the unsearchable riches of Christ" (3:8).

The Greek word translated "riches" is *ploutos,* and it simply means 'wealth'. God's wealth has no bounds or constraints, and it is according to this immeasurable and unsearchable bounty that he provides for us. Our needs will never outweigh or drain God's riches. Further still, our needs could never contain the fulness of God's provisions, and so he gives out of his bounty with an awareness of what we can hold. It is out of the awareness of this bounty and an awareness of the spiritual capacity of the saints at Ephesus that Paul prays this prayer. It is very much in the same line of thought as when Jesus said to his disciples, "I still have many things to say to you, but you cannot bear them now." (Jn.16:12)

On this occasion, he links the word "riches" with the word "glory". Kenneth Wuest, quoting *Expositor's,* described this glory as "the glory is the whole revealed perfections of God, not merely His grace and power … those perfections of God which are revealed now in their glorious fulness and inexhaustible wealth"[1]. Paul also wrote to the believers in Philippi, "And my God will supply every need of yours according to his riches in glory in Christ Jesus." (Phil.4:19) It is not just what God has, but who he is in himself. His glory is revealed in his generous and gentle-with-us giving.

Thought

The immense capacity of God to provide is balanced with our limited capacity to receive.

Prayer

Dear Lord, please gently increase my capacity to receive and understand.

---

[1] Kenneth Wuest, *Wuest's Word Studies,* Vol.1, 'Ephesians and Colossians', (Eerdmans, Michigan, 1953), pp.87.88

DAY ONE HUNDRED AND FIFTY-SIX

Strengthened with Power

Eph.3:16

...that according to the riches of his glory he may grant you to be strengthened with power through his Spirit in your inner being...

Zydrunas Savickas holds the current 'tyre deadlift' record of 1,155 pounds. As for the heaviest absolute weight ever raised by a human being, the incredible amount of 6,270 pounds was raised off the ground by Paul Anderson in a "back lift"[1]. "Hold this for a moment," said the seven-foot, 18-stone, muscular weightlifter, handing over an enormous set of weights to the five-foot teenage girl stood next to him. She lasted less than three seconds.

Paul is starting to pray strong meat into these believers, but in order to be able to receive it, they must first be strengthened. Paul is in effect saying that he needed them to have the inner strength and capacity to receive and hold what he is praying into them. In verse 18, he will write about having the "strength to comprehend". We have to realise our natural inner inability to receive, hold and handle the things of God.

Paul starts to pray that, according to God's riches in glory, the Ephesian believers might be "strengthened". The Greek word he uses here is *krataiōthēnai,* and it is in the passive voice, which, according to Harold Hoehner, "reinforces the idea that it is God who gives the strength; it is not self-endowed"[2]. In other words, we are simply the recipients of this strength, not the manufacturers of it. We don't beef ourselves up to walk with God; we acknowledge our weakness in order to receive his strength.

The very first Beatitude is, "Blessed are the poor in spirit, for theirs is the kingdom of heaven." (Matt.5:3) The "poor in spirit" are those who have come to see that they have no inner strength. Jesus uses the word

---

[1]   Cited in the 1985 *Guinness Book of World Records,* (Sterling Publishing Co., Inc, New York, 1985)

[2]   Harold Hoehner, *Ephesians: An Exegetical Commentary,* (Baker Academic, Michigan, 2002), p.478

ptōchos, which describes an abject poverty and powerlessness. Concerning this Beatitude, William Barclay wrote, "It means the way to power lies through the realisation of weakness; the way to victory lies through the admission of defeat; the way to knowledge lies through the admission of ignorance."[1]

The classic Old Testament story of Gideon illustrates the truth of this text, and is found in Judges 7:1-8. The key thought there is that God does not need human strength to bring about his purposes. This truth is reflected in many passages in the Bible. In fact, seeking to help God out is mostly counterproductive.

The concept of becoming 'God's man or woman of power for the hour' seems to leave many high and dry. In God's economy, which is vastly different from ours, the way to power is through the acknowledgment of weakness. In fact, Paul boasted of his weaknesses. In response to a prayer for deliverance from a debilitating affliction, he records that the Lord said to him, "My grace is sufficient for you, for my power is made perfect in weakness." Paul then responded with the words, "Therefore I will boast all the more gladly of my weaknesses, so that the power of Christ may rest upon me." (2.Cor.12:9)

Thought

The recognition of our inabilities is the first step to being strengthened by God.

Prayer

Dear Lord, grant me a revelation of what I am not, and what I cannot do.

---

[1]   William Barclay, *The Plain Man Looks at the Beatitudes,* (Collins, London, 1963), p.20

DAY ONE HUNDRED AND FIFTY-SEVEN

The Inner Being

Eph.3:16

...strengthened with power through his Spirit in your inner being...

When I was a very young Christian, I remember coming across some words of Paul in his letter to the church in Galatia. He wrote, "I have been crucified with Christ. It is no longer I who live, but Christ who lives in me." (Gal.2:20) I felt presented with a dilemma. If I had 'died', and Christ was alive in me, then where was I? The second half of the verse shed a little light: "And the life I now live in the flesh I live by faith in the Son of God, who loved me and gave himself for me." So, I was obviously still alive, but life as I knew it was going to become incredibly different. I must confess that I still felt a little confused as to the dynamics of this walk with Christ living within me. We both inhabited this body, but how did that work? It was when I spent two years on a mission team in the South of France with Operation Mobilisation that I came across the writings of Watchman Nee, a Chinese pastor. Nee fully saw and understood the workings and dynamics of the inner life and, to be honest, much benefit can be derived from working slowly through his *magnum opus* (his greatest work), his three-volumed book *The Spiritual Man*[1]. He wrote another much smaller but equally powerful book called *Release of the Spirit* and, as I worked my way through it, a spiritual light suddenly switched on. I quickly saw exactly who I was and what the Holy Spirit was up to in me.

In it he wrote:

> *When God comes to indwell us, by His Spirit, life and power,*
> *He comes into our spirit which we are calling the inward man.*
> *Outside this inward man is the soul wherein functions our*
> *thoughts, emotions and will. The outermost man is our*
> *physical body. Thus we will speak of the inward man as the*

---

[1]   Watchman Nee, *The Spiritual Man,* (Christian Fellowship Publishers, New York, 1977)

79

spirit, the outer man as the soul and the outermost man as the body. We must never forget that our inward man is the human spirit where God dwells, where His Spirit mingles with our spirit. Just as we are dressed in clothes, so our inward man 'wears' an outward man: the spirit 'wears' the soul. And similarly the spirit and the soul 'wear' the body.[1]

I learned that I am a living soul, living in a body, having a human spirit.

Over the next few days, I want us to spend time looking at what our 'inner being' is all about. We need to see for ourselves, understand deeply and firmly grasp just how God is at work in us by his Spirit.

Before our conversion we were operating with only two faculties: body and soul. Our spirit was quite dead. Our soul was therefore influenced and shaped from what was going on outside of us. What we saw and heard, experienced and felt, formed us into who and what we became. At our conversion, however, we were 'born again' by the regenerating work of the Holy Spirit. Our dead spirit was resurrected by the Holy Spirit. Something deep within us came alive. Our spirit was 'mingled' and brought into union with the Holy Spirit. And at this point, there came from within another influence upon our souls. This stimulus, this other life – this eternal life – began to empower, envision, challenge and cleanse us. And as we progressed in this walk, we began to realise that the purpose of the indwelling Spirit was to change us to becoming Christ-like in all things – a process that would take a lifetime to bring about.

Thought

Let the shaping of our soul come from within, not from without.

Prayer

Lord, grant me to understand how and what you are doing in me.

---

[1] Watchman Nee, *The Release of the Spirit,* (New Wine Press, Chichester, 2007), p.15

DAY ONE HUNDRED AND FIFTY-EIGHT

The Trinity of Man

1.Thess.5:23

Now may the God of peace himself sanctify you completely, and may your whole spirit and soul and body be kept blameless at the coming of our Lord Jesus Christ.

God is a trinity, and so are we. We are, as the theologians say, tripartite in nature. We are body, soul and spirit. Our text for today inserts the word 'and' between these three totally different dimensions of our humanity. That there is a difference between our soul and our spirit is demonstrated in the letter to the Hebrews, where the unknown writer speaks about the cutting edge of God's word. He writes, "For the word of God is living and active, sharper than any two-edged sword, piercing to the division of soul and of spirit, of joints and of marrow, and discerning the thoughts and intentions of the heart." (Heb.4:12) There he speaks of the division of soul and spirit.

The phrase that the writer used was *achri merismou*. It was an old word derived from *merizō*. Vine says that *merizō* is akin to *meros,* which means "a part, to part, to partition, to divide into"[1]. Thayer says that it means primarily "to separate into parts, to cut into pieces". It carries the sense of both being divided and apportioned into parts. I liken it to a surgeon's scalpel dissecting the 'inner being' and laying the different dimensions on a spiritual table saying, "This is the soul and this is the spirit." Although together they make up 'the inner being', they are separate in their functionality.

I have a physical body. Job described human bodies as "houses of clay, whose foundation is in the dust" (Job 4:19). Describing himself, he said, "I too was pinched off from a piece of clay." (Job 33:6) In the New Testament, Peter used these words: "I think it right, as long as I am in this body, to stir you up by way of reminder, since I know that the putting off of my body will be soon, as our Lord Jesus Christ made clear to me." (2.Pet.1:13,14) Note carefully his words "in the body" and "the putting

---

[1] W.E. Vine, *Vine's Expository Dictionary of Biblical Words,* (Thomas Nelson, New York, 1985), p.178

off of my body". My human body is simply the temporary 'house' or 'tent' that I live in. When my body stops working, I move on and into my new physical, indestructible and perfect resurrection body.

I am a living soul. I have a physical and corporate body, but I am a living and incorporeal soul. When God created Adam, it is written, "The LORD God formed the man of dust from the ground and breathed into his nostrils the breath of life, and the man became a living creature." (Gen.2:7) The Hebrew word translated "creature" in the ESV is *nephesh*, rightly translated 'soul'. My soul is who I am, and is basically made up of my mind, my emotions and my will. Therein I find my thoughts, my feelings and my choices. Here resides my personality and my character, my preferences and desires.

I have a spirit. It is that God-given faculty, deeply within my soul that is touched by the Spirit and also touches the Spirit. Here, I sense and hear God.

To sum up, the soul, through the body, is conscious of the physical world. The soul, in itself, is conscious of itself. The soul, through the spirit, is conscious of God. Put another way, the soul is who I am, the body is the house I live in, and the spirit is that faculty by which I see, hear and know God. My body is temporal, my soul is shapeable and my spirit is eternal.

Thought

A primary step in spiritual growth is to know who we are.

Prayer

Dear Lord, may I this day be filled with wonder in how you have knit me together.

DAY ONE HUNDRED AND FIFTY-NINE

The Inner War

Rom.7:24

Wretched man that I am! Who will deliver me from this body of death?

They often say that becoming a Christian is the beginning of the conflicts. Spiritually, there is a warzone around us, and there is one also within us. A young Christian came to an older, mature Christian and said to him, "I find within me both a wolf and a lamb, and there is constant struggle, and I'm afraid the wolf will win. What should I do?" The answer came, "Feed the one and starve the other."

As we embark and continue on our walk with Christ, we will quickly find that we are often in areas of conflict within ourselves. As the life and ways of the Spirit advance within us, he meets areas of resistance. Our old life, our old attitudes, our old ways of thinking and doing things are deeply entrenched within us, and at times they manifest in thoughts, actions and reactions that give resistance to the advancing of the new life now within us.

Paul wrote to the believers in the Galatian church:

> *But I say, walk by the Spirit, and you will not gratify the desires of the flesh. For the desires of the flesh are against the Spirit, and the desires of the Spirit are against the flesh, for these are opposed to each other, to keep you from doing the things you want to do.*

> Galatians 5:16,17

There are two strong words that he uses in this particular passage. The first is "against", and the second is "opposed". The first word Paul uses is *kata,* which, according to Kenneth Wuest, has the root meaning of "down" and which "thus has the idea of suppression"[1]. The second

---

[1] Kenneth Wuest, *Wuest's Word Studies,* Vol.1, 'Galatians', (Eerdmans, Michigan, 1953), p.154

word is *antikeimai,* and carries the meaning of being "lined up in conflict, face to face, a spiritual duel"[1].

What we have here is a determined and entrenched position that is set in a stubborn resistance. Kenneth Wuest's translation puts it like this:

> *But I say, through the instrumentality of the Spirit, habitually order your manner of life, and you will in no wise execute the passionate desire of the evil nature, for the evil nature constantly has a strong desire to suppress the Spirit, and the Spirit constantly has a strong desire to suppress the evil nature. And these are entrenched in an attitude of mutual opposition.[2]*

Notice the word "entrenchment". Within us we still find pockets of resistance – "I've always done it this way"; pockets of stubbornness – "I'll do it my way"; and pockets of rebellion – "Nobody tells me what to do".

I have some classic books in my library written by A.W. Tozer. Especially stirring is his book entitled *The Divine Conquest.* The theme of the book is that the Holy Spirit wants to take over! In it he writes, "Salvation is from our side a choice, from the divine side it is a seizing upon, an apprehending, a conquest by the Most High God."[3] In another place he writes, "The experiences of men who walked with God in olden times agree to teach that the Lord cannot fully bless a man until he has first conquered him."[4] In order to accommodate this 'gracious to us yet ruthless towards sin' invasion, we must forever capitulate and surrender each area of resistance. Beautiful is a fully yielded soul.

Thought

Allow the Holy Spirit to reveal the pockets of resistance in you and then surrender each one.

Prayer

Dear Holy Spirit, please find in me in both the act and the attitude of full surrender.

---

[1] *Robertson's Word Pictures,* e-sword.net
[2] Kenneth Wuest, *The New Testament, An Expanded Translation,* (Eerdmans, Michigan, 2004), pp.446,447
[3] A.W. Tozer, *The Divine Conquest,* (Oliphants, London, 1965), p.49
[4] Ibid, p.53

DAY ONE HUNDRED AND SIXTY

The Final Separation

2.Cor.4:16

...so we do not lose heart. Though our outer self is wasting away, our inner self is being renewed day by day.

So wrote Paul to a group of Christians in Corinth who were suffering all kinds of trial and hardship. They were being worn down by what life was throwing at them, especially in the areas of persecution from both the unbelieving Jewish and Greek communities and also the Roman authorities.

Here, Paul was saying that in the divine economy of things, although the outer self – the physical body – is being subject to damage, decay and even death, something vastly different is happening in the inner self. It is being renewed. Paul was making a distinction between the outer and the inner life. Dr Martyn Lloyd-Jones wrote, "The inner man is the opposite of the body and all its faculties and functions. It is this other man that is apart from them, the innermost part of our being, the spiritual part of our being."[1]

To understand this distinction is, in the words of Lloyd-Jones, "one of the profoundest discoveries that we can ever make in our Christian experience"[2]. I am not my body but I do live in my body, which, incidentally, is quite temporary! According to this text in 2 Corinthians, my body is wasting away but my innermost being – the truest me – is being renewed! Eventually, there will come a separating of the two. Death then, in biblical terms, is the separating of the body from the soul – the outer shell from the inner life residing within.

This came vividly to me one day as I was driving to visit a man who was suffering painfully with cancer. His wife had called me to come over and speak with him. Normally the perfect gentleman, he was beginning

---

[1] Martyn Lloyd-Jones, *The Unsearchable Riches of Christ,* (Banner of Truth, Edinburgh, 1979), p.127

[2] Ibid.

to become quite irritable with those around him who were seeking to look after him. When I entered, she excused herself to the kitchen, where she deliberately took her time in making a cup of tea, giving us time for some private conversation together. As we spoke, I asked him two questions. The first was, "How are you doing physically?" to which he responded, "I am in terrible pain and it is getting worse." I then asked him the second question, "How are you doing spiritually?" to which he replied, with shining eyes, "I have never felt so close to Jesus." I then gently said to him, "My dear friend, your soul is separating from your body. In the same way that you have fought this cancer with faith and courage, I believe you now need to face the Lord himself – he's taking you home." His wife rang me the very next day to say that he had died peacefully in the Lord in the early hours of the morning.

I was quite shocked by her phone call. It had happened so quickly. My friend had turned his eyes from the fight, and had looked at Jesus. The fight of faith now turned into the fruit of faith. It was as if the Lord had said to him, "Lay down your sword and shield, and come now with me. The fight is over. Enter into your rest, my good and faithful servant."

Paul, writing to the Corinthians, said:

> For we know that if the tent that is our earthly home is destroyed, we have a building from God, a house not made with hands, eternal in the heavens. For in this tent we groan, longing to put on our heavenly dwelling...
>
> 2 Corinthians 5:1,2

Death, then, is the final separation here on the earth of the inner self from the outer self. The good news is that there will be a new house to live in – an eternal one, never to waste away.

Thought

Death is not a destination but a doorway. For the believer, we know what is coming.

Prayer

Dear Lord, help me to fix my eyes on what you are doing within me.

DAY ONE HUNDRED AND SIXTY-ONE

Through His Spirit

Eph.3:16

...that according to the riches of his glory he may grant you to be strengthened with power through his Spirit in your inner being...

Everything that God does in us is by the Holy Spirit, and it is in this deepest part of us that the Holy Spirit does his work. If the sphere of operations is in the human soul, then the one at work is the Holy Spirit. The anointing of power is not in the realms of the physical (although there may be physical reactions), but in the realms of the inner and invisible life.

The Scriptures are replete with examples of ordinary men and women who were anointed, overwhelmed and transported by the Holy Spirit into extraordinary realms of ability and power. Of Gideon it was written, "...the Spirit of the LORD clothed Gideon..." (Judg.6:34) The Hebrew word is *lâbash,* and means 'to wrap around'. The Keil and Delitzsch commentary says that the Spirit "descended upon him, and laid [himself] around him as it were like a coat of mail, or a strong [piece of] equipment, so that he [Gideon] became invulnerable and invincible in [the Spirit's] might"[1]. Of both Samson and David it is written, "Then the Spirit of the LORD rushed upon him..." (Judg.14:6,19; 15:14; 2.Sam.16:13) The Hebrew word used is *tsâlach,* and it mean 'rushed into' or 'penetrated powerfully'. There were many more, and each time their human abilities were almost not considered at all. Everything was done in such a way that it was seen to be God himself at work.

All these were 'outer' manifestations of the Spirit's power, although there were exceptions. David wrote concerning God, "...on the day I called Thou didst answer me; Thou didst make me bold with strength in my soul." (Ps.138:3, NASB)

In the New Testament there is also evidence of the power of the Spirit enabling men and women to do extraordinary things in the name of the

---

[1] Keil and Delitzsch, *Commentary on the Old Testament,* e-sword.net

Lord. Here, it is much more an inner work of the Spirit. I am so fond of Paul's testimony:

> *And I, when I came to you, brothers, did not come proclaiming to you the testimony of God with lofty speech or wisdom. For I decided to know nothing among you except Jesus Christ and him crucified. And I was with you in weakness and in fear and much trembling, and my speech and my message were not in plausible words of wisdom, but in demonstration of the Spirit and of power, that your faith might not rest in the wisdom of men but in the power of God.*
>
> 1 Corinthians 2:1-5

Professor Gordon Fee wrote what for many theologians is the most outstanding and comprehensive book on the working of the Holy Spirit in the New Testament. It is called *God's Empowering Presence.* Commenting on our verse for today he writes:

> *This passage shows that for Paul the "power of the Spirit" is not only for more visible and extraordinary manifestations of God's presence, but also (especially) for the empowering necessary to be his people in the world, so as to be true reflections of his own glory.*[1]

Inner strength is vastly different from outer strength. J.B. Phillips translated our text for today as, "...the strength of the Spirit's inner re-inforcement..."

Thought

The power and strength of God is an inner issue. We rise up from within.

Prayer

Dear Holy Spirit, strengthen me today for whatever you have in store for me.

---

[1] Gordon Fee, *God's Empowering Presence,* (Baker Academic, Michigan, 1994), p.695

DAY ONE HUNDRED AND SIXTY-TWO

The Indwelling Christ

Eph.3:17

...so that Christ may dwell in your hearts through faith...

The believers to whom Paul wrote this letter were having a rough time. Describing the atmosphere around and within the church, Clinton Arnold writes:

There is a hint of ongoing tensions between Jews and Gentiles in the church. Paul has a continuing pastoral concern about helping Christians converted from a background of magical practices and allegiance to other deities become deeply rooted in the relationship to Christ and his power.[1]

However, God did not move them out of those situations; he was going to minister to them within those situations. God does not often change our circumstances; he strengthens us instead by empowering our inner stances. This way we learn steadfastness.

Kenneth Wuest cited Dr Max Reich, who made this statement: "If we make room for the Holy Spirit, He will make room for the Lord Jesus."[2] Wuest then wrote:

...that is, if the saint lives in conscious dependence upon and yieldedness to the Holy Spirit, the Holy Spirit will make room for the Lord Jesus in the heart and life of the saint by eliminating from his life things that are sinful and of the world, and thus enable the saint to make the Lord Jesus feel completely at home in his heart.[3]

The word "dwell" is *katoikēsai,* which means 'to settle down and be at home'. Our life is not to be marked by occasional visitations by the Lord but by his abiding presence within us. 'Encounters' and 'visitations' are temporary words, whereas 'dwelling' is far more permanent. Vivid

---

[1]   Clinton E. Arnold, *Ephesians,* (Zondervan, Michigan, 2010), p.21
[2]   Kenneth Wuest, *Wuest's Word Studies,* Vol.1, 'Ephesians and Colossians', (Eerdmans, Michigan, 1953), p.88
[3]   Ibid.

encounters invariably bring breakthroughs, fresh revelations and steps forward, and these are to be desired. But life is not lived on the mountaintop experiences; life is lived in the valleys of everyday life. Someone has wisely said, "More fruit grow in the valleys than on the mountaintops." We must guard against becoming spiritual adrenalin junkies. The local church must also guard against fostering these existential desires, teaching people how to live seven days a week, nurturing the deep realisation of the living Christ within them at all times.

He may dwell within our hearts, but is he 'at home' there? Do we make him feel comfortable with the things we think, the things we say and the things we do? Further to that, would he be comfortable with the places we go to, the things we watch and listen to? Would Jesus feel comfortable living with us? He does not dwell in church buildings but in our hearts.

Other powerful scriptures are found in John's Gospel. In a conversation with the disciples, Jesus said, "Whoever has my commandments and keeps them, he it is who loves me. And he who loves me will be loved by my Father, and I will love him and manifest myself to him." (Jn.14:21) He further unpacked it by saying, "If anyone loves me, he will keep my word, and my Father will love him, and we will come to him and make our home with him." (Jn.14:23) Of this phrase "make our home" Albert Barnes wrote:

> *This is a figurative expression implying that God and Christ would manifest themselves in no temporary way, but that it would be the privilege of Christians to enjoy their presence continually. They would take up their residence in the heart as their dwelling-place, as a temple fit for their abode.*[1]

Thought

By the Spirit, the eternal Godhead has taken up residence in your heart.

Prayer

Father, Son and Holy Spirit, may my heart welcome you, becoming your permanent home.

---

[1] Albert Barnes, *Notes on the Bible,* e-sword.net

DAY ONE HUNDRED AND SIXTY-THREE

The Holy Abode

Eph.3:17

...so that Christ may dwell in your hearts through faith...

I am not sure that we are fully aware that Christ and the Father, by the Holy Spirit, dwell within us. Somehow, we still think of the Holy Three as being out there somewhere. We seek their presence and we speak to them as if they were up there in heaven. They are, but they are also with us – within us. We could say, with our hands on our heart, with Jacob of old, "Surely the LORD is in this place and I did not know it." (Gen.28:17)

The whole desire of God has always been to dwell with us. Through the work of Christ, our hearts have been cleansed and purified to become a holy temple. To the Corinthian church Paul would write, "Do you [plural] not know that you are God's temple and that God's Spirit dwells in you? If anyone destroys God's temple, God will destroy him. For God's temple is holy, and you [plural] are that temple." (1.Cor.3:16,17) Paul is speaking here in plural language – the two occurrences of "you" are second person plural pronouns, and therefore Paul is speaking of the community of the church. Later in the same letter, however, he uses the singular form in saying, "Or do you [singular] not know that your body is a temple of the Holy Spirit within you, whom you have from God?" (1.Cor.16:9) In both cases he uses the Greek word *eidō,* translated "know". As we have already noted elsewhere, this is a revelatory word, meaning 'to see'.

We must move from the learning of this and the understanding of it to the seeing of it for ourselves. We must 'see' that Christ dwells in our heart. We must ask God for what I would call 'eidetic moments' of revelation. Let me share with you something I have learned from over fifty years of reading the Scriptures. When our disciplined, consistent and attentive reading of the Bible moves into a musing and a meditating on what we are reading, we create the environment for these 'eidetic moments' – these spiritual flashes of insight and enlightenment. I firmly believe that we all grow by what is revealed to us.

Harold Hoehner wrote:

The strengthening of the inner person results in the deep indwelling of Christ by the means of faith ... that Christ may be at home in, that is, at the very centre of or deeply rooted in believers' lives. Christ must be the controlling factor in attitudes and conduct.[1]

All this is in the realm of faith, not feelings. The writer to the Hebrews put it this way: "Faith is the assurance of things hoped for, the conviction of things not seen." (Heb.11:1) Paul also wrote to the Corinthians, "...for we walk by faith, not by sight." (2.Cor.5:7) Vincent describes true faith like this: "Faith apprehends as a real fact what is not revealed to the senses. It rests on that fact, acts upon it, and is upheld by it in the face of all that seems to contradict it. Faith is real seeing."[2] Faith is seeing the invisible and then living in the reality of it.

We must learn to say to ourselves, "I may not feel him dwelling within but I do believe it, and I will walk through each day trusting he is both with me and within me. I thank Jesus for the encounters and visitations, but I thank him more for his abiding presence."

Thought

See your heart as a holy temple wherein the Lord dwells, and learn to live accordingly.

Prayer

Lord, help me to see you there, in my heart, ruling and directing my paths.

---

[1] Harold Hoehner, *Ephesians: An Exegetical Commentary,* (Baker Academic, Michigan, 2002), p.481

[2] *Vincent's Word Studies,* e-sword.net

DAY ONE HUNDRED AND SIXTY-FOUR

Rooted and Grounded in Love

Eph.3:17

...rooted and grounded in love...

Paul loved metaphors. So did Eugene Peterson. Cathleen Falsani, an award-winning religious journalist, interviewed Peterson at a conference in New York in 2012. In response to a question about Paul's writings, he responded, "I love translating Paul. He has these wild metaphors and his syntax gets all tangled up sometimes. ... He's a very poetic writer."[1]

In his book *Eat This Book – a conversation in the art of spiritual reading*, he wrote :

> *A metaphor is a word that bears a meaning beyond its naming function; the 'beyond' extends and brightens our compre-hension rather than confusing it ... Metaphor does not explain; it does not define; it draws us away from being outsiders into being insiders, involved with all reality spoken into being by God's word ... Metaphor sends out tentacles of connectedness.*[2]

A metaphor, then, is a linguistic 'door' that captures our imagination and draws us into a larger story and deeper truth.

And so, Paul is piling up metaphors yet again – "dwelling", "rooted", "grounded". Paul is writing here that the saints are to be "rooted and grounded in love". Adam Clarke wrote, "Here is a double metaphor; one taken from agriculture, the other, from architecture."[3]

Paul uses two Greek words. The first word, *errizōmenoi,* according to Albert Barnes, describes "a tree whose roots strike deep, and extend afar"[4]. Kenneth Wuest wrote that the word has the idea of being

---

[1] *https://sojo.net/articles/lost-translation-eugene-peterson-and-his-message*
[2] Eugene Peterson, *Eat This Book,* (Hodder & Stoughton, London, 2006), pp.96,97
[3] Adam Clark, *Commentary on the Bible,* e-sword.net
[4] Albert Barnes, *Notes on the Bible,* e-sword.net

"securely settled"[1]. The second word that he uses is *tethemeliōmenoi*. Again, Albert Barnes wrote that it describes "a building ... on a foundation. The word is taken from architecture, where a firm foundation is laid, and the meaning is, that he wished them to be as firm in the love of Christ, as a building is that rests on a solid basis."[2] Wuest wrote that the word speaks of that which is "deeply founded"[3].

John Stott captured this beautifully when he wrote:

> *Paul likens them to a well-rooted tree, and then to a well-built house. In both cases the unseen cause of their stability will be the same: love. Love is to be the soil in which their life is to be rooted; love is to be the foundation on which their life is built.*[4]

Deeply rooted trees and houses with strong subterranean foundations cannot be dislodged by the winds and storms of life. It is the same story with those whose lives are deeply rooted and grounded in love. Paul wrote to the Corinthians, "Love is patient ... endures all things." The Message puts it this way: "Love never gives up ... keeps going to the end." (1.Cor.13:4,7) Love has an enduring quality about it.

Thought

Our roots feed from whatever is in our hearts, manifesting in our attitudes, words and deeds.

Prayer

Lord, may your love conquer and put to death every other thing residing in my heart.

---

[1] Kenneth Wuest, *Wuest's Word Studies,* Vol.1, 'Ephesians and Colossians', (Eerdmans, Michigan, 1953), p.89

[2] Albert Barnes, *Notes on the Bible,* e-sword.net

[3] Kenneth Wuest, *Wuest's Word Studies,* Vol.1, 'Ephesians and Colossians', (Eerdmans, Michigan, 1953), p.89

[4] John Stott, *The Message of Ephesians,* (IVP, Leicester, 1979), p.136

DAY ONE HUNDRED AND SIXTY-FIVE

Living In and From Love

Eph.3:17

...rooted and grounded in love...

D r Martyn Lloyd-Jones wrote, "Love should be the pre-dominating and prevailing element in our lives and conduct and experience."[1] How does this work? Firstly, this love is a received love. The apostle John provides the key. He wrote, "We love because he first loved us." (1.Jn.4:19) Our love for him is a reciprocal response to his love for us, and not the other way around. Secondly, this love is supernatural in its source and of a far higher quality than any other human love. We simply do not have it in ourselves to love with this love. Granted that history has shown examples of self-sacrificial love being shown, especially on the battlefields, but this is speaking of a divine norm that heaven wants to set into our hearts.

What we have been used to, and grown up with, can colour, twist and distort, and even prevent the new. Previous experiences of ungodly love can disable people from receiving this pure and powerful love of the Father. A number have been starved of parental love, or savaged by sexual lust, and thus deprived of having and holding deep friendships. They live alone in their hearts, imprisoned by the fear of any love, and when this gentle love of God touches them, they inwardly freeze, unable to believe that God could or would love them.

John, the apostle who probably understood the love of the Father more than most, wrote, "So we have come to know and to believe the love that God has for us." (1.Jn.4:16) It is one thing to know; it is entirely another thing to believe what we know. For John's hearers, the learning of the love of God had progressed into the believing of it, and it had affected the way they lived.

Paul felt that this deeply sacrificial, and indeed sacred, love of Christ needed to both touch them and overwhelm them, becoming deeply rooted into their lives. His love needed to be believed, received and

---

[1]   Martyn Lloyd-Jones, *The Unsearchable Riches of Christ,* (Banner of Truth, Edinburgh, 1979), p.182

understood, not merely mentally, but deeply spiritually – into every nook and cranny of their hearts. Roots are so important. The basic principle of spiritual life is that the putting down of roots precedes the emergence of fruits. This love of God must be allowed to take deep root into our hearts.

The love of God heals our wounded soul. It gently breaks through all the defensive resistances that we, in our distrust and cynicism, muster against it. It pursues us into the shadows of our hiding places, wanting only to cleanse and restore us and then lead us out into the beautiful daylight of trusting and receiving this love and even being able to share it without fear with others.

These new believers in Ephesus had to learn to trust God's astonishing love, allowing it to plunge deeply into their hearts, invading and pervading the core of their inner beings. This deep love then would eventually but surely emerge, becoming both the motivating and inspirational force of their growth and practice as individuals and communities. This love would then start to touch, invade and pervade the world they lived in. Love was going to become the bottom line of everything they said and did. It would become their calling card, expressing the heart of heaven.

Thought

Can you truly believe and deeply receive the Father's love today?

Prayer

Lord, please open my eyes to begin to understand how deep and strong your love for me is.

DAY ONE HUNDRED AND SIXTY-SIX

Strength to Comprehend

Eph.3:18,19

...may have strength to comprehend with all the saints what is the breadth and length and height and depth, and to know the love of Christ that surpasses knowledge...

There is a story told of a man suffering with an acute mental illness, who was living in an isolated room within a hospital. When he eventually died, the staff came to prepare his room for the next patient, and they found these words etched on the wall:

Could we with ink the ocean fill, and were the skies of parchment made – were every stalk on earth a quill, and every man a scribe by trade; to write the love of God above, would drain the ocean dry; nor can the scroll contain the whole, though stretched from sky to sky.

These verses had originally been written in 1050AD by a Jewish poet called Meir Ben Isaac Nehorai,[1] and it is quite possible that the man in his islolation had memorised them and written them in the middle of his darkness.

Paul writes to the church in Ephesus that he is praying that they might have "strength to comprehend" this love. It is truly a love that both defies and surpasses knowledge, and yet he is praying that they might be enabled by the Holy Spirit to comprehend the incomprehensible. The word "comprehend" is taken from the Greek word *katalabesthai,* which means 'to lay hold of so as to make one's own, to seize upon, to take possession of'. It has a sense of urgent purpose about it. It is from the same verb – *katalambanō* – that Paul used to describe how Jesus had arrested and wrestled him to the ground outside the Damascus Gate.

Of ourselves, we would never have the capacity to grasp and make our own this love from heaven. It is like a mighty ocean with which we are seeking to fill our thimble-like hearts. It is astonishing and immense

---

[1] *https://www.ministrymagazine.org/archive/1950/09/the-story-of-the-love-of-god*

and it silences us as we are overwhelmed by it. Some great Christians have talked of a personal baptism – an inundation of love that swept them away.

Its breadth speaks of its extent, which is universal, inclusive and encompassing all who believe. Its length speaks of its duration, which is everlasting, without beginning, pause or end. Its height speaks of its transcendence, which is lofty, sublime, infinite, and not subject to limitations. Its depth speaks of its condescension that reaches right down to where they are, chasing them out of their hiding places, and lifting them up.

How then can we possibly and adequately measure the love of Christ? It is worth reading the words of the old hymn by Mary Shekleton, who was for many years an invalid. The first verse reads, "It passes knowledge, that dear love of thine, my Saviour Jesus; yet this soul of mine would of thy love, in all its breadth and length, its height and depth and everlasting strength, know more and more."[1] The unknowable can become knowable in the realms of the Spirit. Paul wrote to the believers in Rome that "God's love has been poured into our hearts through the Holy Spirit who has been given to us" (Rom.5:5). It is possible to live in this vast ocean of love, letting it make up the ground and foundation for all true Christian speaking and activity. He wrote to the Corinthians, "Let all that you do be done in love." (1.Cor.16:14) Let the love of God – Father, Son and Holy Spirit – inflame our hearts.

Thought

If what we say and sing, respond and do, does not spring from love then it is futile.

Prayer

Dear Holy Spirit, may your divine love inflame my heart, and may others feel the heat.

---

[1] Mary Shekleton, 'It passeth knowledge', *Mission Praise,* (Collins, 2009), no.349

DAY ONE HUNDRED AND SIXTY-SEVEN

The Fulness of God

Eph.3:19 (NASB)

...that you may be filled up to all the fullness of God.

C an I remind you of the words of John Stott, who wrote that this prayer of Paul's was to be likened to a staircase "with which he climbs higher and higher in his aspiration for his readers"[1]. It seems now that we are at the top of the staircase. This part of the prayer is simply astonishing!

But first we need to unpack what it means. It seems to me that the NASB (quoted above) has the best translation of the text. It all hinges around the Greek preposition *eis* which "indicates movement towards a goal"[2]. It is, therefore, not filled with the fulness of God but filled up to the fulness of God. Harold Hoehner wrote, "This implies that believers will never be filled as God is filled but should move towards that goal."[3] As William Hendriksen wrote, "To be sure, believers would never be filled with the fulness of God in the sense that they would become God."[4] The finite could never contain the infinite. Could a cup contain the whole of the ocean? He is not, and cannot be, limited to our capacity.

This then become a goal, an aspiration. John Stott wrote:

> *God's fulness or perfection becomes the standard or level up to which we pray to be filled. The aspiration is the same in principle as that implied by the commands to be holy as God is holy, and to be perfect as our heavenly Father is perfect.*[5]

The sphere, and the only sphere for all this, is 'in Christ'. Paul wrote to the believers in Colossae that "...in him [Christ] all the fullness of God was pleased to dwell..." (Col.1:29) He also wrote in the same letter,

---

[1]   John Stott, *The Message of Ephesians,* (IVP, Leicester, 1979), 'Day Thirty-Three', p.134

[2]   Harold Hoehner, *Ephesians: An Exegetical Commentary,* (Baker Academic, Michigan, 2002), p.490

[3]   Ibid.

[4]   William Hendriksen, *Ephesians,* (Banner of Truth, Edinburgh, 1976), p.174

[5]   John Stott, *The Message of Ephesians,* (IVP, Leicester, 1979), p.138

"...in him [Christ] the whole fullness of deity dwells bodily..." (Col.2:9) Clinton Arnold writes, "Only by virtue of their union with Christ do believers share in the fullness..."[1]

Here is the paradox: he resides in me and I am growing in him. I have him, and I shall have more of him, and he is inexhaustible. We have been filled, are being filled, and shall be filled, yet without arriving. We shall always be finite creatures and he will always be the infinite Creator.

There is a sense where this "fullness" is both the believers being filled to their finite capacity with God himself, alongside the potential of the growth of that finite capacity. Our goal is the inner 'housing' of God by the Spirit, and also the development and growth of that inner 'house' as it learns more and more, is inhabited more and more, and is transformed more and more into his likeness. The process has been started and it will be continued throughout eternity in heaven.

What shall we make of this? He who dwells within us is greater than we are. And this is only the beginning. I'm not sure that we are fully aware of who he is who dwells within. How is all of this possible? How can the temple of my feeble heart be home to the eternal one? We can only bow in wonder.

Thought

God is far greater than our capacity to have him dwelling in our hearts.

Prayer

Dear God, my heart aches with wonder, and lies exhausted by such knowledge.

---

[1]   Clinton E. Arnold, *Ephesians,* (Zondervan, Michigan, 2010), p.218

DAY ONE HUNDRED AND SIXTY-EIGHT

Far More Abundantly

Eph.3:20

Now to him who is able to do far more abundantly than all that we ask or think...

God dwelling within our finite inner being, and us dwelling and growing within the infinite God. Yesterday we asked, how is all of this possible? Maybe that's why Paul wrote these next lines. Paul has asked a lot from God. It is probably one of the biggest prayers in the whole of the New Testament.

Grappling, then, with the enormity of his request, Paul then bursts into what is called a doxology. The careful reader of scripture will find them scattered throughout his writings. A doxology is simply 'an outburst of praise'. Paul would write something utterly profound, then get quite overwhelmed by what he had written, and then he would erupt into praise and worship. This is, in fact, what good theology is designed to do. In 1993, J.I. Packer wrote:

> *The older I get, the more I want to sing my faith and get others singing it with me. Theology, as I constantly tell my students, is for doxology: the first thing to do with it is to turn it into praise and thus honour the God who is its subject, the God in whose presence and by whose help it was worked out.*[1]

T.C. Robinson, in his New Leaven blog on Jim Packer, wrote, "Theology that does not lead to doxology and devotion is nothing but bad theology. The theologian has missed the mark."[2]

Paul has asked a lot, but he now writes that God can grant a lot more than that. Here, the reasoning is accumulative. William Hendriksen wrote:

> *In order to appreciate fully what is implied in these words it should be noted that Paul's reasoning has taken the following*

---

[1]   J.I. Packer, *God has Spoken,* (Hodder & Stoughton, London, 2016), p.7

[2]   *https://nleaven.wordpress.com/2012/07/04/j-i-packer-on-the-goal-of-theology*

steps: a. God is able to do all that we ask Him to; b. He is even able to do all that we dare not ask, but merely imagine; c. He can do even more than this; far more; very far more.[1]

The NASB translation of our text is, "Now to Him who is able to do exceedingly abundantly beyond all that we ask or think..." Let's pick up this phrase "exceedingly abundantly". In the Greek language, it is the compound word *huperekperissou,* which can be translated "the highest form of comparison imaginable"[2]. It is only used by Paul twice more in his first letter to the Thessalonians. (1.Thess.3:10; 5:13) Kenneth Wuest wrote:

> *The compound word is a superlative of superlatives in force. It speaks of the ability of God to do something, that ability having more than enough potential power, this power exhaustless, and then some on top of that. Thus, Paul says that God is able to do super-abundantly above and beyond what we ask or think, and then some on top of that.*[3]

Paul uses the two words "ask" and "think". The first is spoken; the second is unspoken. Our praying and our thinking are often limited by an inadequate knowledge of exactly who God is and how immense is his power. The thought here is that whatever we manage to pray, and whatever we think or imagine, God can do far more and God is far greater. "Can you move this stone?" said the ant to the bulldozer!

Thought

Our prayers and our thoughts are limited by our human understanding.

Prayer

Dear Lord, please enlarge my understanding of who you are, and help me to pray accordingly.

---

[1] William Hendriksen, *Ephesians,* (Banner of Truth, Edinburgh, 1976), p.175
[2] Clinton E. Arnold, *Ephesians,* (Zondervan, Michigan, 2010). p.219
[3] Kenneth Wuest, *Wuest's Word Studies,* Vol.1, 'Ephesians and Colossians', (Eerdmans, Michigan, 1953), p.91

DAY ONE HUNDRED AND SIXTY-NINE

The Power at Work Within Us

Eph.3:20

...according to the power at work within us...

William Hendriksen points out that Paul is not dealing with abstracts here. He wrote, "The omnipotence which God reveals in answering prayer is not a figment of his imagination but is in line with that mighty operation of His power that is already at work within us."[1] This is not the power of God that is out there somewhere to be sought after and reached for. This is his mighty power at work within us.

That phrase "according to" – *kata* – has appeared yet again. In other words, God works under and according to his 'purposeful power' at work within us. He is not veering off on spasmodic tangents and whimsical jaunts with us. He has a definite purpose for our lives and everything will be brought to bear to serve that purpose. The chaotic, messy and sporadic stuff that surrounds us will actually become subservient to his purposes.

Our thinking must progress to realising that if there is no limit to what God himself can do, then there is no limit to what God can do through us. The sad thing, however, is that we can limit God both by the lack of our knowledge of the Almighty and our unyielded-ness to the Holy Spirit. The first stunts our understanding and the second prevents his free working in and through us.

Robert Boyd Munger wrote a little booklet entitled *My Heart, Christ's Home*[2]. In it he paints an allegory about the visit of Jesus to someone's heart. The door of the soul is opened and Christ enters. He then systematically goes through every room in this 'house', challenging, cleansing and even redecorating to his own taste and desires. As he does so, even with the most secret and foulest of the 'rooms', the soul finds

---

[1]   William Hendriksen, *Ephesians,* (Banner of Truth, Edinburgh, 1976), p.175
[2]   Robert Munger, *My Heart, Christ's Home,* (IVP, Downers Grove, Illinois, 2004)

both great peace and great release, thus creating the environment for the easy working and movement of God's Spirit in and through him.

Paul writes that this power is "at work within us". God now does his work in and through us, through our attitudes, words and hands. During the time of Christ's incarnation, God was in Jesus the Man, and he moved powerfully through the Son. Now God is in the church and, under this new covenant, we are now the body of Christ. God touches human lives and ministers to them through us by the power of the Holy Spirit.

However, this work can be hindered. Watchman Nee, in his powerful little book *Release of the Spirit*, wrote, "Anyone who serves God will discover sooner or later that the great hindrance to his work is not others but himself."[1] An unconquered and un-surrendered believer is not a blessing to Christ or his church, rather a stumbling block. The best way to serve the Lord is to allow him free access to every area of our inner lives, thus creating a way of free passage for the Holy Spirit. When this happens to all of us in the church, it becomes the glory of God in the church.

Thought

Personal surrender is the key to personal victory and opens the door to much fruitfulness.

Prayer

Holy Spirit, conquer every part of my life, bringing it into line with what you are doing.

---

[1]   Watchman Nee, *The Release of the Spirit*, (New Wine Press, Chichester, 2007), p.13

DAY ONE HUNDRED AND SEVENTY

Glory in the Church and in Christ Jesus

Eph.3:21

...to him be glory in the church and in Christ Jesus throughout all generations, forever and ever. Amen.

In this superb doxology, Paul is caught up with both the wonder of the church and the wonder of what God in Christ has done. From in his cell, he peers down the ages. His view becomes far-reaching. This is not any 'living for the moment' writing; this is far more than a worldview, this is a seeing of the long-term purpose of God in and beyond human life as we know it. He stares into both time and eternity.

Everything that God has done, is doing and will be doing, is designed to bring glory to his name. And that is right. The ancient Hebrew psalmist wrote, "Not to us, O LORD, not to us, but to your name give glory, for the sake of your steadfast love and your faithfulness!" (Ps.115:1) He understood that God would not share his glory with another. (Is.48:11) John Stott wrote, "The power comes from him; the glory must go to him."[1] Interestingly, this is the only doxology where both the church and Christ are mentioned in bringing glory to God.

Firstly, to God will be glory in the church. The church is the sphere of the outworking of God's purpose on earth. It is the body of Christ, and through the church, the local embassies of the kingdom of heaven, God makes himself known. Clinton Arnold wrote:

> *As the church maintains its vital unity with Christ, becomes more like the Father in holiness, defeats the influence of the power of supernatural enemies, fills the world with the good news of the Son resulting in numerical growth, and offers continual praise to God, the church brings glory to God.*[2]

Secondly, to God there will be glory in Christ Jesus, the Founder and Head of the church. His coming and his work was both planned by the Father and pleasing to the Father. He completed what the Father sent

---

[1]   John Stott, *The Message of Ephesians,* (IVP, Leicester, 1979), p.140
[2]   Clinton E. Arnold, *Ephesians,* (Zondervan, Michigan, 2010), p.220

him for. The glory of God shines in his face. (2.Cor.4:6) Harold Hoehner wrote: "God is to be glorified in the church because his power and splendor are displayed there and he is glorified in Christ Jesus because Christ's work, which pleased the Father, made the church possible."[1]

The phrase "throughout all generations, forever and ever" is unique to Paul. William Hendriksen wrote, "It refers to the flow of moments from past to present to future, continuing on and on without ever coming to an end."[2] This glorifying of God will traverse through time into eternity.

Here ends the theology. Paul will now move into the outworking and the practice of what the saints believe. He is anxious that their understanding of God and his purpose in Christ should not remain solely in their heads and within the four walls of the church, but that it should affect the mission, the morals, the marriage, the family and work relationships, and the street. Faith needs to have not only a voice but feet and hands. If our believed theology does not become a practised theology, in whatever setting we find ourselves in, then we are walking in circles through our spiritual life with one leg pinned down.

Thought

Only when the glory of God becomes our sole focus are we fully alive and functioning.

Prayer

Father in heaven, may my life both reflect and point to your glory.

---

[1] Harold Hoehner, *Ephesians: An Exegetical Commentary,* (Baker Academic, Michigan, 2002), p.495
[2] William Hendriksen, *Ephesians,* (Banner of Truth, Edinburgh, 1976), p.176

Day One Hundred and Seventy-One

Therefore

Eph.4:1

I therefore, a prisoner for the Lord...

L arge doors swing on small hinges. The word "therefore", according to Eugene Peterson, is a hinge word, moving us from "an exuberant exploration of who God is and the way he works to a detailed account of who we are and the way we work"[1]. Using an engineering analogy, we now move from the architect's office to the shop floor.

This, then, is where we come to the dividing line of the letter. The first three chapters have dealt with doctrine – the things we need to believe; the remainder of the letter will deal with the things we should be doing, and how we should be living as a result of what we believe. There is something drastically wrong if what we believe does not translate into our daily living. W. Graham Scroggie wrote:

> *The subject of the first three chapters is the Church; and the subject of the second three is the Christian. The first is an institution, and the second is an individual. The Church must look to its creed, and the Christian to his conduct.[2]*

The first half tells us who we are, the second half tells us how to live.

Having said that, Dr Martyn Lloyd-Jones wisely pointed out that "as we reach this transition, we must not make too much of it, we must not press it too hard"[3]. He went on to make the remark that in the fourth verse of this chapter "the Apostle goes back to doctrine. It is a characteristic of his that he never indulges in absolute divisions and for the simple reason that, in the last analysis, we cannot and must not

---

[1] Eugene Peterson, *Practise Resurrection,* (Hodder & Stoughton, London, 2010), p.166

[2] W. Graham Scroggie, *The Unfolding Drama of Redemption,* Vol.3, (Pickering & Inglis, London, 1970), p.191

[3] Dr Martyn Lloyd Jones, *Christian Unity,* (Banner of Truth, Edinburgh, 1980), p.11

separate doctrine and practice."[1] This is sound wisdom. Our walk with the Lord must always be mingled with doctrine and practice. As we make progress, we will continually be learning new things and then working them out by practice, and into our lives by long experience. Learning and practice is not meant to be a linear experience but a cyclical one. 'Learn, practice and absorb – learn, practice and absorb – learn, practice and absorb' is a truly Christian mantra.

Our encounters with Christ, and what we subsequently believe, will, or should, alter and determine our behaviour. The "therefore" links the two halves of the letter. Having laid out some pretty powerful theology, Paul is now saying, "Christ has made you a saint, now live like one." Put another way, he is saying, "Having now learned what to believe, earth it all and authenticate it all in your behaviour."

When Peter the fisherman saw Jesus of Nazareth walking towards him on the beach, he had no idea of how much his life was about to change. And when Jesus said to him, "Follow me," it became apparent that Jesus was not interested in becoming the senior partner of Peter's fishing business. Firstly, Peter had to make the move from being in charge of his own fishing business affairs to becoming a follower in the deep-sea fishing affairs of the Lord. Then he had to learn that not only circumstantial changes were in the air, but deep internal changes were also to come. His change of beliefs was going to morph into a change of lifestyle. It was the same with Saul of Tarsus, the hard-nosed religious zealot whom Jesus toppled to the ground outside Damascus. For him, life was not going to be the same again – ever.

Thought

Authentic faith demonstrates itself in everyday living.

Prayer

Dear Lord, help me this day to demonstrate what I believe to those around me.

---

[1] Ibid, pp.11,12

Day One Hundred and Seventy-Two

A Prisoner of the Lord

Eph.4:1

I therefore, a prisoner for the Lord...

As we noted yesterday, we must not introduce clinical divisions in our thinking about theology and lifestyle. They are not to become isolated from each other, compartmentalised in different boxes. They must be constantly interwoven together so that we learn about our faith as well as practise our faith. Think of it like this: doctrine and theology are the roots of our faith and the absorbing and practice of it produces the fruit of our faith.

Mark Roberts adds to our thinking by stating that "although chapters 4-6 contain rich theological content, they emphasise not so much what God has done as what we should do in response to God's actions"[1]. This is another strong principle that we need to get hold of. Our faith is a responsive faith. We respond to his love, and we respond to what he has done and also what he is doing. I am not convinced that God is looking for people of initiative who then enlist the Lord's backing for their spiritual enterprises, as much as for people who are responsive and then obedient to his directions. The former requires little seeking of the Lord, the latter requires much seeking of the Lord.

Paul describes himself again as a prisoner for the Lord. It is somewhat poignant that the one who in his previous life had feverishly put people behind bars because of their faith, was now behind bars himself because of his faith and his burning passion for Christ. The fact that he was chained and restricted, however, did not limit God or his work, but rather it focused and enhanced it. In fact, in his second letter to Timothy, he wrote about being "bound with chains as a criminal". And went on to add, "But the word of God is not bound!" (2.Tim.2:9) In his letter to the church at Philippi, he made the astute observation that "what has happened to me has really served to advance the gospel, so that it has become known throughout the whole imperial guard and to all the rest

---

[1]   Mark D. Roberts, *Ephesians,* (Zondervan, Michigan, 2016), p.116

that my imprisonment is for Christ" (Phil.1:12,13). Faith sees possibilities and opportunities in whatever circumstances we find ourselves.

A somewhat different scenario is recorded in the book of Daniel, where we read about the three friends of the prophet who had been cast into a fiery furnace by the ego-inflated king of Babylon. Daniel records:

> *Then King Nebuchadnezzar was astonished and rose up in haste. He declared to his counsellors, "Did we not cast three men bound into the fire?" They answered and said to the king, "True, O king." He answered and said, "But I see four men unbound, walking in the midst of the fire, and they are not hurt; and the appearance of the fourth is like a son of the gods."*
>
> Daniel 3:24,25

Here, in these distressing circumstances, there was also the presence of the divine. Possibilities, opportunities and the liberating presence of the Lord were found within the confinements of life.

Paul is an apostle of Jesus Christ whether he is preaching and teaching in synagogues, houses, market places or halls; even when he is writing behind prison bars, chained to a Roman soldier. Our circumstances do not, and must not, define us. Rather, it is the One who walks with us, who envisions us in our darkness, who defines us. We are his, and there is no place that we may find ourselves that he will not be present to us.

Thought

Your circumstances should not define you; the One who walks with you defines you.

Prayer

Dear Lord, please turn my prison into a platform where you can be seen at work in me.

110

DAY ONE HUNDRED AND SEVENTY-THREE

Walk in a Manner Worthy

Eph.4:1

I therefore, a prisoner for the Lord, urge you to walk in a manner worthy of the calling to which you have been called...

Imagine Paul, sitting in his cell, visualising these Ephesians believers. He has been laying before them an incredibly beautiful and powerful picture of the activity of the Holy Three, and now he yearns that they would walk into it all. All his pastoral heart is coming out in the words that are to follow. He uses a tender word *parakalō,* which literally means 'to call to one's side'. It also carries the sense of 'begging, pleading, entreating, beseeching'. Kenneth Wuest captured this well when he translated it as, "I beg of you, please..."[1] We can almost feel the gentle but firm urgency of Paul's longings for them in this word.

All this is set in the context of his imprisonment for Christ. Paul, the incarcerated one, is saying to those who are outside and walking free that they can walk these truths out in their various settings of life. He, however, has only the one setting – a prison cell. All he can do is write, and pray, and seek to exhibit utmost patience in his sufferings. It's a strong argument that he is using. It is as if he is saying, "Please come near, if you can, to my heart in this cell. You have a freedom that I do not have. Therefore, take hold of this understanding of who God is and what he has purposed and accomplished in Christ, and then walk it out strongly and clearly in the visible market places of your lives."

His heart cry for them also comes out in these words: "...walk in a manner worthy of the calling to which you have been called..." Clinton Arnold points out that the word translated "walk" is the Greek word *peripateō,* and is "a common metaphor in Jewish circles for one's conduct in everyday life"[2].

Paul then uses another important word – *axiōs.* This word is found five times in his writings. The picture is that of an old-fashioned set of

---

[1] Kenneth Wuest, *The New Testament, An Expanded Translation,* (Eerdmans, Michigan, 2004), p.453

[2] Clinton E. Arnold, *Ephesians,* (Zondervan, Michigan, 2010), p.130

scales. Harold Hoehner wrote that the word literally means "bringing up the other beam of the scales" or "bringing into equilibrium"[1]. Paul is therefore saying that their calling must be in perfect balance with their walking. Kenneth Wuest wrote, "...the saints should see to it that their Christian experience, the Christian life which they live, should weigh as much as the profession of Christianity which they make."[2] In other words, what they believed needed to balance beautifully and accurately with what they practised. Many a magnificent profession of truth and faith has been seriously undone by a lack of the absence of godly practice. Paul then writes of "the calling". For him, this was not simply a weekend pursuit or a part-time job, it was a 'vocation'; yet it was much, much more than a vocation. It was a summons to walk before God in his presence, having fellowship with the Father, Son and Holy Spirit, and participating in what heaven is actively doing in the earth – a calling that is both wonderful, all-consuming and awesome, and it is something that will last forever, touching the world for generations to come. These believers, called and commissioned by God, were to become ambassadors of heaven, and they were to live and act like it.

Thought

The truly balanced Christian life is one of deep belief and consistent practice of that belief.

Prayer

Grant me, Lord, never to become a hypocrite – pretending to be someone I am not in reality.

---

[1] Harold Hoehner, *Ephesians: An Exegetical Commentary,* (Baker Academic, Michigan, 2002), p.504

[2] Kenneth Wuest, *Wuest's Word Studies,* Vol.1, 'Ephesians and Colossians', (Eerdmans, Michigan, 1953), p.93,94

DAY ONE HUNDRED AND SEVENTY-FOUR

Humility

Eph.4:2,3

...with all humility and gentleness, with patience, bearing with one another in love, eager to maintain the unity of the Spirit in the bond of peace.

Paul now begins to explain what he means by the walk that is worthy of our calling. As we think deeply about these words before us, we find that there is a strong resemblance to Jesus and the way he walked among us. Producing Christlikeness in the life and walk of a believer is the specific goal of the Holy Spirit, and we should concur with that goal, agreeing with him in it, and allowing him to pursue it in us.

An important thing to consider at this stage is that Paul is writing out of a context of unity. God, in Christ, is bringing people together from all walks of life and creating one people – the family of God. The word "together" is so important. The qualities that he is about to mention are all relational qualities. Clinton Arnold rightly says, "Because God's calling is not to a private relationship with him but to a life in community with other believers, it is essential for Christians to display the kind of qualities that enhance this life together."[1] Let's be clear: our private devotions before God must outwork themselves in our relationships with others. The 'God and me only' lifestyle is tainted with a kind of spiritual narcissism that is often rooted in an inability or lack of desire to connect meaningfully with those around us. In fact, the Scriptures are quite candid about this. Solomon wrote, "Whoever isolates himself seeks his own desire; he breaks out against all sound judgment." (Prov.18:1)

The first word that Paul uses is "humility". This is a word with a huge history in the Scriptures. The Greek word is *tapeinophrosunē,* which literally means 'a lowliness of mind'. To a Greek mind, however, this word was not regarded as a virtue but something to be despised and looked down upon. F.F. Bruce wrote that "lowliness or humility was

---

[1]   Clinton E. Arnold, *Ephesians,* (Zondervan, Michigan, 2010), p.229

regarded more of a vice than a virtue in pagan antiquity"[1]. On the other hand, in the Hebrew Scriptures, it was something that God loved and responded to. In Isaiah 66:2, we read, "...this is the one to whom I will look: he who is humble and contrite in spirit and trembles at my word."

The humility that Paul is writing about here is in the realms of not so much our social status, but how we think about ourselves and about others. It is important to get this right. Paul wrote to the believers in Rome, "I say to everyone among you not to think of himself more highly than he ought to think, but to think with sober judgment..." (Rom.12:3) A genuine humility will have an accurate reading of oneself – knowing and acknowledging both one's weaknesses and strengths. A true humility will be unconscious of itself. G. Campbell Morgan wrote, "Real humility never knows that it is humble; mock humility is proud of its humility."[2]

Concerning others, Paul wrote to the believers in Philippi, "Do nothing from selfish ambition or conceit, but in humility count others more significant than yourselves." (Phil.2:3) How we think of others matters much in the kingdom. A true humility will elevate others above ourselves.

Thought

True humility will foster and encourage unity; pride will dismantle it.

Prayer

Dear Lord, open my eyes to see and get an accurate reading of who I really am in your sight.

---

[1]   F.F. Bruce, *The Epistle to the Ephesians,* (Pickering Paperbacks, Glasgow, 1983), p.75

[2]   G. Campbell Morgan, *The Gospel of Matthew,* (Oliphants, London, 1929), p.23

DAY ONE HUNDRED AND SEVENTY-FIVE

Gentleness

Eph.4:2,3

...with all humility and gentleness, with patience, bearing with one another in love, eager to maintain the unity of the Spirit in the bond of peace.

Into the present climate of pushing for prestige, position and power, it would be good to hear a powerful nudge in the opposite direction from the Augustinian monk Thomas à Kempis. He wrote, "If thou wouldst learn anything of lasting benefit, seek to be unknown and little esteemed of men."[1] It is worth meditating on this little jewel and then letting it cut across and affect our thinking.

Paul now adds another word to the mix. It is *praotēs,* which means 'gentleness, mildness, meekness'. The ESV translates it as "gentleness", whereas the KJV uses the word "meekness". The word "meekness" describes an inner condition of heart and mind, whereas "gentleness" is appropriate rather to outward actions. As we are in our heart, so we ought to be in the things we do and say in our relationships with others.

The word is always associated, however, with strength. Meekness is not weakness, but the power to be gentle. Eugene Peterson taught that the word spoke of a torrent of energy that is focused and used for purpose. He called it "energy sanctified" – energy that is channelled and directed. It is not reactive, but directed.[2] Another concept is that of a wild horse that has been tamed and is now quietly under the control of its master.

In one of his lectures, Peterson mentioned G.K. Chesterton, who would speak of the difference between crustaceans and vertebrates.[3] Crustaceans (crabs, lobsters) are not nice creatures. Their 'bones' are on the outside and are visible and deliberately scary. They are 'crusty'

---

[1] Thomas á Kempis, *The Imitation of Christ,* translated by George F. Maine, (Collins, London, 1971), p.35

[2] Eugene Peterson, *Lectures on the Beatitudes,* lecture 5, Regents College, Vancouver

[3] Ibid.

individuals. Vertebrates, on the other hand, have their bones on the insides. They are soft to the touch, but their strength in on the inside. They are flexible, but have inner strength. They can be handled and held without people getting hurt.

From a Hebrew point of view, the word meant a commitment to God in perfect trust and obedience. From a Greek point of view, it meant a man who has every instinct and passion under the control and mastery of the Holy Spirit and, as such, he is totally content in whatever circumstances he finds himself. (cf. Phil.4:11.12)

Albert Barnes wrote:

> *Meekness produces peace. It is proof of true greatness of soul. It comes from a heart too great to be moved by little insults. It looks upon those who offer them with pity. He that is constantly ruffled; that suffers every little insult or injury to throw him off his guard and to raise a storm of passion within, is at the mercy of every mortal that chooses to disturb him.*[1]

Gentleness and meekness are expressed in a submissiveness to the will of God and to others. It reveals itself in being teachable and correctable, and is noticed in its ability to absorb whatever is thrown at it without a negative or violent reaction. This takes the power of God for it to be achieved.

Thought

'Crusty' individuals do not represent the kingdom of heaven very well.

Prayer

Dear Jesus, please work on my sharp edges and hard-nosed attitudes, softening them.

---

[1] Albert Barnes, *Notes on the Bible,* commenting on Matthew 5:5, e-sword.net

DAY ONE HUNDRED AND SEVENTY-SIX

Patience

Eph.4:2,3

...with all humility and gentleness, with patience, bearing with one another in love, eager to maintain the unity of the Spirit in the bond of peace.

There is a strong determination coming from the Holy Spirit, and it is directed at bringing all sorts of people together into a deep unity of heart and soul. God, in Christ, has broken the dividing walls, and he speaks to us, compelling and urging us to come together as the body of Christ.

For those of us who have been in church life for decades, it is obvious that this is not easy. We are all individuals, from different backgrounds, with different temperaments and with different viewpoints on life. The church is God's idea, but participating in church life is often difficult because people are difficult. We somehow want to cling on to our independence and defend our positions. As a father with five grown-up kids, I have watched them during their formative years argue over both little and large things, and also grow up together. I have learned that despite my lack of patience at times, God is incredibly patient – with us all.

And this leads us to the next word that Paul introduces into this section – "patience". Some versions use the word "long-suffering". The Greek word is *makrothumias,* and it means 'long-tempered'. Kenneth Wuest describes it as the "steadfastness of the soul under provocation"[1]. William Hendriksen wrote, "It characterizes the person who, in relation to those who annoy, oppose, or molest him, exercises patience. He refuses to yield to passion or to outbursts of anger."[2] It is a long holding out against the passions that could be so destructive. The opposite is the 'short temper' that easily flies off the handle, and 'loses it' under the

---

[1] Kenneth Wuest, *Wuest's Word Studies,* Vol.1, 'Galatians', (Eerdmans, Michigan, 1953), p.160

[2] William Hendriksen, *Galatians*, (Banner of Truth, Edinburgh, 1968), p.224

slightest provocation. This has everything to do with our relationships with each other.

The word is actually stronger than "patience" because it also carries the idea of endurance. It acts in a passive sense – that of bearing up under the stresses and strains of life. You can most certainly see this quality in the life of Christ. When he endured such violent abuse and rejection, he kept his mouth shut. When all hell was breaking out upon him, he entrusted himself to his heavenly Father.

And so *makrothumias* is also a trust word. It believes that all of our days, events and encounters are in the hands and timing of God. Nothing is unseen to him and everything that 'gets through' to us has design to it. "All things are your servants," said the psalmist in Psalm 119:91. Paul wrote to the church in Rome, "And we know that for those who love God all things work together for good." (Rom.8:28) The long-tempered man is the long-sighted man. Much of what comes our way is specifically designed to teach us spiritual warfare, to toughen our spirit and to build up our faith.

The word *makrothumias* is a maturity word. When we are easily 'put out of joint' by a word or circumstances, it reveals our shallow rooted-ness in the constant love and watchful care of God. Faber wrote, "We must wait for God, long, meekly, in the wind and the wet, in the thunder and the lightning, in the cold and the dark. Wait and he will come. He never comes to those who do not wait."[1]

Thought

Patience is not a gift; it is a practised virtue – practised on others.

Prayer

Lord, help me to treat each difficult encounter as a personal learning opportunity.

---

[1] *https://www.goodreads.com/quotes/5756657-we-must-wait-for-god-long-meekly-in-the-wind*

DAY ONE HUNDRED AND SEVENTY-SEVEN

Forbearance

Eph.4:2,3

...with all humility and gentleness, with patience, bearing with one another in love, eager to maintain the unity of the Spirit in the bond of peace.

All these words that Paul is introducing are, in a nutshell, about the imitating of Christ. Christ-likeness is the great goal of our calling. Paul wrote to the members of the church in Corinth, "Be imitators of me, as I am of Christ." (1.Cor.11:1) To be like Christ was Paul's deepest passion.

Thomas à Kempis, according to the preface of the translators of a new edition of his famous book *The Imitation of Christ*, was "a teacher and writer whose life was devoted to patterning his life after Jesus Christ"[1]. In the first book and the first chapter, Thomas himself wrote that "we are advised to imitate his life and habits, if we wish to be truly enlightened and free from all blindness of heart"[2].

We should also reflect that all this is to be worked out in the company of others. Becoming like Jesus has to be worked out in personal relationships. And so, into this array of words, Paul now inserts another relational word: 'forbearance'. The ESV has it "bearing with one another"[3]. Clinton Arnold has translated this as "putting up with one another". Harold Hoehner cites A.T. Robertson as suggesting that the meaning is "holding yourself back from one another"[4]. Hoehner himself writes that "in other words, differences between believers are to be tolerated"[5].

---

[1] Aloysius Croft and Harold Bolton, preface to *The Imitation of Christ,* (Hendrikson, Massachusetts, 2004), p.xii

[2] Thomas á Kempis, *The Imitation of Christ,* (Hendrikson, Massachusetts, 2004), p.3

[3] Clinton E. Arnold, *Ephesians,* (Zondervan, Michigan, 2010), p.230

[4] Harold Hoehner, *Ephesians: An Exegetical Commentary,* (Baker Academic, Michigan, 2002), p.509; cf. A.T. Robertson, *A Grammar of the Greek New Testament,* (Hodder & Stoughton, New York, 1914)

[5] Ibid.

The Greek word is *anechomenoi,* which means 'to hold up, to sustain, to bear with even-ness of mind and temper'. It means bearing with one another, making allowances for mistakes and failures, and giving room for imperfections. It is bearing with one another's weaknesses without inwardly boiling!

Here is another piece of wisdom from Thomas à Kempis:

> *Try to bear patiently with the defects and infirmities of others, whatever they may be, because you also have many a fault which others must endure. If you cannot make yourself what you wish to be, how can you bend others to your will? We want them to be perfect, yet we do not correct our own fault. We wish them to be severely corrected, yet we will not correct ourselves.*[1]

Doesn't this remind you of the words of Jesus, who said, "Why do you see the speck that is in your brother's eye, but do not notice the log that is in your own eye?" (Matt.7:3)

To sum up, Theodore Epp, the founder director and speaker of the 'Back to the Bible' broadcasts, wrote:

> *This has to do with lovingly putting up with all that is disagreeable in other people. Our attitude toward them should be love and patience even though they do things with which we cannot agree. Impatience tends to destructive criticism.*[2]

Thought

Reproducing God's patience with us, as we deal with difficult others, is a life-long quest.

Prayer

Father, this is a difficult task. Help me to love, tolerate and give space to others as you do.

---

[1] Thomas á Kempis, *The Imitation of Christ,* (Hendrikson, Massachusetts, 2004), p.16

[2] Theodore Epp, *Living Abundantly – Studies in Ephesians,* (Back to the Bible, Nebraska, 1973), p.146

Day One Hundred and Seventy-Eight

Love

Eph.4:2

...with all humility and gentleness, with patience, bearing with one another in love...

Many years ago, I remember our three children, Ruth, Joseph and Simon, sitting on our bed, having wonderful fun with each other. It was a special moment. Mo, my wife, then left the room and came back with our newly born fourth child, Sarah. All of a sudden, I was suddenly filled with a strong sense of parental responsibility. It was more than love; it was the knowledge that we had been given the responsibility of nurturing these young lives into adulthood.

The Lennon/McCartney song *All You Need Is Love* summed up the hippy culture of the 60s. Hippy love has been defined as "the idea of a relationship without responsibility"[1]. I was part of that culture and sang the song with feeling and gusto. But the love that they were writing about, and I was singing about, had very little to do with the kind of love that we have been thinking about over these last few days.

Eugene Peterson wrote that the word 'love' "is probably the most frequently used word in our vocabulary for saying what we like, what attracts us, what we hunger for. In common use it is stripped of theological connotations and personal reciprocities."[2] He continues by saying that the phrase "I love you" "is a life-transforming, life-deepening, life-saving sentence. Spoken by God it is. And spoken in God's name it is. But with its God-origins and God-content removed, it is a hollow word, hopelessly trivialised, endlessly banalised."[3]

God's love is deeply relational and filled with responsibility. We were responsible for our sins, but he took responsibility for our redemption. He did not ignore us in our plight. The apostle John records that "God

---

[1] *https://www.urbandictionary.com/define.php?term=Hippie%20Love*
[2] Eugene Peterson, *Practise Resurrection,* (Hodder & Stoughton, London, 2010), p.209
[3] Ibid, p.210

so loved the world, that he gave his only Son, that whoever believes in him should not perish but have eternal life" (Jn.3:16). God, in his love, not only observed our fallenness but gave himself in his Son, sacrificially, to save and restore us. Jesus went on to say, "This is my commandment, that you love one another as I have loved you. Greater love has no one than this, that someone lay down his life for his friends." (Jn.15:12,13) The love of God has others well and truly in its sights.

The 'marks' that we have been looking at are also deeply relational – "humility and gentleness, with patience, bearing with one another". These qualities determine how we interact with those around us. We are not designed to be passive recipients of the intentions of others and the swelling surges of circumstances. We are to think through, speak and act in the name of the Lord. If our calling card is indeed love, then we are called to have a divine and Christlike effect on the broken humanity amongst whom we live.

All these relational qualities come to perfect fruition when they are rooted and grounded in love. Paul, writing something similar in his letter to the Colossians, rounded off the qualities by saying, "…above all these put on love, which binds everything together in perfect harmony." (Col.3:14)

Thought

The love of God has a totally unselfish spirit behind it.

Prayer

Dear Lord, let your love melt and mould my heart.

Day One Hundred and Seventy-Nine

Maintaining the Unity

Eph.4:3

...eager to maintain the unity of the Spirit in the bond of peace.

The unity of the Spirit is not something to be acquired. It cannot be manufactured by human endeavours. People can unite around a cause, an ideal or ideology, but that is not the unity of the Spirit. It is not even the blending of doctrinal or theological stances, seeking to find the lowest common denominator in order to bring churches together. It is something directly imparted and constructed by the Holy Spirit.

According to Paul, the unity of the Spirit was already there, and it was something to do with being in the twice-born family of God. The Jewish and Gentile believers had been reconciled to God by the blood of Christ and had, by virtue of the new birth, been made into one body by the one Holy Spirit. It was an act that had been accomplished by heaven, but can be, in the words of Clinton Arnold, "easily wrecked"[1] by those living on the earth. Arnold adds, "Although we might expect Paul to encourage his readers to attain unity in the church, he actually implores them to maintain a unity that already exists."[2]

We are, then, to preserve and maintain what God has already done for us. We have been brought into, and made, a family, so we should endeavour at all costs to stay close to each other.

Paul writes that they were to be "eager" in preserving this unity. The NASB uses the word "diligent". The Greek word that Paul uses is *spoudazontes,* which means 'taking care, making haste, doing one's best'. Maintaining unity takes hard work and determined effort, and the enemy loves to discourage believers in this. We need to be jealous for the family that God had placed us in. There's an urgency about it.

The word "maintain" is a translation of the Greek word *tērein* which means 'to keep by guarding, to guard by exercising watchful care'. In

---

[1]   Clinton E. Arnold, *Ephesians,* (Zondervan, Michigan, 2010), p.231
[2]   Ibid.

other words, they were to be on the lookout for anything that would divide them. Weeds are not cultivated; they grow because of neglect. On the other hand, the unity of the Spirit must be cultivated and preserved.

We must not always blame the Devil for disunity. He loves to fuel disunity, but when we foolishly listen to him, we end up making divisive choices. Jesus said, albeit in the context of marriage, "What therefore God has joined together, let not man separate." (Mk.10:9) The principle is nevertheless the same. Jesus also said, "...a family splintered by feuding will fall apart." (Mk.3:25, NLT)

Paul wrote to the Galatian believers that "the deeds of the flesh are enmities, strife, jealousy, outbursts of anger, disputes, dissensions, factions" (Gal.5:20). He also wrote to the Corinthians, "...since then there is jealousy and strife among you, are you not just fleshly, and are you not walking like mere men?" (1.Cor.3:3) Division among the saints is childish immaturity.

Let us then be bound to each other, rooting for each other, tolerating each other, forgiving each other, defending each other, sticking with each other. This is what makes for peace, and has quite an impact!

Thought

The responsibility of the church is to demonstrate this divine and unique unity of the Spirit.

Prayer

Father, fill me with a passion to cherish, nurture and guard this unity that you have given.

DAY ONE HUNDRED AND EIGHTY

One

Eph.4:4-6

There is one body and one Spirit – just as you were called to the one hope that belongs to your call – one Lord, one faith, one baptism, one God and Father of all, who is over all and through all and in all.

It's hard not to notice the repetition of the word "one" in the passage that we are looking at today. It's mentioned seven times! Sadly, as we survey church history, much of what we see is fragmentation, and it feels like a million miles away from the prayer of Jesus on his way to Gethsemane. As he walked, he prayed for his disciples and then he said:

"I do not ask for these only, but also for those who will believe in me through their word, that they may all be one, just as you, Father, are in me, and I in you, that they also may be in us, so that the world may believe that you have sent me. The glory that you have given me I have given to them, that they may be one even as we are one, I in them and you in me, that they may become perfectly one, so that the world may know that you sent me and loved them even as you loved me."

John 17:20-23

Notice again the repetition of the word "one". It is an important word to God.

When Paul wrote about the "unity" of the Spirit, he used an unusual word – *henotēta*. It appears only twice in the whole of the New Testament, and only in this letter. (4:3,13) The root of *henotēta* is *heis*, which means 'one'. It also carries a strong sense of uniqueness. This oneness that the Spirit has created is absolutely unique. Clinton Arnold writes, "So we are to eagerly preserve oneness because our oneness is anchored in the manifold oneness of divine reality."[1]

---

[1]   Clinton E. Arnold, *Ephesians,* (Zondervan, Michigan, 2010), p.120

The Greek word for Spirit is *pneuma*, and the technical name for the study of the Holy Spirit is called pneumatology. Professor James Dunn wrote a two-volumed work entitled *The Christ and the Spirit*. In his second volume he wrote these words: "Paul experienced the Spirit as a centrifugal as well as a centripetal force."[1] That statement stopped me in my tracks. Let me explain.

The term 'centripetal' comes from the Latin words *centrum* (centre) and *petere* (tend towards, aim at). It is a pulling in towards a centre or axis, bringing it to a unity. The term 'centrifugal' comes from the Latin words *centrum* (centre) and *fugere* (to flee). It is a propulsion away from a centre or axis. In a nutshell, the centripetal force draws in and the centrifugal force thrusts out. One tends inwards and the other tends outwards. Unity and mission are the lub-dub (double sound) of the heartbeat of God.

This centripetal work of the Spirit is constantly drawing the twice-born children of God together into a single unity. This drawing is towards each other. According to Paul, by the Spirit we have all been baptised into the body of Christ, into a oneness. If, then, I find something in me that is resisting fellowship with others, then I am resisting this centripetal movement of the Spirit. In the mind of God, the thought that people say that they love him whilst finding their brother or sister repugnant, is utterly incongruent.

Professor George Caird wrote, "The corporate unity of the church is not a desirable end, but a datum to which the behaviour of its members must conform."[2] Now there's a thought!

Thought

The unifying Spirit of God is exerting an influence on me that I must not resist.

Prayer

Dear Holy Spirit, draw me closer, willingly, not only to the Father, but to his children.

---

[1] James D.G. Dunn, *The Christ and The Spirit,* Vol.2, (Eerdmans, Cambridge, 1998), p.16

[2] Cited by Francis Foulkes, *Ephesians,* (IVP, Leicester, 1999), p.119

DAY ONE HUNDRED AND EIGHTY-ONE

The Oneness of the Three

Eph.4:4-6

There is one body and one Spirit – just as you were called to the one hope that belongs to your call – one Lord, one faith, one baptism, one God and Father of all, who is over all and through all and in all.

Concerning the sevenfold use of the word "one", Eugene Peterson wrote, "The repetitions in this context are not, I think, a nagging insistence on monotheism as a dogma to be believed; this is a gentle pastoral reassurance that we are involved in a life of basic simplicity."[1] The word "one" brings us back from our sporadic and anxious multiplication of things we feel we need to believe and practise.

William Hendriksen wrote, "It is as clear as daylight and universally admitted that this section, especially in its opening verses, emphasises unity. This unity, moreover, is not external and mechanical, but internal and organic."[2] This unity is a given from heaven, and it is a *fait accompli* – it has already been given and established in Christ. If you like, a seed has been planted in the earth, and it is down to us to protect and nurture it. The church has been born – the body of Christ has become apparent – it needs loving, appreciating and cultivating.

Many commentators agree that these words are derived from either a fragment of an early Christian hymn or a primitive credal statement. They are constructed of three triads, each containing three unities. Dr Skevington Wood noticed that, "In three groups of three items each, Paul's thought ascends from the realization of unity in the Spirit to the focus of unity in the Son and thence to the source of unity in the Father."[3] We cannot but notice the strong inference to the uniqueness of the three persons of the Holy Trinity of God – one Spirit, one Lord and one Father.

---

[1] Eugene Peterson, *Practise Resurrection,* (Hodder & Stoughton, London, 2010), pp.176,177

[2] William Hendriksen, *Ephesians,* (Banner of Truth, Edinburgh, 1976), p.181

[3] A. Skevington Wood, 'Ephesians', *NIV Bible Commentary,* Vol.2, (Hodder & Stoughton, London, 1994), p.767

As we find our way around this new life in the kingdom of heaven, we will experience both the influence and the activity of the Trinity. Trinity is far more than a mysterious dogma; it is a mysterious, yet deeply warm, intimate and intense relationship – a life into which we enter. As we read our way through the Scriptures, we will find the Father, the Son and the Spirit emerging in various places and in various ways. The Christian life is a life immersed in the Trinity.

In his book *Christ Plays in Ten Thousand Places*, Eugene Peterson wrote what for many theologians is the most definitive description of what we call the Holy Trinity. He put it this way:

> *Trinity is the most comprehensive and integrative framework that we have for understanding and participating in the Christian life. Early on in our history, our pastors and teachers formulated the Trinity to express what is distinctive in the revelation of God in Christ. This theology provides an immense horizon against which we can understand and practise the Christian life largely and comprehensively.*[1]

He added:

> *Trinity reveals the immense world of God creating, saving, and blessing in the name of Father, Son, and Holy Spirit with immediate and lived implications for the way we live, for our spirituality.*[2]

Thought

We must learn to live in the warm embrace of the Trinity.

Prayer

Most Holy Three in One, please draw me into your beautiful life.

---

[1] Eugene Peterson, *Christ Plays in Ten Thousand Places,* (Hodder & Stoughton, London, 2005), p.45

[2] Ibid.

DAY ONE HUNDRED AND EIGHTY-TWO

One Body

Eph.4:4-6

There is one body and one Spirit...

Paul was steeped in the Old Testament Scriptures yet he was an innovative thinker. It was Paul who first coined the word "body" to describe the church. It was a concept never imagined by the Jewish people. Clinton Arnold wrote, "Paul himself is the originator of the specific metaphor of the church as the body of Christ..."[1] Creative thinking must always be rooted in deep truth and wisdom.

Professor James Dunn feels that "this in fact is the dominant theological image in Pauline ecclesiology"[2]. Paul saw the body of Christ as the embodiment of Christ. Dunn says that it enables "corporeal encounter and relationship"[3], adding, "The point being that, as it is human embodiment that makes society possible, so the church is the means by which Christ makes actual tangible encounter with wider society."[4] Jesus makes contact today through ordinary people who make up his church, the body of Christ. It is we who express who he is.

This one body is not a nation that is tied to a geographical place on the earth; it is not even a dispersed nation that is held together by a shared genealogy and national culture. It is not a political body that is held together by a shared ideology and belief system. This one body is a completely different entity, imagined and purposed by God before the foundation of time, paid for by the blood of his Son on the cross and created and empowered by the Spirit of God. This one body engulfed and established both Jews and Gentiles, Romans and barbarians into one brand new body.

It goes without saying that what Paul is seeing is not the multitude of denominations that litter the world today, most caused by divisions and

---

[1] Clinton E. Arnold, *Ephesians,* (Zondervan, Michigan, 2010), p.233
[2] James D.G. Dunn, *The Theology of Paul the Apostle,* (T&T Clark, London, 1998), p.548
[3] Ibid, p.563
[4] Ibid, pp.563,564

arguments. Jesus envisioned the one church, and so did Paul. Neither is Paul thinking about the purely outward and organisational church that is entered by mental assent to doctrine and practice. Paul sees a living, functional embodiment of Jesus himself, through the indwelling Spirit, where the order of the day is not conformity to a system *per se*, but conformity to Jesus the Head of the church. (I'm racing ahead of myself!)

The body he sees has various functions, different ministries and a multitude of expressions. This body is exemplified by the term 'variety in unity'. He wrote to the church in Rome, "For as in one body we have many members, and the members do not all have the same function, so we, though many, are one body in Christ, and individually members one of another." (Rom.12:4,5) In his teaching to the Corinthians, he stressed that "just as the body is one and has many members, and all the members of the body, though many, are one body, so it is with Christ" (1.Cor.12:12).

The body of Christ is a deeply spiritual organism that is at the heart of all true churchmanship. We may leave a church, or a denomination, but to cut oneself off from the body results in the decomposition of one's spiritual life.

Thought

In the one body of Christ, his life flows through each member to each member.

Prayer

Help me to see the value of this one body, of which I am a participating member.

DAY ONE HUNDRED AND EIGHTY-THREE

One Spirit

Eph.4:4-6

There is one body and one Spirit...

He was there before the beginning, in deep and silent converse with the Father and the Son. No one knows how long that conversation took because we are talking about an eternal dimension that has no beginning and no end. The conversation comes to a conclusion – the purpose was formed. Then God spoke, but we have no record of what he said. What we do have, however, are these scriptures: "By faith we understand that the universe was created by the word of God..." (Heb.11:3) That "word" is the Greek word *rhēmati* – 'a living and spoken word'. He spoke, and the whole universe suddenly came into being. It was now created, but it remained in total darkness. Speaking specifically of the earth, it was "without form and void" (Gen.1:2). There is an interesting piece of Hebrew poetry here – *tôhû vabôhû* – 'unshapen and empty'. Almost like an unformed child in the darkness of a womb. (cf. Ps.139:16)

He was there in the darkness, hovering. The word "hovering" (Gen.1:2) is from the Hebrew word *râchaph,* and speaks of "the hovering and brooding of a bird over its young, to warm them, and develop their vital powers"[1]. The Hebrew word is only used again in the song of Moses:

> *He found him in a desert land, and in the howling waste of the wilderness; he encircled him, he cared for him, he kept him as the apple of his eye. Like an eagle that stirs up its nest, that flutters over its young...*
>
> Deuteronomy 32:10-11

In this passage, the word "flutters" is that same Hebrew word *râchaph.* There is a mother's love being expressed here, a warm and deep love that seeks to nurture. Derek Kidner wrote, "The picture is that of a

---

[1]   Keil and Delitzsch, *Commentary on the Old Testament,* e-sword.net

mother eagle stirring up her nest, fluttering over her young, bringing what is immature into more active life."[1]

Notice the words and phrases "encircled", "cared for", "kept as the apple of the eye", "fluttered". This is the very heart of the Spirit of God. A profound, tender, nurturing and cultivating love. As he hovered, there was an atmosphere of expectation – of something about to happen.

He was there in the incarnation. Raymond Brown, a world-renowned Catholic scholar, wrote, "The earth was void and without form when that Spirit arrived; just so Mary's womb was a void until the Spirit of God filled it with a child who was His Son."[2] The Spirit's loving activity brought the Christ-child into the womb and then into the world. He then grew under his nurture, and became the Saviour of the world.

He is here now in the church, the body of Christ. The same loving Spirit now inhabits the church, seeking to nurture her into maturity – into the fulness of the image of the Son of God. All his working in us is to this effect. His influence is always lovingly restorative, always lovingly nurturing, always lovingly encouraging, always bringing things together. That's how he is recognised. Other spirits, both human and demonic, are noted, incidentally, for their destructive and divisive nature.

Throughout the history of this earth, and in the children of Adam and Eve, he has sought to lovingly nurture and develop all that God has created. He is the same Spirit – the timeless Spirit – the one Spirit.

Thought

Walking and working with the Spirit brings deep and refreshing fruit.

Prayer

Dear Holy Spirit, fold me into your nurturing processes in the church and in the earth.

---

[1] Derek Kidner, *Genesis,* (IVP, Leicester, 1990), p.26
[2] Raymond Brown, *The Birth of the Messiah,* (Doubleday, New York, 1977), p.314

DAY ONE HUNDRED AND EIGHTY-FOUR

One Hope

Eph.4:4

...just as you were called to the one hope that belongs to your call...

Paul's roots were deep in the Hebrew faith and he was soaked in the Hebrew Scriptures. The Jewish faith was established firmly in the *Shema* – "Hear, O Israel: The LORD our God, the LORD is one. You shall love the LORD your God with all your heart and with all your soul and with all your might." (Deut.6:4,5) The numerical value of "one" is huge in Jewish thinking and theology. And so is the number seven – through both Old and New Testaments. Eugene Peterson feels that the seven ones that are used in this passage are like Monet's paintings of the lilies in his water garden.

Claude Monet was one of the most influential French painters of the nineteenth century. In 1883, he settled at Giverny, about some 65 kilometres west of Paris. It was here that he created his famous water garden. In the garden he built a Japanese bridge, and his painting of the bridge is called *Le Bassin aux Nympheas.* It was auctioned at Christie's of London in 2008, and sold for £40.9 million. After painting the gardens around his house, he then turned his attention to the water gardens. Between 1897 and his death in 1926, he produced more than 250 oil paintings of his lily ponds and his Japanese bridge. They were all painted from different angles and at different times of the day. Similarly, Paul is giving us seven portraits, seven variations on the one theme – God and his activities.

Today, we are looking at the "one hope" and, like the others words, it is rich in texture and meaning. Paul uses the Greek word *elpidi,* which means 'to anticipate, to have an expectation'. In the Greek Old Testament, the word is used 116 times. In the New Testament, the word is used 53 times. Paul used it 36 times. Harold Hoehner wrote, "The NT's concept of hope is built on the OT and has the elements of expectation, a trust in God, and the patient waiting for God's outworking of his plan."[1]

There is nothing worse in life than living with no hope. I have conducted funerals for those who had no hope, and the despair and fear are often palpable. When there is nothing at all in view, we live in a perpetual darkness of soul.

Theologians are in agreement that the hope that Paul is writing about here (and in 1:18) is a subjective hope rather than an objective hope. It is linked to, empowered by and inspired by the calling. Harold Hoehner felt that it could be better translated "the hope produced by your call"[2]. Clinton Arnold concurs, writing, "...the calling is what produces the hope."[3] Hope, therefore, is not our goal but our experience.

The fact is that you and I have been called not so much into a personal hope as into the great hope of God, that sees the immense picture of people of all walks of life, cultures and nations being reborn into a kaleidoscopic unity in Christ. This is something that both inflames and sustains the heart and imagination.

Thought

Our calling into the purpose of God originates and inspires a deep hope within us.

Prayer

O Lord, all my personal hopes and dreams find their ultimate fulfilment in your great hope.

---

[1] Harold Hoehner, *Ephesians: An Exegetical Commentary*, (Baker Academic, Michigan, 2002), p.264

[2] Ibid, p.516

[3] Clinton E. Arnold, *Ephesians*, (Zondervan, Michigan, 2010), p.233

DAY ONE HUNDRED AND EIGHTY-FIVE

One Lord

Eph.4:5

...one Lord, one faith, one baptism...

At the very heart of walking with Jesus is the immutable fact that he called us to follow him. We are not designed, as some would have it, to follow our own inclinations, or our own desires and dreams. We were not called to forge our own destinies. All these are laid down and left behind as we take our place following the Master. My personal agenda had to die on the table when I saw his. There is a huge cost in all this; when we follow him, we leave things, people, dreams and personal visions behind us.

Gordon MacDonald tells the story of a man who was struggling with the concept of 'accepting Christ'. He was making the point that accepting someone was not a big deal. Acceptance could mean simply tolerance. MacDonald went on to change the idea to that of 'following Christ'. A first century audience would understand that concept. MacDonald said to the man, "Apparently, they knew exactly what that meant because it was a familiar invitation on the part of teachers. In practical terms it meant living with the man for a while and learning to look at all of reality from the way he saw it." The man's response is notable: "That's an improvement. I can see some sense in that concept. And it certainly makes clear as to who's on top and in the lead."[1]

The word "Lord" is hugely significant. The Greek word is *kurios* and, according to Thayer, it means "he to whom a person or thing belongs, about which he has power of deciding"[2]. In other words, the word describes someone who has ultimate authority over our lives. Therefore, he is more than a Saviour, he is a Sovereign, before whom we walk and to whom we give loving and obedient service. Our wills are swallowed up in his and, to be honest, we are most fulfilled when we allow him to lead us.

---

[1] Gordon MacDonald, *Forging a Real World Faith,* (Highland Books, East Sussex, 1990), pp.45,46

[2] *Thayer's Greek Definitions,* e-sword.net

In the Roman world in which these believers lived, to express openly that Jesus is Lord was tantamount to treason of the highest order. Living under the popular Roman belief and insistence that Caesar is Lord, the early Christians often found themselves in direct conflict with the authorities. In fact, many died in amphitheatres and colosseums simply because they refused to recant of their belief that Jesus was the one true Lord of all.

In a world of many 'lords', the believers insisted that there was only one – the Lord Jesus Christ. Paul, in writing to the Philippians, put it this way: that in the light of his humbling himself to become one of us and taking on the sufferings and death on the cross...

> *God has highly exalted him and bestowed on him the name that is above every name, so that at the name of Jesus every knee should bow, in heaven and on earth and under the earth, and every tongue confess that Jesus Christ is Lord, to the glory of God the Father.*
>
> Philippians 2:9-11

He is Lord of the universe, he is Lord of all the earth, he is Lord of the church, and he is my Lord and your Lord too. All allegiance is owed to him. There is no other to whom we should give our hearts and our lives. And the key marker that this has happened is that there rises up within us a willing and genuine desire to obey him, and follow him wherever he chooses to lead us.

Thought

We need to transition from simply being forgiven to become forgiven followers.

Prayer

Lord Jesus, that is your rightful title. I will follow you, and obey your leadings.

DAY ONE HUNDRED AND EIGHTY-SIX

One Faith

Eph.4:5

...one Lord, one faith, one baptism...

L et me blind you with some statistics. You can find a lot of information on the Internet. For example, according to Wikipedia, some statisticians estimate that there are roughly 4,200 religions in the world.[1] And according to *infoplease.com:*

> *...the world's faithful account for 83% of the global population; the great majority of these fall under twelve classical religions – Baha'i, Buddhism, Christianity, Confucianism, Hinduism, Islam, Jainism, Judaism, Shinto, Sikhism, Taoism, and Zoroastrianism.*[2]

This in itself paints a picture of confusion.

Another site, *Twelvetribes.com,* notes:

> *According to a report published by the Center for the Study of Global Christianity at Gordon-Conwell Theological Seminary, in mid-2014 there were over 45,000 Christian denominations worldwide. Furthermore, that number is increasing at the rate of 2.2 new denominations per day.*[3]

Yet another site, *learnreligions.com,* says:

> *In 2015, Christians still comprised the largest religious group in the world (with 2.3 billion adherents), representing nearly a third (31%) of the total global population.*[4]

Yet for all this, Paul writes to the Ephesians saying that there is "one faith", and that still holds true today. Although Christianity is not the oldest religion, nevertheless, according to the apostle John, Jesus was "the true light, which gives light to everyone, [that] was coming into the

---

[1]   *https://en.wikipedia.org/wiki/List_of_religions_and_spiritual_traditions*
[2]   *https://www.infoplease.com/world/religion/major-religions-world*
[3]   *https://www.twelvetribes.com/articles/why-are-there-45000-denominations*
[4]   *https://www.learnreligions.com/christianity-statistics-700533*

world. He was in the world, and the world was made through him, yet the world did not know him." (Jn.1:9,10) In another place Paul wrote to Timothy, "...for there is one God, and there is one mediator between God and men, the man Christ Jesus, who gave himself as a ransom for all, which is the testimony given at the proper time." (2.Tim.2:5,6)

This "one faith" separates itself from, and towers above, all other faiths. Only here do we have a God who enters our world in human form as one of us, but also dies for our sins and rises from the dead. Only here do we have a God who desires to enter into a deep and personal relationship with us, teaching us to hear his voice, and challenging us to walk closely with him. Only here do we have a God who regularly breaks into our lives with provision, healing and deep love.

The only way that the "one faith" can ever be achieved is by getting close to the "one Lord". It will never be by finding the lowest common denominator in our belief systems. And when you look at the Christian church today with all of its particular denominations, one must wonder if heaven despairs. It seems that almost 'at the drop of a hat' we will find something to disagree with or be offended by, and that will be our cue to join something else that better suits our style of church, or we will form something else that is more to our spiritual taste. What we have today in large measure is 'faith according to our taste'. "One faith" and "one church" is not easy, but it is the Jesus way. We must find a way to live with great tolerance with and for each other, aiming purposefully at maintaining the unity already given to us in Christ.

Thought

Turning away from each other equals turning away from the Christ who lives in us.

Prayer

Dear Lord, help me to surrender my own perspectives and find yours instead.

DAY ONE HUNDRED AND EIGHTY-SEVEN

Simplicity

Eph.4:5

...one Lord, one faith, one baptism...

Into our thinking of these seven portraits of the one theme of God in all his activities, I want to introduce a pause. In these verses Paul is streamlining everything. Into a world that was full of spiritual pluralities and religious options, he was inserting a deep simplicity.

Simplicity is different from simple. If something is simple, then it takes very little effort or cost to achieve. On the other hand, a true simplicity requires the drastic and sometimes painful pruning of the superfluous in our lives in order to enhance the important. Dallas Willard describes it as "the arrangement of life around a few consistent purposes, explicitly excluding what is not necessary to human well-being"[1].

The phrase "one thing" is mentioned 14 times in the Scriptures. I want to pick out three of them. The first is found on the lips of David, when he writes, "One thing have I asked of the LORD, that will I seek after: that I may dwell in the house of the LORD all the days of my life, to gaze upon the beauty of the LORD and to inquire in his temple." (Ps.27:4) The second is found on the lips of Jesus as he reproved an over-anxious Martha. He said, "Martha, Martha, you are anxious and troubled about many things, but one thing is necessary. Mary has chosen the good portion, which will not be taken away from her." (Lk.10:41,42) Then Paul writes himself to the Philippians, "...one thing I do: forgetting what lies behind and straining forward to what lies ahead, I press on toward the goal for the prize of the upward call of God in Christ Jesus." (Phil.3:13,14) True simplicity brings a sharp focus.

In 2012, Eugene Peterson was invited to share in a conference entitled 'Cultivating Your Inner Life in an Age of Distraction'. One of his sessions was on the subject of simplicity. It was noted by an attendee that...

---

[1]   Dallas Willard, *The Spirit of The Disciplines,* (Harper & Row, San Francisco, 1988), p.170

Peterson started with a confession. Not only was simplicity the hardest discipline for him to talk about, but it has never personally been something that he has found easy to live out. But from everything I've seen, his life would suggest otherwise. He moves gently, and has a soft-spoken demeanour, that almost makes you think of a monk – misplaced.[1]

What he was inside was exhibited in his deportment.

Richard Foster is the professor of Spiritual Formation at Azusa Pacific University. On the subject of simplicity, he wrote that the Christian discipline of simplicity "is an inward reality that results in an outward life-style"[2]. He added, "To attempt to arrange an outward life-style of simplicity without the inward reality leads to deadly legalism."[3] Simplicity, then, is not a technical thing, rather it is a matter of the heart.

Paul is insisting that the Christian faith does not become complicated and full of personal preferences and diversions. For him there is "one body, one Spirit, one hope, one Lord, one faith, one baptism, one God and Father of all, who is over all and through all and in all". Paul is saying, "Reduce and simplify!"

Thought

Clearing the superfluous from our lives allows us to see spiritual reality more clearly.

Prayer

Father, please point out those things that clog me up, so I can walk without impediments.

---

[1] *https://faithoncampus.com/blog/eugene-peterson-on-simplicity/*
[2] Richard Foster, *Celebration of Discipline,* (Hodder & Stoughton, London, 1989), p.99
[3] Ibid, pp.99,100

DAY ONE HUNDRED AND EIGHTY-EIGHT

One Baptism

Eph.4:5

...one Lord, one faith, one baptism...

I remember well the Sunday evening I was baptised in my local Baptist Church. I had been out the night before doing some 'coffee bar' evangelism in the Lanes in Brighton. All was going well until about six or seven Hell's Angels walked in. At that point my ministry suddenly and fearfully changed from engaging people in conversation to serving coffee from behind the relative safety of the coffee bar counter! Sad to say, but I went home thoroughly ashamed of myself.

On that Sunday evening, prior to the service, I was in a prayer meeting with those being baptised. I found myself confessing my fears, and asking God to baptise me also with the Holy Spirit. As the service proceeded, I falteringly gave my testimony and then entered the baptismal pool. As I went under the water, I remembered my prayer, and suddenly it happened! The Spirit of God touched me profoundly and I came out of the pool shouting, "Hallelujah!" very loudly indeed! I was filled with a holy joy and a boldness. The following Saturday night's 'coffee bar' evangelism was noticeably different! I couldn't wait to get at those Hell's Angels. For me, the text in the first chapter of Acts had come alive – "But you will receive power when the Holy Spirit has come upon you, and you will be my witnesses..." (Acts 1:8) Paul writes that there is "one baptism". My experience was that the two were rolled into one!

The "one baptism" that he was speaking about is, of course, the baptism in water. It is a significant part of the discipling of new believers. Jesus commissioned his own disciples, "Go, therefore and make disciples of all nations, baptising them in the name of the Father and of the Son and of the Holy Spirit..." (Matt.28:19) This trinitarian baptism is an identification of the new believer with the family of God. When Jesus was baptised, it was in order to identify with fallen mankind. When we are baptised, we are identifying ourselves as the children of God. We are, to use the current language, 'coming out' with our faith, bringing it into the public eye. For many believers in the Near and Middle East, that could prove to be a fatal move. Such a public declaration of faith puts their livelihoods, and at times their lives, at risk.

But it is deeper than that. Paul, writing to the believers in Rome, put it this way:

> *Do you not know that all of us who have been baptised into Christ Jesus were baptised into his death? We were buried therefore with him by baptism into death, in order that, just as Christ was raised from the dead by the glory of the Father, we too might walk in newness of life. For if we have been united with him in a death like his, we shall certainly be united with him in a resurrection like his.*

Romans 6:3-5

In other words, the old me – with all my attitudes, belief systems, habits and perceptions – was buried in the baptismal pool, a very wet and watery grave! I must confess that I know more about the significance of baptism now than I did back in 1970, and sometimes wish that I could do it again in the light of what I now understand.

A compelling image is supplied by Kenneth Leech: "It is a symbolic drowning of the old life; the baptismal pool becomes tomb and womb, grave and mother, and from it emerges a new child of the resurrection."[1]

Thought

The external water burial is a public demonstration of the death that has happened within.

Prayer

Dear Lord, help me to come out of my hiding and to go public with my faith in you.

---

[1] Kenneth Leech, *Soul Friend – a Study of Spirituality,* (Sheldon Press, London, 1980), p.122

DAY ONE HUNDRED AND EIGHTY-NINE

One God and Father

Eph.4:6

...one God and Father of all, who is over all and through all and in all.

Just to add to yesterday's thinking about the "one baptism": according to the Scriptures, new life emerges out of the death of the old one and, to quote F.F. Bruce, "Burial sets the seal on death; so the Christian's baptism is a token burial in which the old order of living comes to an end, to be replaced by the new order of life-in-Christ."[1]

Paul now rounds up his thinking on the seven portraits of the triune God and his activities. He writes that there is "one God and Father of all, who is over all and through all and in all". Paul repeats this kind of 'rounding up' elsewhere in his writings. To the believers in Rome he wrote, "For from him and through him and to him are all things. To him be glory forever. Amen." (Rom.11:36) To the church in Colossae he wrote of Christ, "He is the image of the invisible God, the firstborn of all creation. For by him all things were created, in heaven and on earth, visible and invisible, whether thrones or dominions or rulers or authorities – all things were created through him and for him. And he is before all things, and in him all things hold together." (Col.1:15-17)

Concerning our text for today, Eugene Peterson wrote, "The underlying and all-encompassing oneness that is church flows from the understanding and all-encompassing oneness that is God."[2] He went on to write:

> *The repetitions in this context are not, I think, a nagging insistence on monotheism as a dogma to be believed; this is gentle pastoral reassurance that we are involved in a life of*

---

[1] F.F. Bruce, *Romans,* (IVP, Michigan, 1983), p.138
[2] Eugene Peterson, *Practise Resurrection,* (Hodder & Stoughton, London, 2010), p.176

basic simplicity ... this basic and inherent oneness is at hand wherever we look and whatever we touch.[1]

It is we who complicate things, dividing them up into our boxes of preference and practice. God is a unity, and if we truly follow him, we will be drawn into that unity.

Here, he is the God and Father of all. This is primarily in the sense of our origins. Without God, no one or nothing would exist. This is "the Father, from whom every family in heaven and on earth is named" (Eph.3:15). Clinton Arnold writes that it is best "to view it as a confession of God's sovereignty, his omnipotence, and his presence in all of his creation"[2].

This is not pantheism, where God is taken to literally live in all things, but the biblical thought that he is "involved in all things, working his will in all things, and ultimately uniting all things in Christ"[3]. Neither is this an expression of universalism, that insists that ultimately all will be saved. These old chestnuts have torn the motivation, the passion and the urgency for evangelism out of the heart of many churches.

The Creator is also the saviour, the restorer and the gatherer. Where Satan brings disintegration and destruction, God integrates us into a deep unity and fulfilment with himself, his people and his creation.

Thought

The river of God gathers. The rivers (plural) of evil scatter. Get in the right river.

Prayer

Dear Father, draw me to yourself, and through me draw others to each other and to you.

---

[1]   Ibid, pp.176,177
[2]   Clinton E. Arnold, *Ephesians,* (Zondervan, Michigan, 2010), p.236
[3]   Mark D. Roberts, *Ephesians,* (Zondervan, Michigan, 2016), p.122

DAY ONE HUNDRED AND NINETY

Each One of Us

Eph.4:7

But grace was given to each one of us according to the measure of Christ's gift.

We are now moving from thinking about the whole church, immersed and wrapped up in the unity of the triune God, to the grace that is given to each individual. There is variety and diversity found in unity. There is one body that consists of many members, each playing different roles. True unity is realised in harmony, not uniformity or conformity. The only conformity that is valid is conformity to Christ.

Just as the unity of the Spirit is supernatural in source and activity, so it is with God's diverse grace given to individuals. Clinton Arnold writes that…

> …*this diversity has nothing to do with the various ethnicities, background, and natural talents of the individual members. It has to do with Christ's sovereign distribution of divine gifts and abilities among the different members.*[1]

In other words, both the unity and the giftings of grace are God-given – the natural has nothing much to do with it, except to cooperate with the Holy Spirit in order to nurture and express what God has graciously conferred. It is true that often a gift of God is wrapped up in a human gifting or ability, but nevertheless it is a grace-gift of God, and it is to him that we must look for its nurture and manifestation. If you like, a natural gift is like an engine in a car, but the grace of God is the fuel.

From another angle, Harold Hoehner makes this observation: "Every single believer is included, no one is excluded, it is not only for the leaders of the assembly."[2] Paul will treat leadership giftings, or more accurately, gifts of specifically graced individuals, later. Here, Paul is looking at every

---

[1] Clinton E. Arnold, *Ephesians,* (Zondervan, Michigan, 2010), p.243
[2] Harold Hoehner, *Ephesians: An Exegetical Commentary,* (Baker Academic, Michigan, 2002), p.522

individual. As Arnold rightly notes, "To each individual God has given a gift to contribute to the growth of the body."[1]

The grace that Paul is writing about is not the grace of salvation, but the grace to function as a contributing believer and member of the body of Christ. This grace enables.

I have observed over the years that some people end up doing things in the church that they are not actually graced to do. The result of that is intense stress and sometimes burnout. They find themselves being round pegs in square holes. God's grace is identified by a smooth and easy manifestation and fruitfulness. Eugene Peterson's rendering of the word of Jesus to stressed people is, "Walk with me and work with me – watch how I do it. Learn the unforced rhythms of grace. I won't lay anything heavy or ill-fitting on you. Keep company with me and you'll learn to live freely and lightly." (Matt.11:29,30, MSG) I like that very much – "the unforced rhythms of grace" – it says it all.

This grace of God lifts us up and empowers us to contribute to the growth of the church – the body of Christ. It doesn't matter who you are or where you come from – God has placed you, and is empowering you to bring something to that which he is building, and only you can bring it. One little boy brought his lunchbox and it fed more than 5,000 people. (Jn.6:1-13)

Thought

God has given you something with which to serve the church. Identify it and give it.

Prayer

Help me to see that I am a significant member of your body with something to contribute.

---

[1] Clinton E. Arnold, *Ephesians,* (Zondervan, Michigan, 2010), p.246

DAY ONE HUNDRED AND NINETY-ONE

According to the Measure

Eph.4:7

But grace was given to each one of us according to the measure of Christ's gift.

God has a very long-term view of the church. As each age passes, he has had individuals lined up to enter each generation in order fulfil a particular ministry in, to and through the church. From an eternal perspective, God had ordered it so from before the foundation of the earth. From a historical perspective, however, these folks are graced and gifted, sometimes at birth, where it begins to manifest very early, and sometimes upon their new birth, where again it begins to show itself, often to the surprise of the individual. Looking back, however, after many years, it can be seen that a grace-seed had been sown and, over much time, had been lovingly nurtured and developed.

As we noted yesterday, this is not grace for salvation but grace for service. This is functioning grace. John Stott called the difference "saving grace" and "serving grace".[1] Paul, in his letter to the church in Corinth, wrote that "according to the grace of God given to me, like a skilled master builder I laid a foundation" (1.Cor.3:10). In other words, he was enabled by the grace of God to function as a church builder. He wrote of his ability to work harder than his apostolic contemporaries, attributing the energy to do so to the grace of God. His own testimony was, "But by the grace of God I am what I am, and his grace toward me was not in vain. On the contrary, I worked harder than any of them, though it was not I, but the grace of God that is with me." (1.Cor.15:10)

This empowering grace comes by measure, and it is Christ who allocates both the gift and the measure. This is very much in line with what Paul shared with the church in Rome. He felt that there was a measure of faith given to each individual, and that we ought to think carefully about that, writing, "For by the grace given to me I say to everyone among you not to think of himself more highly than he ought to think, but to think with sober judgment, each according to the measure

---

[1] John Stott, *The Message of Ephesians,* (IVP, Leicester, 1979), p.155

of faith that God has assigned." (Rom.12:3) He then wrote that "having gifts that differ according to the grace given to us, let us use them" (Rom.12:6).

There is a specific measure of grace for each one of us, a specific size of sphere of service, and the choice of that measure has been made by Christ himself. We need to seek the Lord about this, and also be open to the wise counsel of others who see in us what we do not see in ourselves. We are to know it and grow into it. I have also seen those who have shied away from any kind of ministry, thinking that they were not able or worthy, but they have robbed themselves and the church of the grace-gift that God had given them. We are to grow into it but not exceed it. I have also seen too many tragic occurrences of those who thought their ministry was larger than it actually was, and they have floundered and caused pain to the church. There is a balance in all this.

Whatever measure God has given to us, we need to live in that measure to the full. Let me reiterate here that Paul is talking about every child of God, not just leaders in the church. Your sphere of service in your place of employment is equally valid to that of the preacher in the pulpit. Let God grow you into your gift and cause your gift to grow. Be content with your placement and with what he has given you.

Thought

God has his people everywhere – in churches, offices and shop floors. They are everywhere.

Prayer

Lord, help me to recognise both the gift and the sphere that you have given me to serve you.

DAY ONE HUNDRED AND NINETY-TWO

The Captive Becomes the Gift

Eph.4:8

Therefore it says, "When he ascended on high he led a host of captives, and he gave gifts to men."

Today is going to be a thinking day. Paul now breaks into another parenthesis, another of his literary tactics. It's like he wants to set another stage for what is coming next, and so he now introduces a text from the book of Psalms – "You ascended on high, leading a host of captives in your train and receiving gifts among men, even among the rebellious, that the LORD God may dwell there." (Ps.68:18)

Here's the thing: David, in this psalm, wrote that the conquering king received gifts. Paul, on the other hand, wrote that the resurrected Christ gave gifts. Eugene Peterson called this "a creative and deliberate misquotation"[1]. Let's think about this.

Two of the oldest translations of the Old Testament are the Aramaic *Targum* and the Syriac *Peshitta*. The Aramaic *Targum* was literally a free paraphrastic (the expressing of the meaning by other words – today we use the word 'paraphrase') rendering of the Hebrew Scriptures into Aramaic. They date from around the second century AD. Also, the spread of Christianity into Syria brought about the need for a translation in their own language, hence the Syriac *Peshitta*. The word *peshitta* means a 'simple version'. Both these ancient versions have the word "gave" instead of "receive". They were in use in Paul's day, and thus reflected what was probably the traditional interpretation.

John Stott wrote:

> *...we need to remember that after every conquest in the ancient world there was invariably both a receiving of tribute and a distributing of largesse. What conquerors took from their captives, they gave away to their own people.[2]*

---

[1] Eugene Peterson, lectures on 'Soulcraft: The Formation of a Mature Life in Christ', Regents College, Vancouver

[2] John Stott, *The Message of Ephesians,* (IVP, Leicester, 1979), p.157

H.G. Leupold, a professor of Old Testament exegesis, wrote:

Paul's use of this verse in Eph.4:8 is somewhat free ... but entirely in the spirit of the passage. He apparently regards the Lord's victorious entrance into Jerusalem as a type or figure of Christ's triumphant entry into the heavens, laden with the fruits of his encounter, fruits which he is ready to bestow on his own.[1]

Keil and Delitzsch, in their very technical commentary on the Old Testament, wrote, "What the Victor has gained over the powers of darkness and of death, He has gained not for His own aggrandisement, but for the interests of men. [They are] ... gifts which He now distributes among men..."[2]

Eugene Peterson went on to say, "This switch gets our attention. Jesus surprises us. Instead of receiving, He gives gifts. Instead of hoarding, He shares them out to the church."[3] Someone has put it like this: "Jesus captivates people. He captured Saul and reconditioned him, and then gave him back to the church. What God conquers he does not keep. He transforms them into gifts for the church." Service is at the heart of God, and the service he gives to the church is through redeemed, sanctified and specifically shaped individuals.

Thought

One of the principles of heaven is that we receive in order to give.

Prayer

Lord, reshape my surrendered heart in order that I may become your effective servant.

---

[1]   H.G. Leupold, *Exposition of the Psalms,* (Evangelical Press, London, 1972), p.495
[2]   Keil and Delitzsch, *Commentary on the Old Testament,* e-sword.net
[3]   Eugene Peterson, lectures on 'Soulcraft: The Formation of a Mature Life in Christ', Regents College, Vancouver

DAY ONE HUNDRED AND NINETY-THREE

The Deep Descent

Eph.4:9,10

(In saying, "He ascended," what does it mean but that he had also descended into the lower regions, the earth? He who descended is the one who also ascended far above all the heavens, that he might fill all things.)

Apart from Mary and Joseph, John the apostle was probably the closest individual to Jesus who really understood who he really was and is. On a number of occasions in his Gospel, John records Jesus dropping strong hints about his home turf – heaven. For example, he said, "For I have come down from heaven, not to do my own will but the will of him who sent me." (Jn.6:38) Later in the same chapter he said to some grumbling disciples, "Do you take offence at this? Then what if you were to see the Son of Man ascending to where he was before?" (Jn.6:62) He then said to the unbelieving Pharisees, "I will be with you a little longer, and then I am going to him who sent me. You will seek me and you will not find me. Where I am you cannot come." (Jn.7:33,34) Christ did not originate in Mary's womb. In fact, Christ did not originate. He is the eternal Son. He said to some other Pharisees, "You are from below; I am from above. You are of this world; I am not of this world," (Jn.8:23) and then later, "Truly, truly, I say to you, before Abraham *was, I am.*" (Jn.8:58, emphasis added) Note the tenses in this last text.

The Christian faith is the only one that takes Christ's incarnation seriously. It is the only faith where the God of all creation came down to the earth where humanity lived, took on human form, lived and then died among us and for us. As Eugene Peterson put it in The Message, "The Word became flesh and blood, and moved into the neighbourhood." (Jn.1:14)

The King of heaven came into our darkness, treading our earth, breathing our air and suffering our sufferings. The sinless one took upon himself the sin of the world – the root cause of all suffering and pain – and paid the just penalty for it in our stead on the cross. Paul, in his letter to the Philippians, put it like this: "He took the humble position of a slave and was born as a human being. When He appeared in human form, He

151

humbled Himself in obedience to God and died a criminal's death on a cross." (Phil.2:7,8, NLT) You and I, wherever we are found, were included in that death. In that one act he wiped out all of our sins.

Christ descended from the highest place to the lowest of all places. There has been a measure of debate about the phrase "the lower regions, the earth". It should read more literally "the lower parts of the earth". Clinton Arnold wrote, "The view of the early Church Fathers and the consensus view throughout the centuries has been that it refers to a descent of Christ to the underworld (or, Hades)."[1] This finds a resonance with something the apostle Peter wrote in his first letter: "For Christ … went and proclaimed to the spirits in prison..." (1.Pet.3:19) The Apostles' Creed says, "He descended into hell..."

There are no depths to which Jesus cannot, and does not, descend with the good news of the gospel of the kingdom. No matter how low one has got or become, Christ reaches there with salvation in his hands.

Thought

His eye beholds the deepest darkness and finds us there.

Prayer

Lord, all my darkness is as day to you. I am so grateful that you found me, and still find me.

---

[1]   Clinton E. Arnold, *Ephesians,* (Zondervan, Michigan, 2010), p.253

DAY ONE HUNDRED AND NINETY-FOUR

The Huge Ascent

Eph.4:9,10

(In saying, "He ascended," what does it mean but that he had also descended into the lower regions, the earth? He who descended is the one who also ascended far above all the heavens, that he might fill all things.)

Yesterday we looked at the deep descent of Christ. He came to where all of humanity had bottomed out. No one is too deep in sin and shame for him to touch and rescue with his redeeming love.

The Christian faith is the only one that takes Christ's ascension seriously. It is the only faith where the God who came down to earth also went back to where he came from. As Luke records, "And when he had said these things, as they were looking on, he was lifted up, and a cloud took him out of their sight." (Acts 1:9) The Message has it, "As they watched, he was taken up and disappeared in a cloud. They stood there, staring into the empty sky."

After the deep descent, Christ made his ascent – to the highest place – "far above the heavens". This is where God lives. The heavens that we can all see – the heavens that science attempts to measure – are the creation of God. Paul, in his letter to the church in Corinth, spoke of a third heaven. Speaking, we believe, of himself, he wrote, "I know a man in Christ who fourteen years ago was caught up to the third heaven..." (2.Cor.12:2) Philip Hughes, in his commentary on Second Corinthians, cites the German Lutheran theologian Johann Albrecht Bengel (1687-1752) as explaining "that the first heaven was that of the clouds, that is, of the earth's atmosphere, the second that of the stars, and the third a heaven which is spiritual"[1]. This third heaven is unseen; it is the totally different realm that is over and above creation, and yet in which all creation is somehow located. It is to here, the third, invisible heaven, to which Christ ascended.

---

[1] Philip E. Hughes, *The Second Epistle to the Corinthians,* (Eerdmans, Michigan, 1977), p.433

The purpose was that "he might fill all things". Harold Hoehner wrote, "...the object of Christ's ascension was to allow him to enter into a sovereign relationship with the whole world, and in that position he has the right to bestow gifts as he wills."[1]

Hoehner also sums up these verses that we have been looking at by writing, "Christ's descent enabled him to gain victory over Satan, sin, and death, followed by his ascension where as conqueror he has the right to bestow gifts to the church."[2]

Thus Paul has set the scene from Psalm 68, which Eugene Peterson describes as "a long song, a collection of fragments, mostly to do with warfare. The psalm describes the triumph of God, an atmosphere of worship..."[3] Paul reinterprets by saying this had a prophetic dimension, describing how the King of heaven would enter our world, breaking all the power of our three deadly enemies – Satan, sin and death – and would ascend triumphantly back into the wonderful realm from where he emerged.

Thought

The stage has been set, the King is waiting for you to walk on and play your part.

Prayer

Lord, show me my part to play, and grant me to play it well, to the applause of heaven.

---

[1] Harold Hoehner, *Ephesians: An Exegetical Commentary*, (Baker Academic, Michigan, 2002), p.537
[2] Ibid, p.538
[3] Eugene Peterson, lectures on 'Soulcraft: The Formation of a Mature Life in Christ', Regents College, Vancouver

DAY ONE HUNDRED AND NINETY-FIVE

The Gifts of Christ (1)

Eph.4:11

And he gave the apostles, the prophets, the evangelists, the shepherds and teachers...

We now encounter another of Paul's long sentences. In the original Greek there are 124 words in this sentence; it runs from verse 11 right through to verse 16. One can feel the excitement of the apostle as he warms to his subject.

The stage has been set, and now Paul is going to introduce some of the players. Firstly, the phrase "he gave" – *autos edōken* – contains an intensive pronoun in the Greek language. It is better translated 'he himself gave'. These were not appointments by men, but by the Head of the church – Christ himself. Neither were these advancements in one's spiritual career. These people were specifically named, called and grown for an express purpose. Paul always saw his apostleship as a specific calling from God, having nothing to do with human machinations. He wrote to the Galatians, "Paul, an apostle – not from men nor through man, but through Jesus Christ and God the Father..." (Gal.1:1) His apostleship was not conferred, rather it was recognised.

Secondly, these were some, not all, of the players. The ESV reading above misses the important word 'some'. Harold Hoehner translates it more literally: "Namely, he gave some to be apostles, and some to be prophets, and some to be evangelists, and some to be pastors and teachers."[1]

Still using the analogy of a theatre production, these five are the main players. But, as in every production, there is the vast army of other functionaries, many of them unseen to the public view. In the world of films, one only has to look at the long list of credits that fill the screen after each movie. Without them, the production and the film would grind to a halt. If we change the analogy to that of an army, these five represent the special forces in the frontline of an assault on enemy territory. And it

---

[1] Harold Hoehner, *Ephesians: An Exegetical Commentary,* (Baker Academic, Michigan, 2002), p.540

is well worth considering that, as such, they are the prime target of the enemy.

Many have desired to be the main players, desiring the visible successes and the recognition, adulation and attention that follows. They have not, however, considered the cost. I remember being quite challenged by the words of Charles Spurgeon, deemed to be the prince of preachers in his time. Commenting on the scripture, "O LORD, my heart is not lifted up; my eyes are not raised too high; I do not occupy myself with things too great and too marvellous for me," (Ps.131:1) he wrote:

> *Many through wishing to be great have failed to be good: they were not content to adorn the lowly stations which the Lord appointed them, and so they have rushed at grandeur and power; and found destruction where they looked for honour.*[1]

The main thing to point out here is that these gifts are not so much spiritual endowments that are given to individuals; they are the individuals themselves. These gifts of Christ are people who have been crafted and shaped by God over the years and, functioning in a certain way, they themselves have become the gifts that Christ gives to the church.

Thought

Frontline ministries attract frontal attacks. Pray for and protect such ministries.

Prayer

Lord, whatever role you have for me to play, let me be content and thereby fruitful in it.

---

[1] Charles H. Spurgeon, *Treasury of David,* Vol.6, (Marshall Brothers, London), p.137

Day One Hundred and Ninety-Six

The Gifts of Christ (2)

Eph.4:11

And he gave the apostles, the prophets, the evangelists, the shepherds and teachers...

In the church, there is a whole variety of ministries. Paul wrote to the Corinthians, "Now there are varieties of gifts, but the same Spirit; and there are varieties of service, but the same Lord; and there are varieties of activities, but it is the same God who empowers them all in everyone." (1.Cor.12:4-6) He also wrote:

For as in one body we have many members, and the members do not all have the same function, so we, though many, are one body in Christ, and individually members one of another. Having gifts that differ according to the grace given to us, let us use them...

Romans 12:4-6

As we read carefully through the New Testament, we cannot help but notice that there are many players in God's great production. There are many different kinds of giftings and levels of functions. Some are very visible and many are well behind the scenes.

When it comes to the leadership structures in churches, there are some leadership roles that are pertinent to the local church. To use the English terminology, these are the 'elders' and 'deacons'. To use the Greek words, they are the *presbuterois* and the *diakonois* – those who spiritually presided over the local church, and those who supervised the practical activities of the local church. These were rooted in, and functioned within, their own local church.

However, when it comes to what is commonly called 'the five-fold ministries gifts' of apostles, prophets, evangelists, pastors and teachers, these are ministries that are translocal. In other words, they function not only within a local church but elsewhere as well. They can be placed or sent anywhere, and they will function according to who and what they are. They need to be based and rooted in a local church, but they are ministries that can be sent. They are gifts, not so much to a local church, but to *the* church – national and international.

According to the late Professor Emeritus J. Rodman Williams, regarded as the father of modern renewal theology, they are "limited in number"[1]. He adds, "Not every Christian shares in them. Unlike *charismata* gifts, in which all believers participate, these *domata* gifts are of the few."[2]

In the book of Acts, we read of apostles being sent by their local church in Antioch to another local church at Jerusalem. The text reads:

> *Paul and Barnabas and some of the others were appointed to go up to Jerusalem to the apostles and the elders about this question. So, being sent on their way by the church, they passed through both Phoenicia and Samaria, describing in detail the conversion of the Gentiles, and brought great joy to all the brothers. When they came to Jerusalem, they were welcomed by the church and the apostles and the elders, and they declared all that God had done with them.*

Acts 15:2-4

These 'five-fold ministries' are intrinsically peripatetic (itinerant) in nature. Wherever they find themselves, they function and fulfil their ministry. And it's not so much that they have a ministry; they have become, and are, the ministry.

Thought

These few are tasked with a wide-reaching responsibility, seeing beyond the local walls.

Prayer

Lord, help me to see and recognise these individuals and to uphold them in my prayers.

---

[1] J. Rodman Williams, *Renewal Theology,* Vol.3, (Zondervan, Michigan, 1996), p.164
[2] Ibid.

DAY ONE HUNDRED AND NINETY-SEVEN

The Gifts of Christ (3)

Eph.4:11

And he gave the apostles, the prophets, the evangelists, the shepherds and teachers...

Today, I want us to think about the word 'process'. In reflecting over these five ministry gifts to the church, it has to be said that none of them appeared overnight. Each one was forged over time by the hands of God. No man laid hands on Paul, saying, "Receive the gift of apostleship." Chosen and called before time began, the child named Saul was born in whom the embryonic apostolic ability already resided. He would write years later to the Galatians:

> *But when he who had set me apart before I was born, and who called me by his grace, was pleased to reveal his Son to me, in order that I might preach him among the Gentiles, I did not immediately consult with anyone...*

Galatians 1:15,16

Over the years, subject to many providential activities, the zealot Saul was shaped and honed into his calling. He grew from the inside into becoming the apostle Paul. Talking of the apostle Paul, the Cistercian monk Thomas Merton wrote, "He was qualified to be an apostle by the depths of his interior life."[1]

If we use the analogy of a blacksmith creating a sword, we can truly understand the process. Imagine with me: drawn from the dark depths of the earth, the iron is hammered and cut into a rough bar. It is then introduced to the furnace where the blazing heat enters deeply into the iron, both purifying it and making it malleable to the hammer. The process begins of repeated heating and hammering. The fire cleanses and softens the iron. The hammer knocks it into shape. When he has finished the heating and beating, it is still not finished. If the sword, at this point,

---

[1] Thomas Merton, *Merton on St Bernard,* (Michigan, Cistercian Publications, 1980), p.32

was taken into battle, it would bend and become blunt very quickly under the pressure. When the shape is right, it is heated again until it glows bright red, and then plunged into cold water, the molecules within the metal changing, thus 'hardening' it.

Even now it is not ready. One strong encounter and the blade would shatter. The blacksmith then puts the sword back into the fire, but carefully this time. He watches for a blue colour to appear, and then he plunges it, not into water, but oil. The steel is now 'tempered' – not so much hard, but toughened. The brittleness has been removed and durability has been introduced. It is now ready for the clash.

The imagery is strong and full of meaning. This is how it goes with those whom God works on to become his ministry gifts to the church. This work is done over time, with plenty of fire and plenty of hammering, knocking and moulding his servants into the right shape and the right constituency.

These five ministry gifts are God's veteran soldiers and master craftsmen for the planting, the building and the shaping of the church. Each one brings a well-seasoned ministry to the church. They are to function together as a team, each having different perspectives and life-flows. Someone has written, "The apostle sees the whole picture; the prophet sees the mind of God; the evangelist sees the lost; the pastor sees the flock and the teacher sees the mature church." They forge their way into new territories under divine direction, creating and establishing churches, which are the light-emitting embassies of the kingdom of heaven in a dark world. They bring challenges and movement; they feed, nourish and equip the saints, enabling them to function well and efficiently in their own spheres.

Thought

There is no such gift as the gift of durability – it is forged over time.

Prayer

Dear Lord, grant me patience, and receptivity to your dealings in my life.

DAY ONE HUNDRED AND NINETY-EIGHT

The Five Perspectives

Eph.4:11

And he gave the apostles, the prophets, the evangelists, the shepherds and teachers...

As we continue looking at these five ministries, we can see a wonderful model of team. Each one of these individuals has a particular gifting, and also a different perspective, yet all of them are needed for a fully balanced church life.

As we noted yesterday, "The apostle sees the whole picture; the prophet sees the mind of God; the evangelist sees the lost; the pastor sees the flock and the teacher sees the mature church." Another way of putting this is that if you put an apostle in the pulpit, you'll get the big picture – their agenda is governing, strategy and vision. If you put a prophet in the pulpit, you'll get the big direction – their agenda is hearing from God, guiding and direction. If you put an evangelist in the pulpit, you'll get the big harvest – their agenda is gathering and growth. If you put a pastor in the pulpit, and you'll get the big heart – their agenda is caring, nurturing, guarding and security. And if you put a teacher in the pulpit, you'll get the big feed – their agenda is grounding, strengthening and maturity.

Yet another way of looking at this is to say, "The apostles construct the church; the prophets communicate the mind of God; the evangelists cast nets to catch men and women; the pastors care for the flock; and the teachers confirm and establish the church."

The different perspectives have to flow together in order to create a beautiful harmony, not a sharp cacophony. On occasions, however, there will be clashes of perspective. For me, the worst-case scenario is found in the argument between Paul and Barnabas. Paul wanted to revisit the churches that he and Barnabas had planted. Luke records:

Now Barnabas wanted to take with them John called Mark. But Paul thought best not to take with them one who had withdrawn from them in Pamphylia and had not gone with them to the work. And there arose a sharp disagreement, so that they separated from each other.

Acts 15:37-39

Here Paul, with the apostolic mindset, saw the big picture and cared passionately about it. Barnabas, with the pastoral mindset, saw the least worthy brother, Mark, and cared passionately about him. We need to think about a lot of the words we use – vision, strategy, purpose, direction. All these mentioned are important, but I would suggest that they are all impersonal. Perhaps we need to think also about people: Mark, and Barnabas and Paul. Both aspects make for a healthy balance.

Here's a thought: the apostolic, prophetic and evangelistic ministries reach out and plant churches; the pastoral ministry then turns them into homes; and the teaching ministry ensures that they are well fed and strong.

Just a final thought on all this... Eugene Peterson said in one of his lectures, "All our work is 'word work'. All these are 'workers of the word'. It's the word that shapes who we are and what we do."[1] In whatever way we present the good news of the kingdom, we must never forget that the power for change lies in the ministry of the word of God that is saturated and enabled by the Spirit of God.

Thought

Whatever the 'perspective', it is the word of God that is living and life-changing.

Prayer

Dear Lord, wherever I am and whatever I do, may I be a carrier of your word and Spirit.

---

[1]   Eugene Peterson, lectures on 'Soulcraft: The Formation of a Mature Life in Christ', Regents College, Vancouver

DAY ONE HUNDRED AND NINETY-NINE

Apostles

Rom.1:1

Paul, a servant of Christ Jesus, called to be an apostle, set apart for the gospel of God...

Today I want to insert one final thought about these five ministry gifts. They are not at 'the top of the tree', but rather, they reside around the roots. You see, the principles and values of the kingdom of heaven are totally different to the way we do life here on earth. Ponder these words of Jesus:

> *"You know that the rulers of the Gentiles lord it over them, and their great ones exercise authority over them. It shall not be so among you. But whoever would be great among you must be your servant, and whoever would be first among you must be your slave, even as the Son of Man came not to be served but to serve, and to give his life as a ransom for many."*
>
> Matthew 20:25-28

In this context, let me now introduce the first of these five 'ministry servants' – the apostle. Paul wrote to the Corinthians, who were a little over-fascinated by status, "I think that God has exhibited us apostles as last of all, like men sentenced to death, because we have become a spectacle to the world, to angels, and to men." (1.Cor.4:9) The Message puts it bluntly:

> *It seems to me that God has put us who bear his Message on stage in a theatre in which no one wants to buy a ticket. We're something everyone stands around and stares at, like an accident in the street. We're the Messiah's misfits.*

The apostle is intrinsically, in Paul's words, "a skilled master builder" (1.Cor.3:10). The Greek word translated "skilled" here is *sophos,* and means 'skilled, wise, expert'. The Greek word for "master builder" is *architektōn,* from which we get our word 'architect'.

Dr Robertson wrote that "this is the only New Testament example of the old and common word *architektōn,* our architect. *Tektōn* is from *tiktō,* to beget, and means a begetter, then a worker in wood or stone, a carpenter or mason."[1] The prefix *archi* simply means 'primary'. Gordon Fee, in his notes, describes the role as "the one who serves as both architect and chief engineer"[2]. Professor F.W. Grosheide put it this way: the *architektōn* is the "one who knows his profession. Such a man knows which foundation should be laid and how best to do it."[3] The word "apostle" is a transliteration of the Greek word *apostolos,* and is literally 'a sent one'. This, therefore, gives the strong sense of someone who is working under authority and who is directed by another. Let me be clear: a biblical 'apostle' is not someone whose authority lies within himself.

The apostle, then, is a well-seasoned craftsman in God's house, sent by God to work on his house. Behind this individual are decades of spiritual formation. The apostle pioneers into uncharted territories, plants churches, structures leadership and acts as a spiritual consultant. He thinks strategically and always sees the big picture. This ministry has never ceased and is desperately needed today. The apostle's ministry is saturated with sagacity, signs and sufferings. There are wonderful days and there are painful days. Apostles were then, and sometimes are now, respected, fruitful, imprisoned, executed and later honoured. We must firstly pray that God raises up more and more of them and secondly pray *for* them, asking God to both anoint and protect them.

Thought

Identify those true apostles among the churches and then bring them to God in prayer.

Prayer

Dear God, thank you for those who exercise such a pioneering and foundational ministry.

---

[1] *Robertson's Word Pictures,* e-sword.net
[2] Gordon Fee, *The First Epistle to the Corinthians,* (Eerdmans, Michigan, 1987), p.138
[3] F.W. Grosheide, *Commentary on the First Epistle to the Corinthians,* (Eerdmans, Michigan, 1980), p.84

DAY TWO HUNDRED

Prophets

1.Cor.12:28

And God has appointed in the church first apostles, second prophets, third teachers, then miracles, then gifts of healing, helping, administrating, and various kinds of tongues.

T he word 'apostle' has some history in the Old Testament. In the Greek version of the book of Psalms, we read of both Joseph and Moses who were "sent" by God. The Greek words used are *apesteilen* and *exapostellō,* both of which mean 'to send away from or to send forth', and both of which contain the root word *apostellō.* Neither Joseph nor Moses went of their own accord.

The word 'prophet' has a much larger history in the Old Testament. In a nutshell, a prophet was someone who took great interest in what God was saying and doing. The ancient word for a prophet was "seer", from the Hebrew word *râ'âh* (pronounced 'raw-aw'), which simply meant 'to see'. It is written, "(Formerly in Israel, when a man went to inquire of God, he said, 'Come, let us go to the seer,' for today's 'prophet' was formerly called a seer.)" (1.Sam.9:9)

The prophet's familiar habitat was in the Spirit, gazing at, and listening to, the activity around the throne of God. A very clear picture of this is found in the case of Micaiah the prophet. The writer of the book of Kings and Chronicles records, "And Micaiah said, 'Therefore hear the word of the LORD: I saw the LORD sitting on his throne, and all the host of heaven standing beside him on his right hand and on his left...'" (1.Kgs.22:19 & 2.Chr.18:18) Men such as this meditated deeply in the Scriptures and were often drawn into profound conversations with God, seeing and hearing what he was doing or about to do. Amos the prophet wrote, "For the Lord GOD does nothing without revealing his secret to his servants the prophets. The lion has roared; who will not fear? The Lord GOD has spoken; who can but prophesy?" (Am.3:7,8)

This was the background that became the setting for the New Testament prophets. The gift of prophecy was released into the church, and many began to exercise it. Paul gave clear guidance concerning the wise management of the gift (e.g. 1.Cor.14). As individuals progressed in their use of this gift, it became apparent to leadership that a number of them were not only accurately bringing the mind of God to the congregations, but that their ministry was getting stronger and carrying more weight. They began to become recognised, not only as individuals who exercised well and precisely the gift of prophecy, but in whom the gift seemed almost permanently resident. Over the years, the practice of prophecy had saturated and soaked them to the extent that they themselves had become the gift. Time tells.

The first occurrence of the New Testament prophet appears in the book of Acts. Luke records:

> *Now in these days prophets came down from Jerusalem to Antioch. And one of them named Agabus stood up and foretold by the Spirit that there would be a great famine over all the world (this took place in the days of Claudius).*
>
> Acts 11:27,28

As we continue to work through the book of Acts, we begin to note that their ministry involved the accurate predicting of future events, the identifying and releasing of people into ministries, and the strengthening and encouraging of churches. It also becomes very clear that they operated both in local and translocal settings.

How the church needs such prophets among us today! It starts with a serious heart that looks to see and hear God, then gets deeply and prayerfully into the Scriptures, becoming sensitive to his voice.

Thought

God has not stopped speaking and he is looking for those who will learn to listen.

Prayer

Dear God, please nudge me from bringing good advice to bringing the word of the Lord.

DAY TWO HUNDRED AND ONE

Evangelists

Acts 21:8

On the next day we departed and came to Caesarea, and we entered the house of Philip the evangelist, who was one of the seven, and stayed with him.

I shall never forget the time I first time I heard an evangelist. He was speaking in a tent mission near Worthing in Sussex. I was a very young Christian and I had brought an unconverted friend with me. The evangelist spoke clearly about the gospel and then he gave an appeal. It was then that I felt the power of God through the evangelistic gift. It was like a divine magnet, drawing people to respond and give their lives to Christ.

I also remember the first time I saw and heard Billy Graham. He preached a simple message, and then he said, "I want you to get up and come out of your seats, and come to Christ." I then felt the same drawing power go like a wave around and across the football stadium. An elderly gentleman called Ron sat next to me. He had survived a concentration camp during the Second World War and was a regular attender at the church I was pastoring. As I turned to him, I saw tears rolling down his cheeks as he, too, sensed the Spirit of God beckoning people to Christ.

As with the prophetic gift, where there are many who prophesy and a few who go on after some time to be recognised at prophets, so it is with the evangelistic gift. All are called to witness to their faith wherever they find themselves, and many do in fact lead others to Christ. The evangelistic gift, however, begins to be recognised when an individual is found to be leading people to Christ in ever increasing numbers. For them, it's what they feel called to do, and their primary focus and burden in life is centred in seeing people become Christians.

Our scripture today references Philip. He was one of the seven men who were selected to be deacons in the Jerusalem church. (Acts 6:1-6) He faithfully discharged that ministry, but later, when persecution came upon the church, he was scattered along with many others (Acts 8:2) and found himself in the city of Samaria. Luke records that...

Philip went down to the city of Samaria and proclaimed to them the Christ. And the crowds with one accord paid attention to what was being said by Philip when they heard him and saw the signs that he did. For unclean spirits, crying out with a loud voice, came out of many who had them, and many who were paralysed or lame were healed. So there was much joy in that city.

Acts 8:5-8

Hearing of this magnificent move of God in Samaria, the apostles, who were still resident in Jerusalem, sent Peter and John...

...who came down and prayed for them that they might receive the Holy Spirit, for he had not yet fallen on any of them, but they had only been baptised in the name of the Lord Jesus. Then they laid their hands on them and they received the Holy Spirit.

Acts 8:15-17

This is a wonderful example of where the team of the five ministry gifts kicks in, working together to see people, not only coming to Christ, but being established in their new-found faith by the activity of the Spirit.

In the middle of all this, Philip was commanded by an angel to travel south to the road that goes from Gaza to Jerusalem. There, under the Holy Spirit's guidance, he met an Ethiopian and, after some conversation, led him to Christ. (Acts 8:26-39) This is the essence of an evangelist. Where God leads him, he will lead people to Christ, whether they be in numbers or just an individual. His is a gift ministry, he understands and is sensitive to 'the appointments of God'.

Thought

The evangelist exercises a ministry with one burden only – to see people come to Christ.

Prayer

Lord, help me to see that my platform may not be in church, but in my place of work.

DAY TWO HUNDRED AND TWO

Pastors (1)

Ps.78:70-72

He chose David his servant and took him from the sheepfolds; from following the nursing ewes he brought him to shepherd Jacob his people, Israel his inheritance. With upright heart he shepherded them and guided them with his skilful hand.

Many years ago, I used to preach over weekends at a church in Barnoldswick in Lancashire, led by a man called Bryon Linguard who became a good friend. I remember him once telling me, "You can always tell a shepherd in the making; people flock around him because they feel comfortable around him, feeling that they can talk to him about their deepest feelings." I have never forgotten that.

We are all called to be gentle and sensitive to each other, but there are certain individuals who seem to stand out. They have a genuine heart for people. This ministry gift is indeed a heart gift. The Greek word found in Ephesians 4:11 is *poimenas,* from a root word meaning 'to protect'.

Our text for today highlights David, the shepherd boy who became a much-loved king of Israel. As we read his story, we realise fairly quickly that he was far from perfect, but nevertheless was a great shepherd of the nation. A number of things stand out from the passage. Firstly, he was taken from the sheepfolds. In other words, he was already exercising a caring ministry, albeit to sheep. Secondly, he was taken from "the care of the sheep" (NASB); "tending the sheep"(NIV); "following the sheep" (ESV). The ESV has it literally. The Hebrew word used is *'achar,* and it means 'the hind, the following part'. The same sense is found in Genesis 33:14, 2 Samuel 7:8 and Isaiah 40:1.

From this we learn that David was not so up front that the sheep lost sight of him; he was not driving them so hard that it became oppressive. His prime concern was for the care of the sheep, not so much the route or the speed. He obviously loved the sheep because at times he would carry the weaker ones. He had patience because he was able to go at their pace and was gentle with them. Some of them were expectant mothers and others were youngsters. The picture thus created here in Scripture is of a shepherd who both leads and follows. He knows where he is going, and he also ensures that the flock is coping with the pace and direction of the journey.

David was also a shepherd who recognised that the flock did not belong to him. The people of Israel were God's people, God's inheritance. This brought about a sense of responsibility and accountability, not ownership. He was simply a steward. He was a shepherd who operated out of integrity of heart. In other words, what he was in public is what he was in private. He sought to be honest at all levels.

David was a shepherd whose hands were skilful. Note the order of integrity before skills. He knew how to treat the flock. The Hebrew word used here is *tebûnâh,* and it means 'understanding, discerning'. David not only had a shepherd's heart but he also had the skill of a good shepherd. This, then, was not only a gift, but a skill to be developed. He was intrinsically a 'people person', who did not, out of ignorance or personal agendas, rough-handle the flock. Dr Martyn Lloyd-Jones once said, "The most sensitive thing God ever made was a human soul…"

A real shepherd, then, is one with a heart for people, who is skilful in his understanding and handling of them, especially with those who struggle. He is both gentle and firm in his care for them. They feel safe under his care, and they feel loved and protected under his shepherding. Shepherds function wherever there is a flock.

Thought

A good shepherd bears somewhat of a resemblance to Christ, the Good Shepherd.

Prayer

Lord, wherever I find myself, give me a real heart for people.

DAY TWO HUNDRED AND THREE

Pastors (2)

Jn.10:11

I am the good shepherd. The good shepherd lays down his life for the sheep.

I would like us to stay with this for another day. This is probably the gift ministry that is most experienced by people in the life of the church. Each church will have someone exercising a pastoral gift and, as with the others, there are some who exercise this gift wherever they are. Their whole drift is the care and nurture of people, and they can operate translocally. For many years I operated as a peripatetic shepherd, based in my local church in Lincoln, but sent for seasons to shepherd other churches around the Lincolnshire area.

In my own journey in this ministry I was greatly helped by the ministry of Eugene Peterson, who truly understood the shepherd's heart. His book *Working the Angles* is seminal. He taught that the pastoral ministry is totally "people orientated". It is so important to note at this point that all ministry has to do with words and with people. When the apostle John wrote, "For God so loved the world..." he wasn't referring to the scenery. People skills are not about structures, about administration, or even about preaching or teaching. All these are necessary in church life, but they are not ends in themselves; they all cater for people.

Peterson said that the pastoral ministry will give dignity to individuals. He wrote:

> *The culture conditions us to approach people and situations as journalists: see the big, exploit the crisis, edit and abridge the commonplace, interview the glamorous. But the Scriptures and our best pastoral traditions train us in a different approach: notice the small, persevere in the commonplace, appreciate the obscure.*[1]

---

[1] Eugene Peterson, *Working the Angles,* (Eerdmans, Michigan, 1897), p.149

Shepherds will give attention to the small details of life. They take seriously what others dismiss as irrelevant.

Shepherds will always give attention to what God is doing in individuals. No one is the same, for they all have different backgrounds, temperaments and ways of doing life. Using the first few verses in the book of Genesis, each individual is a 'Genesis project', where the Spirit of God is nurturing order and fruitfulness out of darkness and disorder. God, by his active grace, is at work, recreating and reshaping every individual life.

Each person is unique. Peterson cited Nicholas Berdyaev, who wrote, "In a certain sense, every single human soul has more meaning and value than the whole of history with its empires, its wars and revolutions, its blossoming and fading civilisations."[1] We must learn to see the worth of every individual.

Shepherds treat individuals with respect. Peterson wrote:

> *This face before me, its loveliness scored with stress, is in the image of God. This fidgety and slouching body that I am looking at is a temple of the Holy Spirit. This awkward, slightly asymmetrical assemblage of legs and arms, ears and mouth, is part of the body of Christ.*[2]

Shepherds learn to see the face of Christ in each individual in their flock and they minister to them accordingly.

Thought

Throughout the Scriptures is the principle that sheep without a shepherd scatter.

Prayer

Dear great Shepherd of the church, give me a heart to pray for the shepherds in my church.

---

[1] Ibid, p.159
[2] Ibid, p.188

Day Two Hundred and Four

Teachers

Jas.3:1

Not many of you should become teachers, my brothers, for you know that we who teach will be judged with greater strictness.

There has been much discussion on whether a pastor is one thing and a teacher is another. Some feel that the gift is a merged gift – a pastor-teacher. I have seen pastors who have a great heart for people but are not great teachers. I have also seen great teachers who are not so great in dealing with people. Is it fair to say that generally (tongue in cheek) pastors will have 'how to grow your church' books on their bookshelves, whereas teachers will have study books and commentaries?

The person that springs to mind from the Old Testament is Ezra. It is written of him that "he was a scribe skilled in the Law of Moses that the LORD, the God of Israel, had given" and that he "had set his heart to study the Law of the LORD, and to do it and to teach his statutes and rules in Israel" (Ez.7:6,10). Ezra was firstly "skilled in the Law". More literally, he was "a ready scribe in the law of Moses" (ASV). The phrase "ready scribe" in the Hebrew language is *sopher machir,* and refers to one who is "eminently skilful in expounding the law"[1]. John Gill wrote, concerning the law of God, that Ezra "was well versed in the knowledge of it; had studied it thoroughly, well instructed in it, and was abundantly qualified to teach it others; he was an eminent doctor of the law"[2].

Secondly, there was a process with him. It was setting his heart to study the Scriptures, then to practise what he had learned from the Scriptures and then, and only then, to teach the Scriptures. "Study, practice, teach" was his mantra – and in that order.

The character that I think of from the New Testament is Apollos. It is written of him that he was "an eloquent man ... and he was mighty in the scriptures" (Acts 18:24). The Greek word translated "eloquent" is *logios* and is used only here in the New Testament. It means someone

---

[1]   Adam Clark, *Commentary on the Bible,* e-sword.net
[2]   John Gill, *Exposition of the Whole Bible,* e-sword.net

who is "learned, a man of letters, skilled in literature and the arts, especially versed in history and the antiquities, skilled in speech, eloquent, rational, wise"[1]. The word translated "mighty" is from the Greek word *dunatos* which means 'able, powerful, mighty, strong'. The overall picture is of one who has studied long and thoroughly, and has become very articulate in the presentation of truth.

Teachers are those who have spent long hours in the Scriptures. They are their delight (Ps.1:2) and they are disciplined in their reading. They find books that help them understand more fully the Book. They think through theological issues and are able to present their findings clearly. As they open up the Scriptures, light springs forth to enlighten their listeners, causing their hearts to burn. (Lk.24:32) Their mantra is, "...the unfolding of your words gives light; it imparts understanding to the simple." (Ps.119:130) The Hebrew word translated "unfolding" is *pêthach,* and means 'opening, unfolding, entrance, doorway'. Teachers 'open up' and 'unfold' the Scriptures and thereby create 'an entrance', 'a doorway' into the things of God. These are the ones who have a heart for the mature church, who love to spread a nourishing and satisfying feast before the people of God, laying a deep foundation of truth in their lives.

Thought

Great responsibility is laid upon the teachers of the church.

Prayer

Dear Lord, thank you for those who have faithfully taught me the word of God.

---

[1] The NAS New Testament Greek Lexicon,
https://www.biblestudytools.com/lexicons/greek/nas/logios.html

DAY TWO HUNDRED AND FIVE

Ups and Downs

Jn.15:20

"Remember the word that I said to you: 'A servant is not greater than his master.' If they persecuted me, they will also persecute you. If they kept my word, they will also keep yours."

All these ministries have been first seen and modelled in the life of Jesus. He is the great apostle, the primary prophet, the outstanding evangelist, the compassionate shepherd and the astonishing teacher. These five ministry gifts are a team expression of who he is.

And as it was for him, so it will be with them. As in all of life, there are the ups and the downs. In the early church there were both tears of joy and tears of pain. Apostles were beaten, imprisoned and executed. In fact, apart from Judas Iscariot's suicide, all the apostles, except John, were martyred. Prophets were often ignored, slighted and even stoned. Over the centuries, we have seen evangelists have been subjected to attempts to undermine their personal integrity by accusations of scandals, affairs, marriage breakups and financial improprieties. There have been pastors who have been torn apart by the wolves that were around, and sometimes within, the flock of God. The Scriptures indicate quite clearly on a number of occasions that the way to scatter a flock is by striking the cohesive ministry of the shepherd. Teachers over the centuries who have taught and stood for truth have been silenced by imprisonment or by being burnt at the stake.

One only has to think one's way through Paul's own story. To the Corinthians he wrote, "For we do not want you to be unaware, brothers, of the affliction we experienced in Asia. For we were so utterly burdened beyond our strength that we despaired of life itself." (2.Cor.1:8) He later wrote in the same letter:

We are afflicted in every way, but not crushed; perplexed, but not driven to despair; persecuted, but not forsaken; struck down, but not destroyed; always carrying in the body the death of Jesus, so that the life of Jesus may also be manifested in our bodies.

2 Corinthians 4:8-10

I stress this because the ministries of the apostles, prophets, evangelists, pastors and teachers come with a high risk and deep cost to the individuals themselves. Some look for the glamour, their name in lights, the platforms and the book-signings, whereas the authentic gift ministry is found in a Christlike spirit of humility and sacrifice.

But of course, there are also the ups. The apostles see churches being planted and established. They see the power of God being unleashed and moving gently in the lives of the sick and needy. The prophets see people whose lives are opened up and nudged forward and their callings being confirmed by the living words of God. The evangelists see hundreds and thousands of people trusting Christ for the first time. Pastors see people being shaped into families and finding a spiritual home in the local church. Teachers see people becoming deeply rooted in the knowledge of God and his ways. All this fills heaven with joy, and it should fill us with joy too.

These ministries have never been withdrawn from the church. When they are recognised and released, the church grows numerically, as well as in depth and in stature. It is as if the ministry of Jesus is being manifested again in the earth both in and through the church. At times there will be overlap, but that is fine. The main point is that these are five displays of the life and ministry of Christ to the church. He has given us himself through these wonderful and powerful ministry people.

Thought

One of the great principles of the Kingdom is replication. The ministry of Christ goes on.

Prayer

Lord Jesus, where do I fit in all this? Is there something you want me to do, or become?

DAY TWO HUNDRED AND SIX

Equipping the Saints

Eph.4:12

...to equip the saints for the work of ministry...

There is a natural tendency in us all to leave things to others, to the specialists. One huge mistake the church has made over the centuries is to differentiate between the clergy and the laity – between the spiritual professionals and the ordinary people. John Stott remembers being surprised by the front cover of an American Episcopal church that had been influenced by the charismatic movement. He wrote:

> *On the cover of their Sunday bulletin I read the name of the Rector, the Reverend Everett Fullam, then the names of the Associate Rector and of the Assistant to the Rector. Next came the following line: 'Ministers: the entire congregation'. It was startling, but undeniably biblical.*[1]

As I noted yesterday, one of the great principles of the kingdom of heaven is replication. And so it is with these ministry gifts. These people were not put in place to do all the work of the ministry; they were specifically placed in order to firstly equip the saints for the work of ministry.

The word "equip" is a wonderful word in the Greek language. It is *katartismon,* and it is mentioned only here as a noun in the whole of the New Testament. It means 'a making fit, a restoring, a right ordering and arrangement'. In classical Greek it meant 'the refitting a ship' or 'the setting of a broken bone'. It was also a fishing term, used to describe 'the mending' of nets. (Matt.4:21) In one sense it is basically taking hold of that which has become damaged or broken and working on it to make it whole again.

I remember hearing Jack Hayford, who was the pastor of a large church in Van Nuys in California. He spoke on the fishing aspect of the root verb *katartizō.* He noted that there were different aspects to the 'mending'. Firstly, the net was drawn up onto the beach and laid wide

---

[1] John Stott, *The Message of Ephesians,* (IVP, Leicester, 1979), p.168

open. Secondly, the fisherman then began cleaning out the debris that had accumulated by the net's journey through the sea. Thirdly, he took the strands that had been broken by the journey and began to tie them together. Fourthly, he carefully folded up the net in an orderly fashion so that when it was used again it did not snarl up because of past issues. This is a wonderful picture of how God restores our broken lives. This is a wonderful picture of what God does in our lives through the tender agency of these five ministries.

Many theologians, however, feel the sense that is expressed in this particular text is that it is to with preparing rather than repairing. The ESV translates the meaning as "fully trained" in Luke 6:40. Harold Hoehner translated the text, "...for the preparation of the saints for the work of the ministry..."[1]

These ministries are to be involved in instructing believers to function in their own God-given gifts. That means identifying the gifts that they have, and then teaching them how to operate in them skilfully and effectively. John Stott noted that the sixteenth century saw the restoration of the priesthood of all believers and the twentieth century saw the restoration of the ministry of all believers.[2] That ministry is rich in variety, and the emphasis is most definitely that every saint has an important part to play in the life of the church.

Thought

At the heart of every successful church is a whole congregation eager to serve.

Prayer

Lord, help me find my part to play and to learn from my leaders how to play it well.

---

[1]   Harold Hoehner, *Ephesians: An Exegetical Commentary,* (Baker Academic, Michigan, 2002), p.547
[2]   John Stott, *The Message of Ephesians,* (IVP, Leicester, 1979), p.168

DAY TWO HUNDRED AND SEVEN

Serving the Body

Eph.4:12

...for the work of ministry...

Yesterday we looked at the work of the five gift ministries as equipping the saints for the work of ministry. Clinton Arnold writes, "Christ has given gifted leaders to the church not merely to do the ministry, but to invest their time heavily in developing and preparing fellow believers to engage in ministry to the body."[1]

The word "ministry" is a translation of the Greek word *diakonias*. In this form, the word is used seven times in the New Testament. Other similar word forms are *diakonia, diakonos* and, as Dr Lawrence Richards noted, "these words are distinctive in that their focus is squarely on loving action on behalf of a brother or sister or neighbour"[2]. The word basically means 'to serve'.

The word that we are looking at in our text for today – *diakonias* – basically means 'service'. In all seven occurrences it is a genitive feminine singular noun. This leads me to a couple of thoughts. Firstly, I find it quite significant that it is a feminine noun. A *diakonos* is one who expresses the nurturing aspect of God's kingdom. It is very much a 'hands on' caring ministry. Although it is expressed through both male and female saints, yet it demonstrates the cherishing of God's people and beyond.

Secondly, it is quite different from the five ministry gifts in that all, not some, are called into service – *diakonias* – to love, serve and nurture the body of Christ. We see then that it is a shared ministry. The five ministry gifts major on their primary word-based giftings, whereas the rest of the saints pour their lives into heartfelt taking care of each other in both words and deeds. Most ministry is not word-based.

---

[1] Clinton E. Arnold, *Ephesians,* (Zondervan, Michigan, 2010), p.262
[2] Lawrence O. Richards, *Expository Dictionary of Bible Words,* (Marshall Pickering, Basingstoke, 1988), p.433

Harold Hoehner wrote something quite profound here. He said, "It conveys the idea of serving the Lord by ministering to each other."[1] This is so reminiscent of the words of Jesus, who said to his disciples, "Truly, I say to you, as you did it to one of the least of these my brothers, you did it to me." (Matt.25:40) By serving each other in various ways we are actually serving the Lord Jesus. We need to look out for one another and look after one another.

It is a lowly serving. The word *diakonos* is constructed from two words – *diá,* which means 'thoroughly', and *konis*, which means 'dust'. Put together, the word properly means 'thoroughly raise up dust by moving in a hurry, and so to minister'. A.T. Robertson says that it means "to kick up dust" as one running an errand.[2] My friend Ian Silk shared with me that Alan Krieder, in his book *The Patient Ferment of the Early Church*, makes the point that women were often the most effective in spreading the gospel – caring, messy service 'through the dust'.

Christ touched the lepers, spoke to the outcasts, and served his disciples with a basin and a towel, washing off the dust, leaving them a powerful example of what service is. We have to climb down to serve.

Thought

If the top of the tree is to be found at the bottom, where are you to be found?

Prayer

Lord Jesus, help me to serve you in serving the least of those around me.

---

[1] Harold Hoehner, *Ephesians: An Exegetical Commentary,* (Baker Academic, Michigan, 2002), p. 550

[2] *https://biblehub.com/greek/1249.htm*

DAY TWO HUNDRED AND EIGHT

Building the Body

Eph.4:12

...for building up the body of Christ...

William Hendriksen made this astute observation: "...the *immediate* purpose of Christ's gifts is the ministry to be rendered by the entire flock; their *ultimate* purpose in the building up of the body, namely, the church."[1]

The first function of these five ministry gifts is the equipping of the saints to serve humbly in their local church and surrounding neighbourhood. Eugene Peterson took this a little further when he said in one of his lectures, "The work of ministry is serving others (*diakonias*), and more so outside the thresholds of the church. Your workplace is the primary place for ministry. The church holds it all together."[2]

This helps us to look carefully at the primary function of the church. The church is the place for equipping the saints, helping them to worship, feeding them with the words of God, administering the sacraments of bread and wine, and baptism, encouraging and nurturing them in their own particular spheres of service. In that safe environment they learn to 'practise their serve' with each other, and then they take it out to the community in which they live. As we have noted before, most of this is not word work, but hands-on work. The body is not designed to be all mouth.

The second function of the five ministry gifts is the building up of the body of Christ. The word that Paul uses here is *oikodomēn,* which means 'to build, to reconstruct, to adorn a house'. This 'house-building' takes place in two ways – inwardly and outwardly.

Firstly, the church is grown inwardly by the maturing and building up of individual believers. As we have noted, we have to learn to recognise the work of God in individuals, seeing them as 'one-to-one Genesis projects'. Eugene Peterson said:

---

[1] William Hendriksen, *Ephesians,* (Banner of Truth, Edinburgh, 1976), p.198
[2] Eugene Peterson, lectures on 'Soulcraft: The Formation of a Mature Life in Christ', Regents College, Vancouver

Everyone I meet is someone who is being worked on by the Holy Spirit. This is a comprehensive and integrated approach. Don't clone people, but release them to be themselves in Christ. Christ is not a mould that we fit into. He is someone we walk with.[1]

The apostle Peter wrote that we "like living stones are being built up as a spiritual house" (1.Pet.2:5). Using this analogy, each of us undergoes 'shaping and dressing' in order to be a functional part of the whole. Here, the five ministry gifts work among us, teaching us by word and demonstration, thus equipping us for spiritual growth. Their purpose is to make us healthy so that we can spiritually reproduce. Healthy sheep reproduce.

Secondly, the church is grown outwardly by mission. There are people outside the four walls of our churches who need to be both sensitively and powerfully reached with the good news of the gospel. In this way, the church grows numerically. Under the ministry of the healthy church, "the Lord added to their number day by day those who were being saved" (Acts 2:47).

Thought

Grow and nurture the believers into maturity and the church will be built numerically.

Prayer

Dear Lord, may I become spiritually healthy, and then help me to spiritually reproduce others.

---

[1] Ibid.

DAY TWO HUNDRED AND NINE

Unity of the Faith (1)

Eph.4:13

*...until we all attain to the unity of the faith and of the
knowledge of the Son of God, to mature manhood, to the
measure of the stature of the fullness of Christ...*

Paul now begins to open up even further what needs to be happening
in the church. He highlights four areas in which we are corporately
meant to grow. Francis Foulkes makes the observation that the
spiritual activities found in verse 12 describe a process that leads to a
goal. He points out that the word translated "attain" is the Greek word
katantēsōmen. It is used nine times in the book of Acts "for travellers
arriving at their destination"[1]. In other words, we are all on a journey.
The five ministries accompany us, paving the way, speaking the mind of
God to us, reaching out to others as we travel, teaching us and caring for
us.

There is more than a hint of a long journey here. This work is long,
often tiring, yet deeply satisfying. In Paul's eyes, ministry always has a
goal in mind. The ministry itself is not the goal but simply the means of
arriving at that goal. It is much more than finding personal fulfilment in
what we do; it is about together building God's church and together
reaching out to the lost. It is a corporate view rather than an individual
one.

The first area is "the unity of the faith". John Stott noticed that in
verse 3 there was the injunction to "maintain" the unity of the Spirit –
something already given by God in Christ. Here, we are to "attain" to
the unity of the faith – something to be aimed at. He wrote, "Both verbs
are surprising. If unity already exists as a gift, how can it be attained as
a goal? Perhaps we need to reply that just as unity needs to be maintained
visibly, so it needs to be attained fully."[2]

This responsibility is for all believers, not just for leadership. Unity
should start at leadership level, and then it must filter down to all

---

[1] Francis Foulkes, *Ephesians,* (IVP, Leicester, 1999), p.129
[2] John Stott, *The Message of Ephesians,* (IVP, Leicester, 1979), p.169

members of the church. We all need to work towards attaining this organic unity of the faith.

Paul wrote in verse 5 that there is "one faith". Here he calls it "the faith". That is, this is what we all should be believing. The baleful fact of the matter is, however, that this is not the case. There is such a diversity of beliefs in the church, and many of them come with strong convictions. The truth of the matter, however, is that the body of Christ is quite broken. Over the centuries there have been countless issues, human perspectives, theological interpretations and even personal agendas that have all contributed to the fragmentation of churches.

Clinton Arnold feels that this involves a "unified understanding of the faith"[1]. We have to learn what the truth is, and thereby what to believe. The key to that is found in Christ himself, who said, "I am the truth." (Jn.14:6)

Thought

There has been a major shift from 'what we believe' to 'what I believe'.

Prayer

Lord, delight my heart in the corporate expression of our faith again.

---

[1]   Clinton E. Arnold, *Ephesians,* (Zondervan, Michigan, 2010), p.264

DAY TWO HUNDRED AND TEN

Unity of the Faith (2)

Eph.4:13

...until we all attain to the unity of the faith and of the knowledge of the Son of God, to mature manhood, to the measure of the stature of the fullness of Christ...

Knowledge is so important to our growth. Without it we flounder. According to the book of Proverbs, "An intelligent heart acquires knowledge, and the ear of the wise seeks knowledge," (18:15) and, "By wisdom a house is built, and by understanding it is established; by knowledge the rooms are filled with all precious and pleasant riches." (24:4) Knowledge is not a gift; it is acquired. And the primary way of growing in a knowledge of the Son of God is by diligently reading and studying the Bible.

George Müller, the faith-filled founder of several orphanages in Bristol in the nineteenth century, wrote, "Continuous reading of the Word will in due course throw light upon the general teaching of the Word, revealing God's thoughts in their variety and connection, and will go far to correct erroneous views."[1] One of the main reasons why there is so much disagreement over what we believe is that we don't know what the truth is. Over nearly five decades of ministry, I have seen first-hand that it is only around 5% of those who sit in church on a Sunday who have ever read the Bible in its entirety. The saints seem to be very knowledgeable about what they have never read! A disciplined and continuous reading of the Scriptures will result in an in-depth understanding of the truths of God, and will bring with it a profound unity with others in the things of the faith.

Ralph Shallis was a professor of classical literature who taught in various European countries, and was perfectly fluent in several languages. He used to read the Bible in the original texts. He was a missionary / church planter in North Africa and also in France. It was there in 1971 that I first met him, and he became my first ever mentor.

---

[1] A.T. Pierson, *George Müller of Bristol,* (Pantianos Classics, 1899), pp.168,169

My most challenging experience with him was when he said, "Alan, I have many young people who come to me, telling me about their pet doctrines and theories. To be honest, I won't listen to them at all until they have read the whole Bible for themselves at least 13 times." At first, I was floored, and then I was stirred to dedicate my life to the study of the Scriptures.

As we enter into the world of the Bible, we will find the One whom the Bible talks about – the Lord Jesus himself. To a bunch of Hebrew scholars, Jesus made this comment: "You search the Scriptures because you think that in them you have eternal life; and it is they *that bear witness about me.*" (Jn.5:39, emphasis added) To two disillusioned disciples walking back to Emmaus, Luke records that "beginning with Moses and all the Prophets, he interpreted to them in all the Scriptures *the things concerning himself*" (Lk.24:27, emphasis added). God has given us his word, not to divide us, but to bring us together into the one faith. He is the only way to the Father. He said to Thomas, "I am the way, and the truth, and the life. No one comes to the Father *except through me.*" (Jn.14:6, emphasis added)

Jesus is the unifying factor of our faith. He is the cornerstone against which we all must line up. The Father, the Son and the Holy Spirit yearn for the day when we all believe the same things. We all see Scriptures in our own light – Jesus wants us to see the Scriptures as he sees them. David wrote, "With you is the fountain of life; in your light do we see light." (Ps.36:9)

Thought

Heaven longs for the day when we all 'sing together off the same sheet of music'.

Prayer

Dear Lord, help me to surrender my personal views for the views of heaven.

DAY TWO HUNDRED AND ELEVEN

Knowledge of the Son of God

Eph.4:13

...until we all attain to the unity of the faith and of the knowledge of the Son of God, to mature manhood, to the measure of the stature of the fullness of Christ...

We noted yesterday that knowledge is not a gift but rather it is acquired. If we are to grow in our knowledge of the Son of God, then we must endeavour to find what the Bible teaches about him. We must also learn for ourselves the things that he has said and taught. It is also helpful to discover what other seasoned believers have written about him. It is for us to search these things out and to make use of them. God quite sternly spoke through the prophet Isaiah: "Therefore my people go into exile for lack of knowledge..." (Is.5:13)

If our reading and meditating in the Scriptures points us to Christ, then it follows quite naturally, writes Paul, that we should also attain to "the knowledge of the Son of God". Not only will we find ourselves believing the same things, we will find ourselves being drawn into a deeper relationship with the Lord. This is much more than simply filling our heads with theological data. This is all about being coaxed and nurtured into an intimate awareness of, and a close walk with, Christ himself. The knowledge that Paul writes about is from the Greek word *epignōseōs,* which is "a full and experienced knowledge". This knowledge of Christ leads us to in-depth experience with Christ.

A.W. Tozer's writings played a significant part in my formative years as a Christian. It is well worth saying that it would do you an immense amount of spiritual good both to collect and read his books. In his book *The Pursuit of God* he wrote:

> *The Bible is not an end in itself, but a means to bring men to an intimate and satisfying knowledge of God, that they may enter into Him, that they may delight in His Presence, may*

taste and know the inner sweetness of the very God Himself in the core and centre of their hearts.[1]

Robert Cleaver Chapman, spoken of by Charles Spurgeon as "the saintliest man I ever knew", wrote, "A careless reader of Scripture never made a close walker with God."[2]

If what is being learned, taught and imparted is not deepening our awareness of, and intimacy with, Jesus then it is merely empty words. A.W. Tozer also wrote:

If a man have only correct doctrine to offer me, then I am sure to slip out at the first intermission to seek the company of someone who has seen for himself how lovely is the face of Him who is the Rose of Sharon and the Lily of the Valleys. Such a man and no one else can.[3]

Eugene Peterson wrote:

We obscure the form when we atomize Scripture by dissecting it, analysing it like a specimen in the laboratory. Every detail of Scripture is worth pursuing endlessly; no scholarly attention expended over this text is ever wasted. But when the impersonal objective of the laboratory technician replaces the adoring dalliance of a lover, we end up with file drawers full of information, organised for our convenience as occasions present themselves. It ceases to function as revelation for us.[4]

Thought

Our walk with the Lord must never become a textbook theology.

Prayer

Dear Lord, please place a longing in me to seek and find you in the written word.

[1] A.W. Tozer, *The Pursuit of God,* (STL Books, Bromley, 1984), p.10
[2] Robert Cleaver Chapman, *Choice Sayings,* (Scholar's Choice, United States, 2015)
[3] A.W. Tozer, *The Divine Conquest,* (Oliphants, London, 1964), p.14
[4] Eugene Peterson, *Eat This Book,* (Hodder & Stoughton, London, 2006), p.46

DAY TWO HUNDRED AND TWELVE

Mature Manhood

Eph.4:13

...until we all attain to the unity of the faith and of the knowledge of the Son of God, to mature manhood, to the measure of the stature of the fullness of Christ...

Paul sees the church as being on a journey. Her destination, among other things, is this deep unity of the faith and the profound experiential knowledge of Christ. As we travel under the careful ministry of the apostles, prophets, evangelists, pastors and teachers, we find ourselves developing and growing together. This divine work takes place in our own individual lives and is then expressed and validated in the corporate life of the church.

Paul now mentions the third of the areas we are to grow into, namely, a "mature manhood". The Greek phrase is *andra teleion,* meaning more literally 'a fully-grown man'. Clinton Arnold renders it as "a mature corporate body"[1]. This 'fully grown man' is the "new man" that Paul wrote about in 2:15. There he used the words *hena kainon anthrōpon,* literally 'one new man'. In his view, this is the church. Here, the word 'man' is generic in that there is neither a gender nor a social issue here. All of us who have been saved into Christ – both men and women – form part of this "new man". John the apostle's description of the church is "the bride, the wife of the lamb" (Rev.21:9), and she is composed of both male and female!

And now, this "new" man must become a "mature" man. The freshness of the new must take on the depth of maturity. The word *teleion* means 'pure, fully grown, fully developed or complete'. In other places in the New Testament, it is rendered "perfect". For example, Jesus said, "You therefore must be perfect, as your heavenly Father is perfect." (Matt.5:48) I like the way that Kenneth Wuest translates this:

---

[1]   Clinton E. Arnold, *Ephesians,* (Zondervan, Michigan, 2010), p.265

"...therefore, as for you, you shall be those who are complete in your character, even as your Father in heaven is complete in His being."[1]

Paul wrote to the believers in Colossae, "Him we proclaim, warning everyone and teaching everyone with all wisdom, that we may present everyone mature in Christ." (Col.1:28) Here, Paul's work was towards and with everyone – all the believers – with the goal of seeing a depth of maturity in the whole church. Paul is saying that "we" [plural] – all of us – are to attain to the stature of a mature "man" [singular].

All of this progress is with unity in mind. Harold Hoehner pointed out that "as the body matures, unity results. In fact, a sign of immaturity is the disunity of the body."[2] Kenneth Wuest quoted *Expositor's* as saying, "The state at which unity is lacking is the stage of immaturity; the stage in which oneness in faith and knowledge is reached, is the state of mature manhood in Christ."[3]

The goal is the maturity of the whole church. We all have a part to play in this corporate process. Individuals either contribute to, or detract from, the whole.

Thought

For the mature, diversity is not an issue. In fact, it is greatly valued.

Prayer

Dear Lord, help me to move from what *I* see to what *we* see.

---

[1] Kenneth Wuest, *The New Testament, An Expanded Translation,* (Eerdmans, Michigan, 2004), p.13

[2] Harold Hoehner, *Ephesians: An Exegetical Commentary,* (Baker Academic, Michigan, 2002), p.556

[3] Kenneth Wuest, *Wuest's Word Studies,* Vol.1, 'Ephesians and Colossians', (Eerdmans, Michigan, 1953), p.102

DAY TWO HUNDRED AND THIRTEEN

The Fullness of Christ

Eph.4:13

...until we all attain to the unity of the faith and of the knowledge of the Son of God, to mature manhood, to the measure of the stature of the fullness of Christ...

Imagine the church travelling through life together, growing together in unity, knowledge and maturity. The more we walk with each other in this new sphere called church, the more we become aware of each other, and also of who Jesus actually is, thus becoming quite mellow and grown-up in our attitudes towards life and those we walk with.

Paul now takes us deeper into this journey. He presents to us a picture of the goal that is before us. It is "the measure of the stature of the fullness of Christ". Everything is pointing towards this. It is the goal of every Christian. We are to learn to imitate Christ in everything, to become like him. This is what Paul envisaged as he wrote to the believers in Rome, "For those whom he foreknew he also predestined to be conformed to the image of his Son..." (Rom.8:29) To those in Corinth he wrote, "And we all, with unveiled face, beholding the glory of the Lord, are being transformed into the same image from one degree of glory to another." (2.Cor.3:18) Our lives are to be conformed to Christ and transformed into his likeness. The apostle John put it quite clearly when he wrote, "Whoever says he abides in him ought to walk in the same way in which he walked." (1.Jn.2:6)

When that is happening on an individual basis, one can only imagine what it would look like in the collective life of the church. Paul sees the whole body of Christ taking on the likeness of the Head of the church, moving, speaking, acting, feeling, thinking as he does. All those things that make Jesus what he is are to be imaged, not only in the individual lives of the believers, but also in the church. The goal is Christlikeness in all things.

The language of this phrase – "the measure of the stature of the fullness of Christ" – is spacious. One imagines a reservoir filled to overflowing. Such is the life of Christ that is to be expressed through the church in the earth. Together, we are to present a massive presence of

Christ to the world. All the resources of heaven are stacked up in order to make this happen.

As I write this, however, I am saddened because I know that even after 2,000 years, we still haven't got this right, and we are a long way off the mark. And yet this is the persistent dream of God, the goal of Jesus and the Holy Spirit, and the vision of Paul. To the Galatian believers Paul wrote (and you can sense the pain in his words), "...my little children, for whom I am again in the anguish of childbirth until Christ is formed in you!" (Gal.4:19)

Eugene Peterson's Message translation is wonderful: "...until we're all moving rhythmically and easily with each other, efficient and graceful in response to God's Son, fully mature adults, fully developed within and without, fully alive like Christ."[1] Clinton Arnold wrote, "The goal of the Christian community is to become increasingly like Christ ... [it] must be at the heart of any definition of spiritual formation."[2]

Thought

Among us, his journeying people, the presence and life of Christ should be seen.

Prayer

"Father, make us one, that the world may see the Son."[3]

---

[1]   Eugene Peterson, *The Message,* (NavPress, Colorado, 2002), p.2130
[2]   Clinton E. Arnold, *Ephesians,* (Zondervan, Michigan, 2010), p.276
[3]   Chris Bowater, 'Father, Make Us One', (Sovereign Lifestyle Music, Leighton Buzzard, 1979)

DAY TWO HUNDRED AND FOURTEEN

No Longer Children

Eph.4:14

...so that we may no longer be children, tossed to and fro by the waves and carried about by every wind of doctrine, by human cunning, by craftiness in deceitful schemes.

Children grow up to become adults, or at least they should do. There is something quite wrong if they don't. In a similar manner, the spiritual life also contains a definite transition between childhood and maturity. Paul wrote to the Corinthians, "When I was a child, I spoke like a child, I thought like a child, I reasoned like a child. When I became a man, I gave up childish ways." (1.Cor.13:11)

We have to differentiate between childlikeness and childishness. Jesus commended the former and Paul rebuked the latter. We are called to be childlike but not childish. Childlikeness is evidenced by an innocent receptivity. Childishness is evidenced by peevishness, petulance and moodiness. Childlike people learn easily and quickly. Childish people are easily irritated and easily put out. They are spiritual infants. Paul wrote to the Corinthians:

> *But I, brothers, could not address you as spiritual people, but as people of the flesh, as infants in Christ. I fed you with milk, not solid food, for you were not ready for it. And even now you are not yet ready, for you are still of the flesh. For while there is jealousy and strife among you, are you not of the flesh and behaving only in a human way? For when one says, "I follow Paul," and another, "I follow Apollos," are you not being merely human?*

1 Corinthians 3:1-4

All this was written in the context of divisions in the church. Let us be clear on this: being "merely human" is seen as spiritual infancy. We have been called to something far higher.

Other signs of immaturity were being "...tossed here and there ... carried about by every wind of doctrine..." Clinton Arnold wrote:

...without the firmness and stability that comes from growth stimulated by the ministry of the various members of the Christian community, believers are as vulnerable as a boat adrift on a stormy and tempestuous sea. They are totally at the mercy of the waves and the wind, which can carry them far off course.[1]

The words that Paul uses are so descriptive. The phrase "tossed to and fro" is from the one Greek word *kludōnizomenoi,* which literally means 'the fluctuating, thrown about ones'. It describes "the idea of being thrown around by the waves of the sea and being thrown into confusion"[2]. The phrase "carried about" is again the one Greek word *peripheromenoi,* which means 'the whirled around ones'. One imagines a small child's dinghy in the deep ocean, turning around and around, making the occupants dizzy and disoriented.

The phrase "every wind of doctrine" is *anemō tēs didaskalias,* meaning 'wind of teachings'. Harold Hoehner wrote that the pastors and teachers "bring stability and unity whereas these teachings came from every direction and brought only confusion, turmoil and disunity"[3]. These were like children who are easily moved and swayed by the feelings and opinions of others.

Jesus said of false prophets that they would be known "by their fruits" (Matt.7:15,16). In the same way, good teaching will bring stability and unity whereas false teaching brings disruption and disunity.

Thought

Deeply rooted trees may blow in the wind but they will not fall over.

Prayer

Dear Father, may my life be truly rooted in truth, making me mature and strong.

---

[1] Clinton E. Arnold, *Ephesians,* (Zondervan, Michigan, 2010), p.267
[2] Harold Hoehner, *Ephesians: An Exegetical Commentary,* (Baker Academic, Michigan, 2002), p.561
[3] Ibid.

DAY TWO HUNDRED AND FIFTEEN

Cunning Deceitfulness

Eph.4:14

...so that we may no longer be children, tossed to and fro by the waves and carried about by every wind of doctrine, by human cunning, by craftiness in deceitful schemes.

Today, we will look at the three dimensions of false teaching. In a nutshell, they are cunning, crafty and deceitful. There is an agenda behind false and unbiblical teaching. If you want to destabilise a church, introduce faulty teaching into its life flow. There is such a responsibility upon those who teach. James, the pastor of the Jerusalem church, suggested, "Not many of you should become teachers, my brothers, for you know that we who teach will be judged with greater strictness." (Jas.3:1)

Clinton Arnold writes:

> *In Paul's view, the variant teachings are not innocent errors on the part of their propagators, but are part of a strategy that is designed to lead people astray from the truth of the gospel. Behind it, the fingerprints of the evil one are present.[1]*

The first phrase that Paul uses is "human cunning". The Greek words are *kubeia ton anthrōpōn,* and literally mean 'the dice-playing of men'. The word *kubeia* is from the word *kubos,* which means 'a cube'. The strong inference is that of men playing with loaded dice in order to trick and cheat their way through. The strategy is to make personal gains, causing others to lose what they have. Throughout the ages, immature saints have been duped out of their inheritance.

The second phrase that Paul uses is "craftiness". The Greek word is *panourgia,* and means 'craftiness, cunning, adroitness'. Vincent says that this is "the craft which gamblers use"[2]. Paul wrote to the believers in Corinth, citing the interaction between Satan and Eve:

---

[1]   Clinton E. Arnold, *Ephesians,* (Zondervan, Michigan, 2010), p.267
[2]   *Vincent's Word Studies,* e-sword.net

For I feel a divine jealousy for you, since I betrothed you to one husband, to present you as a pure virgin to Christ. But I am afraid that as the serpent deceived Eve by his cunning, your thoughts will be led astray from a sincere and pure devotion to Christ.

2 Corinthians 11:2,3

Here, the word "cunning" is the Greek word *panourgia*.
Paul also wrote to the Corinthians:

But we have renounced disgraceful, underhanded ways. We refuse to practice cunning [panourgia] or to tamper with God's word, but by the open statement of the truth we would commend ourselves to everyone's conscience in the sight of God.

2 Corinthians 4:2

The word "tamper" is the Greek word *dolountes,* which means 'to ensnare, to corrupt with error'. It is used only here in the New Testament. It was also used of adulterating gold or wine. Clinton writes, "This craftiness and cunning is focused on developing a strategy of deception."[1] One can see clearly a strategy being formed.

The third phrase is "deceitful schemes". In the Greek language this is *methodian tēs planēs,* and means 'tending to the system of error'. Vincent wrote, "Error organizes. It has its systems and its logic. Ellicott remarks that here it is almost personified."[2] These deceitful schemes are demonic in their intent.

Thought

There is a deliberate satanic strategy to destabilise the church of Christ. Become wise to it.

Prayer

Dear Holy Spirit of truth, grant us discernment to see through the words spoken to us.

---

[1] Clinton E. Arnold, *Ephesians*, (Zondervan, Michigan, 2010), p.268
[2] *Vincent's Word Studies,* e-sword.net

DAY TWO HUNDRED AND SIXTEEN

Speaking the Truth in Love

Eph.4:15

...Rather, speaking the truth in love, we are to grow up in every way into him who is the head, into Christ...

One of the most beautiful gifts that God has given to mankind is language. In fact, words play a huge part in the shaping of our lives. With words we can restore and heal a broken spirit, and bring hope and inspiration to a struggling heart.

In a negative sense, and there are always two sides to a coin, we can wreak havoc and destruction with our words. The proverb says, "Death and life are in the power of the tongue, and those who love it will eat its fruits." (Prov.18:21)

Now, in stark contrast to the devilish strategies that lie behind the destabilising of the church with false teachings, Paul writes that the church must be built and established with truth. The phrase "speaking the truth" is a translation of the one Greek word *alētheuontes,* which has quite a wide range of meanings. Harold Hoehner wrote, "In the NT the only other place the verb appears is in Gal.4:16 where it means 'to speak the truth'. However, in Ephesians the concept of 'being truthful' is the best sense of the word."[1] Clinton Arnold translates it as "confessing the truth"[2]. The only other time this word is used in the New Testament is in Paul's letter to the Galatians where he writes, "Have I then become your enemy by telling you the truth?" (Gal.4:16)

Someone has well written that "the best antidote to error is a thorough knowledge of the truth". Truth listened to, read, understood and applied will act as a sure guide through all the myriad versions of error that are thrust upon the church. Truth spoken through men and women whose lives are soaked in truth, and who are living truthful, sincere and transparent lives, has a powerful effect.

---

[1]   Harold Hoehner, *Ephesians: An Exegetical Commentary,* (Baker Academic, Michigan, 2002), p.565

[2]   Clinton E. Arnold, *Ephesians,* (Zondervan, Michigan, 2010), p.268

Paul adds a rider to this: it must be spoken and manifested in love. As Harold Hoehner puts it, "Paul adds '*en agapē*' to temper truth."[1] John Stott, with keen perception, wrote these words:

Thank God there are those in the contemporary church who are determined at all costs to defend and uphold God's revealed truth. But sometimes they are conspicuously lacking in love. When they think they smell heresy, their nose begins to twitch, their muscles ripple, and the light of battle enters their eye.[2]

He added that there are others who, intent on keeping and exhibiting love, sacrifice truth in doing so. He concluded, "Truth becomes hard if it is not softened by love; love becomes soft if it is not strengthened by truth."[3]

Hoehner also noted that deception "is used for selfish ends whereas truth with love considers the interests of others supremely important." The *agapē* love that Paul writes of here is that divinely inspired love that considers the welfare of others far above their own personal concerns. Truth must be spoken and manifested "with a heart that is tender and concerned about the feelings, growth, and well-being of fellow believers"[4].

Thought

It is important that I speak the truth. It is just as important how I say it.

Prayer

Dear Lord, you brought grace and truth. May these virtues characterise my life too.

---

[1] Harold Hoehner, *Ephesians: An Exegetical Commentary,* (Baker Academic, Michigan, 2002), p.565

[2] John Stott, *The Message of Ephesians,* (IVP, Leicester, 1979), p.172

[3] Ibid, p.172

[3] Harold Hoehner, *Ephesians: An Exegetical Commentary,* (Baker Academic, Michigan, 2002), p.565

[4] Clinton E. Arnold, *Ephesians,* (Zondervan, Michigan, 2010), p.269

Day Two Hundred and Seventeen

Growing into Christ

Eph.4:15

...we are to grow up in every way into him who is the head, into Christ...

Lack of knowledge stunts our growth. Misleading teaching distorts our growth. On the other hand, truth that is bathed in love will both encourage and stimulate our growth. And there is something about a healthy and mature body that quickly recognises and seeks to defeat the disease of deception.

Paul now begins to finalise this section of his teaching. He writes that "we are to grow up in every way into him who is the head, into Christ". Every gift and every ministry that God has given the saints in the church has been specifically designed for their personal and corporate growth. Just as a growth gene has been built into the human body, so growth is built into the DNA of heaven. Paul uses the Greek word *auxēsōmen*, which means 'to grow or to increase'. In verse 14 he wrote that we were to be no longer like children. That is negative. Here he says that we are to positively grow up.

This growth is not so much about numerical growth but rather it is a growth in wisdom, knowledge, maturity and stability. Paul is writing firstly about a growth "into Christ", where he becomes both the model for living and the source of that living. It is about becoming Christ-like in all aspects. Yet it is more than that: it is about developing and progressing into a deep intimacy with him. It is a plunging of strong, penetrating roots into his life and his heart. Christ is not simply to be learned about but he is to be loved. Absolutely everything must lead here.

The growth is, secondly, to be in "all things". Harold Hoehner pointed out:

> *...[in the same way] as it is preferable for a child to develop in all areas of his life rather than just one or two areas, so is the child of God to develop in all areas of spiritual life. For*

example, an increase in knowledge must be accompanied by an increase in love and developments of proper attitudes...[1]

Paul now begins to use the metaphor of a body. It is probably the most powerful and functional image of the church that he uses in his writings. Professor James Dunn writes, "This in fact is the dominant theological image in Pauline ecclesiology."[2] Professor Thomas Schreiner calls it the "most famous metaphor for the church in Pauline writing"[3].

The part of the body that he emphasises here is "the head". For Paul, Christ is the Head of the body – which is the church. He is both the source and the directive agent of his body. We all derive our life and our coordination, both personally and corporately, directly from him. If the Head is removed from the body, all we will have left is a fully formed but decapitated corpse. Therefore, it is essential that we are in a deep and living relationship with him, and actively maintaining and nurturing that relationship. A church that is operating without the vital and applied headship of Christ is not a living expression of the Lord, but a religious museum that is simply full of memories of the past. Using a different analogy, Jesus said, "I am the vine; you are the branches. Whoever abides in me and I in him, he it is that bears much fruit, for apart from me you can do nothing." (Jn.15:5) We must be, and stay, connected to our Head!

Thought

Growth emerges from meaningful connectedness with the Head and the rest of the body.

Prayer

Lord Jesus, help me to see that relationship comes before function.

[1] Harold Hoehner, *Ephesians: An Exegetical Commentary,* (Baker Academic, Michigan, 2002), p.567
[2] James D.G. Dunn, *The Theology of Paul the Apostle,* (T&T Clark, London, 1998), p.548
[3] Thomas Schreiner, *Paul, Apostle of God's Glory in Christ,* (IVP, Leicester, 2001) p.335

DAY TWO HUNDRED AND EIGHTEEN

Joined and Held Together (1)

Eph.4:16

...from whom the whole body, joined and held together by every joint with which it is equipped, when each part is working properly, makes the body grow so that it builds itself up in love.

Harold Hoehner rightly said, "Christ is the origin as well as the goal of the body's growth."[1] We need to hold both aspects in perfect harmony, never forgetting our root source and never letting go of our future.

The growth of the church comes from the life of Christ who is the Head of the church. Paul also wrote to the believers in Colossae that it was Jesus, the Head of the church, from "whom the whole body, nourished and knit together through its joints and ligaments, grows with a growth that is from God" (Col.2:19).

The growth of the church does not then come primarily through human agency but through the divine agency of God. It is God who adds to the church. Luke recorded that in those early days "the Lord added to their number day by day those who were being saved" (Acts 2:47). As we are vitally connected to our Head, there is a life flow, a direction and an ability to function.

The emphasis here is primarily on 'corporate' growth rather than the expansion of any 'personal ministry'. The believers had to see "the body" growing rather than the size of their own platform. The sphere of the church should never be used to promote our own ministries. Our ministries are to serve the church, and as the church grows, we will find ourselves growing in the same process. John Calvin wrote, "That man is mistaken who desires his own spiritual growth. For what would it profit

---

[1] Harold Hoehner, *Ephesians: An Exegetical Commentary,* (Baker Academic, Michigan, 2002), p.569

a leg or an arm if it grew to an enormous size?"[1] We grow in proportion to the body we serve.

Paul loves his very long words! He writes here that we are to be "joined and held together". The Greek phrase that he uses is *sunarmologoumenon kai sumbibazōmenon* which, according to Kenneth Wuest, literally translates as "constantly being joined closely together and constantly being knit together"[2]. In the Greek text, this is a present participle that describes an ongoing action. This means that in Christ we were joined together by the Spirit and that work is now continuing into the future. We are participating in a constant process that will culminate when Christ returns. To use another analogy, his bride will be ready, having been beautifully and carefully prepared for that day.

Let me start to unpack the first large word – *sunarmologoumenon*. The word is found only here and in 2:21, and fully means 'to be carefully and closely joined together with words'. In the first instance the joining is of God. He carefully and skilfully selects different people and gently brings them together. We have to see the Father's choice in this and learn to be happy with it. We may not get along with certain individuals that worship with us in our church but it was the Father's choice that they should be there – alongside you and me. Spiritual maturity sees the awkward others, and themselves, as indispensable features of the magnificent work of art that God is working on.

Thought

The church is not a pile of isolated stones but a carefully and skilfully constructed body.

Prayer

Lord, help me to see those around me as encouragements, not impediments, for my growth.

---

[1] John Calvin, *Epistles of Paul the Apostle to the Galatians, Ephesians, Philippians and Colossians,* (Calvin's New Testament Commentaries) (Eerdmans, Michigan, 1960), p.185

[2] Kenneth Wuest, *The New Testament, An Expanded Translation,* (Eerdmans, Michigan, 2004), p.454

DAY TWO HUNDRED AND NINETEEN

Joined and Held Together (2)

Eph.4:16

...from whom the whole body, joined and held together by every joint with which it is equipped, when each part is working properly, makes the body grow so that it builds itself up in love.

We preachers often tell a joke about knowing a little Greek. We say, "He runs a fish and chip shop in the High Street." Here's another little Greek lesson: not only are these present participles describing an ongoing process, but they are also in the passive voice. In other words, we are being acted upon and God is the active agent. He is behind all this, actively nurturing the unity and the growth. We have to let him construct, submitting to his providences.

Harold Hoehner is excellent here:

> *Today with mortar it is easy to fit stones together, but in that day, with no mortar, the stones were cut and smoothed by an elaborate process so that they fit exactly with each other. As the ancient masons used an elaborate process of fitting stones together, it is certain that God's grace carefully fits together persons with one another in order to bring inner unity that can allow them to grow together. The emphasis is on the skilful fitting of each member to the other, as opposed to being thrown together haphazardly.[1]*

When God brings people together there is invariably a chafing that occurs. In 'body dynamics' we find that, over time, rough edges are knocked off so that we fit together. Much of it is done by the Lord himself, but the 'fine tuning' is done in the community of the saints. If our brother rubs us up the wrong way, it is usually because the Lord wants to teach us how to turn around and learn from it.

---

[1] Harold Hoehner, *Ephesians: An Exegetical Commentary,* (Baker Academic, Michigan, 2002), p.569

In this sense stones are always reduced in size in order to achieve a close fitting together. Humility is a major key to bringing about the unity that God is working towards.

William Hendriksen translates *sunarmologoumenon* as being "harmoniously fitted together"[1]. Harmony is achieved by different musicians playing different notes on different instruments – all playing together at the same time from the same sheet of music.

As we have observed before, the church of God is built and joined together with constructive words. What we say to each other, and how we say it, is of paramount importance. Careless, angry, resentful and unforgiving words have torn people apart. On the other hand, gracious, kind and loving words have drawn people together. Our craft is primarily a word craft, enhanced by loving and caring 'hands on' service to the saints and beyond.

The second large word that Paul uses is *sumbibazōmenon,* which means 'to cause to coalesce, to join together, to put together, to unite or knit together'. We are to be "held together". The Greek grammar indicates that this again is an ongoing process as it is also in the passive voice. There is a strong causation from heaven taking place. God is at work, 'entwining' our lives together so that we become inseparable.

Thought

We are not known by our thoughts but our words, and how we say them.

Prayer

Dear Father, help me to speak restorative and gracious words today.

---

[1] William Hendriksen, *Ephesians,* (Banner of Truth, Edinburgh, 1976), p.203

DAY TWO HUNDRED AND TWENTY

Joined and Held Together (3)

Eph.4:16

...from whom the whole body, joined and held together by every joint with which it is equipped, when each part is working properly, makes the body grow so that it builds itself up in love.

When we were courting, Mo, my fiancée, knitted a scarf. After what seemed a long time in the making, it grew so long that eventually we both used to wear it at the same time! Because it was knitted, it couldn't be pulled apart, only unravelled. And that is the way that the enemy of our souls often works. He wants to unravel, bit by bit, what God has knitted together. A word here, an action or reaction there...

Paul, writing to the saints at Colossae, spoke of them as "being knit together in love" and "nourished and knit together" (Col.2:2,19). The KJV uses the word "compacted". The NASB uses the words "held together". The literal sense is that of 'being drawn together' in the sense that we would draw a conclusion after having considered all the various arguments. It is also in the same way that a lawyer would draw together all his arguments in order to make a strong and watertight case. What God is bringing and drawing together is of immense spiritual strength and it is designed to be watertight!

Harold Hoehner wrote of the believers that...

> *...they grow by being carefully fitted and held together, rather than growing individually apart from each other. Thus, it is not self-initiative that causes the growth but the gracious action of God who is responsible for the 'fitting and holding' together of believers.*[1]

Paul then mentions these words: "by every joint with which it is equipped". The NASB translates this as "that which every joint

---

[1] Harold Hoehner, *Ephesians: An Exegetical Commentary,* (Baker Academic, Michigan, 2002), p.570

supplies". Just as all the moving parts of my body are held together by joints, so it is with the body of Christ. The Greek word for "joint" is *haphēs*, which describes that which connects, fastens or secures. Hoehner translated it as "every supporting connection"[1]. He also wrote that the best word for *haphēs* is "contact". He wrote, "When applied to the body of believers it is clear that the union and growth of the body can only come where there is contact with other members of the body."[2] In his *Word Studies*, Professor Marvin Vincent wrote, "The word means primarily touching, and is used in classical Greek of the touch upon harp strings, or the grip of a wrestler."[3]

For the body of Christ to grow, there must be a certain tactility among the various members. We must get over our fears, our inabilities and our reserve, and start learning instead to reach out and touch others, and be touched by them. We must not, and cannot, do spiritual life alone. God has specifically designed the body in such a way that we need the life-communicating touch of others.

What then do we give to each other? What do we receive from each other? Is it good? Is it wholesome? Is it uplifting? It should be a giving and a receiving of that complementing flow of grace, energy and love – the animating life of Christ. It should be Christ in me, ministering his goodness to you, and vice versa. See yourself as a channel of the life of Christ to those around you, and also be happy to receive from them.

Thought

Ask God to help you become a 'carrier of the Spirit', infusing divine life to others.

Prayer

Dear Lord, help me to 'connect' well, bringing the blessing of Christ to those around me.

---

[1] Ibid.
[2] Ibid, p.573
[3] *Vincent's Word Studies*, e-sword.net

DAY TWO HUNDRED AND TWENTY-ONE

Working Properly (1)

Eph.4:16

...from whom the whole body, joined and held together by every joint with which it is equipped, when each part is working properly, makes the body grow so that it builds itself up in love.

Some time ago I had a couple of fuses malfunction in my car, taking out the fan, rear wipers and screen wash among other things. Two little parts managed to disable the effective running of the whole vehicle. We can draw strong messages here: firstly about how little things can affect either positively or negatively the smooth running of the whole body, and secondly how the smallest parts of the body can play such an important part in the growth of the whole body.

Bishop Westcott made this observation:

Whenever one part comes into close connexion with another, it communicates that which it has to give ... Each part as it is brought into contact with other parts, fulfils its own office and contributes to the growth of the whole.[1]

What he meant by that was that each member of the body of Christ has a specific gift that is peculiar to him or her. We are graced for a particular function, and it is tied up with who we are and how we have been shaped as an individual.

The older I have become, and the more I have walked with Christ and his body, the church, the more I have realised that there is the "one thing" that I have been gifted with and that I should focus on, and there are also many things that I could do but are actually outside my sphere of grace.

We are all called to love and serve with gentle humility – that is a general calling on each of us. But there is also the specific serving gift given that only we, and others like us, can fulfil. 'Ears' don't talk very well, and 'mouths' don't listen too well either. It is therefore essential that

---

[1] B.F. Westcott, *Saint Paul's Epistle to the Ephesians,* (MacMillan and Co, London, 1906), pp.64,65

in order to function well in the body of Christ, we must realise that we are not called to be a 'jack of all trades and master of none', but that we are to seek that for which he has primarily called us. We must set ourselves to seek the Lord to discover what our primary gifting is. Very few will be 'platform' giftings.

There are some good resources out there that can help us identify what our primary gifting is.[1] Once we realise what our gifting is, we then begin to exercise it, submitting to the honing and shaping of it. This can take several years, both in solitude and in fellowship with others.

Paul writes that all this is "according to the proper working of each individual part". The Greek phrase here is *energeian en mētro,* literally meaning 'working in measure'. Clinton Arnold translates this as "the powerful working by the measure of each individual part"[2]. He wisely adds, 'The expression ... points to divine enablement, not to any inherent power and ability possessed by the individual members."[3] It is by his power at work in us that we are enabled to serve the Lord by ministering to each other. Our daily walk with him, and our contributions to the body of Christ, must always be dependent upon his grace and strength. Our own strength is mostly unproductive and creates unwanted pressure. Ministry, of whatever sort, must never rely upon our own abilities. A striving soul chafes the body of Christ, but one who is moving easily and freely by the enabling grace of God is constantly gifting the church.

Thought

God loves to show us the "one thing" that we are to occupy ourselves with.

Prayer

Lord, help me to become more dependent upon you rather than on my own resources.

---

[1] e.g. *www.freeshapetest.com*
[2] Clinton E. Arnold, *Ephesians,* (Zondervan, Michigan, 2010), p.271
[3] Ibid.

DAY TWO HUNDRED AND TWENTY-TWO

Working Properly (2)

Eph.4:16

...from whom the whole body, joined and held together by every joint with which it is equipped, when each part is working properly, makes the body grow so that it builds itself up in love.

The giftings of God are embryonic at first. They are usually built into our human DNA before birth, and slowly emerge as we grow older. Sometimes the deep seeds are activated by our new birth, and brought into a more profound clarity. The rain from heaven causes them to spring up.

A gift or ability that is left to its own devices can either wilt, or fly off into undisciplined and unproductive areas. God's gifts need nurturing and gentle discipline. As we noted yesterday, the gifts of God need honing and shaping. It is God who supplies the gift but it is personal discipline, study and application that will sharpen the gift; and the saints around us will help to shape the gift.

This means then that we will learn to work to capacity, fully playing our part. It is in the spirit of 'becoming the best we can be' in our particular field. In descending order, we seek to excel at the best coffee making, the best hospitality, the best stewarding, giving, administrating, caring, preaching and teaching. We must become the best husband, the best wife, the best parents. Children should seek to excel in becoming the best kids for their family. Even in secular employment we must seek to be the best employee that the company has. Whoever we are, and whatever we do, by the grace and nurture of God, we aim at becoming the best we can be. Because of who empowers us, our ministry to each other should be above world class.

All this is possible as we are sourced by Jesus, the Head of the church, and maintain the relationship, firstly with him, and then with my fellow believers. We need to state again that relationships are at the heart of our faith. An isolated member is slowly dying on the inside, and a divisive member is destructive to the relational life of the church.

Kenneth Wuest put it this way:

...the degree to which this life of the Head flowing through the members operates, joining the members of the body more closely together in a more compact organic unity, is determined by the individual saint's fellowship with the Lord and with his fellow saints.[1]

The effectiveness of this wonderful ministry to each other depends on our relationship with Christ and with each other. A fracturing in either relationship severely affects the whole.

Wuest also noted that "the life of the Head flowing through the bands of supply is constantly joining together and causing to grow together the individual members"[2]. There is a divine causing taking place here. The influences of heaven are concentrated on gathering people and things together. If we walk closely with him, we will feel the nudges of God within us, inspiring and enabling us to reach out, to build up, to forgive and, where necessary, to restore. The human body has an inbuilt capacity and propensity to minister and heal itself. Likewise, the body of Christ has within it a divine capacity to heal and restore itself. That is the intended flow of things. This is the direction of the Spirit, and therefore we must reject, and refuse to participate in, anything that does otherwise.

Thought

Actions and words become known by the fruit they produce.

Prayer

Dear Lord, help me to think ahead about the fruit my words and actions will produce today.

---

[1] Kenneth Wuest, *Wuest's Word Studies,* Vol.1, 'Ephesians and Colossians', (Eerdmans, Michigan, 1953), p.105
[2] Ibid.

DAY TWO HUNDRED AND TWENTY-THREE

The Growth of the Body

Eph.4:16

...from whom the whole body, joined and held together by every joint with which it is equipped, when each part is working properly, makes the body grow so that it builds itself up in love.

One of our favourite programmes on the television is *The Repair Shop*. It is filmed in a barn at the Weald and Downland Living Museum, Singleton, West Sussex. It has been described as the venue where "expert craftsmen pool their talents and resources to restore heirlooms and treasured antiques such as music boxes, vases and clocks to prove that anything can be restored to their former glory".

One of the team is Steve Fletcher, a horologist (watchmaker/restorer), who gains deep pleasure in taking broken antique clocks apart and lovingly restoring them to full working order. When every part is repaired and restored to its working order, the clock functions as it was designed to do. In the same way, when all the members of the body of Christ are functioning properly, the body grows as it is designed to do.

Paul goes on to write that when the saints are in full fellowship with Christ and with each other, and in good working order, the body grows. He goes on to state that when everything is working well, the church builds itself up. In the same way that the human body is wired to grow by itself into full maturity, so it is with the body of Christ. Growth genes are running around the veins of the church.

Here is the clear message: feed the church and the church will grow by itself. A church that is cherished and nurtured with the words and life of Christ is a church that is growing in confidence and a winsome beauty. A church that is harassed by constant vision-casting, challenges and exhortations soon becomes a tense and tired church.

This growth dynamic is not human, it is divine. If we look only to our own ideas to enhance the growth of the church, we shall become disappointed. We must never lose sight of the divine dynamic. In his letter to the Colossians, Paul wrote of Christ the Head, "from whom the whole body, nourished and knit together through its joints and ligaments, grows with a growth that is from God" (Col.2:19). He states quite clearly that the growth is from God. In his letter to the Corinthians, Paul stated that though it was he and Apollos who were ministering, it was actually God who gave the growth. He went on to write, "So neither he who plants nor he who waters is anything, but only God who gives the growth." (1.Cor.3:6,7)

In Mark's Gospel there is the parable of the growing seed. Jesus said:

> *"The kingdom of God is as if a man should scatter seed on the ground. He sleeps and rises night and day, and the seed sprouts and grows; he knows not how. The earth produces by itself, first the blade, then the ear, then the full grain in the ear."*

> Mark 4:26-28

In this story, we have firstly the fact that the farmer does not know how the growth occurs. To him it is a mystery. He has his natural knowledge of farming but this dynamic is beyond him. Secondly, he notices that the earth produces "by itself". The phrase is the one Greek word *automatē*, and means 'self-moved, moved by one's own impulse, or acting without the instigation or intervention of another'. It is the word from which we derive our word 'automatically'.

There is a dynamic at work in the church that we do well to recognise and defer to. It will resist our interferences and our seeking to stimulate it. In fact, if we overstimulate it, it will weaken and shrivel.

Thought

The activity of God must be recognised and worked with, not directed or pushed.

Prayer

Dear Holy Spirit, teach me at times to stand back and allow you to work silently.

DAY TWO HUNDRED AND TWENTY-FOUR

The Environment of Love

Eph.4:16

*...when each part is working properly, makes the body grow
so that it builds itself up in love.*

Deon Jackson used to sing *Love Makes The World Go Around*,
and that sentiment still resonates much of the shallow thinking
of this world today. The word 'love' has become an 'anything
goes as long as it makes you feel happy' notion.

When it comes to the church, the word 'love' takes on a powerful,
pure and costly nature. Real love is not getting my needs or wants met;
rather it is the noticing and then giving of oneself to the needs of others.
And it is precisely in this environment of *agapē* love that the church
grows. Kenneth Wuest's translation says that the church builds itself up
"in the sphere of love"[1]. F.F. Bruce wrote, "The bond that unites the
members one with another is the bond of love ... so that only by love can
the church be built up to his stature."[2] Only by love, and in an
atmosphere of love, can the church be built. People grow in an
environment of love. A church that is used, or even abused, will wither
on the inside. On the other hand, a church that knows and experiences
the *agapē* love of Christ, expressed through the leadership and each
member, will feel cherished and will find itself responding to those inner
workings of God that promote growth.

In this respect, feelings are significant. Our feelings are sensitive God-
given facilities that enable us to recognise danger, and they are very
accurate. They can be subjected to being beaten down, or they can be
nurtured to greater precision. How we make people feel is as important
as the truths we speak. Often it has been said, "It wasn't what you said,
or what you did, it was how you made me feel."

---

[1]   Kenneth Wuest, *The New Testament – An Expanded Translation*,
      (Eerdmans, Michigan, 2004)
[2]   F.F. Bruce, *The Epistles to the Colossians, to Philemon, and to the
      Ephesians,* (Eerdmans, Michigan, 1984), p.353

One of our primary needs is to feel safe. As the children of God, we need to feel safe and secure in his presence, and we need to feel safe and secure around each other. Concerning the former, God will always make us feel safe – he is our refuge. We also need to feel safe around others, and make them feel safe as well.

I need to qualify that a little. The truth is that God is both safe and scary. Now there's a 'good scary', and there is a 'not good scary'. There is the famous conversation between Lucy and Mr Badger in C.S. Lewis' book *The Lion, the Witch and the Wardrobe* that goes like this: Mrs Badger has just said that "if there's anyone who can appear before Aslan without their knees knocking, they're either braver than most or else just silly". "Then he isn't safe?" said Lucy. "Safe?" said Mr. Beaver; "don't you hear what Mrs. Beaver tells you? Who said anything about safe? 'Course he isn't safe. But he's good. He's the King, I tell you."[1] In the presence of God, one feels both fearful and joyful.

The sphere of *agapē* love is the most fertile of environments. Clinton Arnold writes that "love is the most conducive atmosphere in which the growth takes place"[2].

Thought

The atmosphere of the house speaks louder than the words we say and the songs we sing.

Prayer

Lord Jesus, help me to be a contributor to building a safe house for your children.

---

[1]   C.S. Lewis, *The Complete Chronicles of Narnia,* (HarperCollins, London, 1998), p.99
[2]   Clinton E. Arnold, *Ephesians,* (Zondervan, Michigan, 2010), p.272

DAY TWO HUNDRED AND TWENTY-FIVE

Don't Walk Like That

Eph.4:17

Now this I say and testify in the Lord, that you must no longer walk as the Gentiles do, in the futility of their minds.

When the love and power of Jesus Christ touches our lives, we can never be the same again. However, if we see Christ merely as an addition to our lives, then we have missed the point completely. Meeting Jesus will mean the end of our old way of living and, instead, embarking on a completely new way of living. Anything short of that is at best shallow and at worst counterfeit.

We now come to a section that others have called "the personal conduct of the Christian", where what we have believed actually starts to outwork itself in the way that we live. Harold Hoehner notes that there are five sections in this letter that are based around the injunctions to walk in the light of what we have just learned.[1] The first section was about unity (4:1-3); this section is about practical holiness.

We must allow the truths of heaven to infiltrate our lives and have their full impact in us. The thinking and the ways of God must start penetrating our thinking, thus directing our behaviour. The proverb says, "For as a man thinks within himself, so he is." (Prov.23:7) The way we think and the contents of our thoughts are so important. John Stott wrote, "Scripture bears an unwavering testimony to the power of ignorance and error to corrupt, and the power of truth to liberate, ennoble and refine."[2] Scripture must deeply influence and affect us, thereby shaping our thinking. That in turn will form our spirituality, which will then be fully authenticated in our everyday living with those around us.

This is so important to Paul. He uses the words, "Now this I say and testify in the Lord..." For Paul, this is not a mild suggestion, but a strong imperative. He uses the Greek word *marturomai,* which is often

---

[1] Harold Hoehner, *Ephesians: An Exegetical Commentary,* (Baker Academic, Michigan, 2002), p.581

[2] John Stott, *The Message of Ephesians,* (IVP, Leicester, 1979), p.176

translated 'witness', but in this context it means 'to insist, to declare solemnly'. For him, what he was about to say was of paramount importance, and needed to be heeded carefully. He added, "...in the Lord..." which was like saying, "I'm not speaking on my own behalf. You need to treat what I am saying as if the Lord himself is saying it to you." There is a spiritual authority that is being exercised here.

It is important how we receive the Scriptures. There are many who shrug them off as 'an opinion on life', whilst there are others who take them with utmost seriousness. Is it possible that God himself speaks through these words? Might I ask, how do you and I receive the words of scripture?

Our spirituality is deeply flawed when we set ourselves up to make judgments on the words of the Bible. If we hold tight control on what we will allow ourselves to believe and respond to, then I suspect that we are not living in a full surrender to the Lord. Insisting on understanding everything he says in order to make a correct response is basically enthroning our minds instead of his. We base our beliefs, not on what we think is right, but on what he says is right. Our finite thinking is no match for the infinite wisdom and decision-making of God. Maybe this – our mind – is one of the important bastions that we need to surrender to him.

Thought

The Bible's verdict on the lofty thoughts of men is that they are a puff of wind. (Ps.94:11)

Prayer

Dear Lord, help me to get myself, and you, in perspective here.

DAY TWO HUNDRED AND TWENTY-SIX

Don't Think Like That (1)

Eph.4:17

Now this I say and testify in the Lord, that you must no longer walk as the Gentiles do, in the futility of their minds.

Some people cannot remember when they crossed the threshold "from death to life", to use Paul's words. Their conversion was a gentle movement, almost unperceptively into the kingdom of heaven. For others, like these Gentiles that Paul is talking about, their conversions were quite dramatic. But, in whatever way it was for us, the values and ways of the kingdom of heaven are vastly different from the values and ways of the world that we were born into and indeed live in. Paul says quite emphatically to these new believers in the Ephesian church, "...you must no longer walk as the Gentiles do..." There obviously was a previous walk, and Paul is saying, "Do not walk that way anymore." When we follow Christ, we do just that. We turn around from where and how we were going and living, and we start following him and his way of doing life.

Because we are called to be one people, we must cultivate unity, and because we are called to be a holy people, we must cultivate holiness. The Ephesians were once pagans, living in a pagan society. But they have become Christians, and Paul is insisting that they live like Christians. They are different, so they should behave differently, according to kingdom standards and lifestyle.

Speaking of Gentiles, Eugene Peterson said in one of his lectures that here the term 'Gentile' is "a generic category for those who do not know the revelation of God"[1]. They are people who are living, yet they are spiritually dead, blind to the revelation of God and deaf to his voice. Peterson went on to say that "sin has a dulling and flattening effect on our lives. There is a sameness about sin. With the word 'saint', we see originality. We are new; we are not copies. Each saint is a unique, new

---

[1] Eugene Peterson, lectures on 'Soulcraft: The Formation of a Mature Life in Christ', Regents College, Vancouver

creation of God."[1] Out of the mud of earth, God is still creating masterpieces, and you and I are included in that.

In this section that we are going to shortly start looking at, we will notice a process that takes both time and lots of inner decisions. We have to see that we are not made perfect the instant we believe. Sanctification, or the process of becoming Christ-like, is an ongoing 'step by step' procedure. The first thing, then, is that we have to put off, like an old stained garment, the 'old self', the 'old me' – in other words, all that I was. The old 'walk' that we had was, and still is to a certain extent, deeply ingrained in us, and therefore it will take more than a lifetime in order to be fully freed from it and changed into the image of Christ. It will be a day by day process, "from one degree of glory to another" (2.Cor.3:8).

Paul is talking about a faulty lifestyle that arose out of faulty thinking, whereby their thoughts determined their values, their words, their actions and also their reactions. So he begins by addressing three areas, the first of which is the state of their reasoning. He speaks of a 'futility of mind', and uses the Greek word *mataiotēti,* which means 'that which is empty, aimless, result-less, fruitless, meaningless'. These were thinking processes that did not produce anything. Natural thinking can be quite fatuous, self-indulgent and self-protective. God's thoughts, on the other hand, are selflessly constructive and productive.

Thought

Look for, and start thinking, thoughts that are selfless, constructive and productive.

Prayer

Lord, your thoughts are not like mine. Help me to train my mind to think your thoughts.

---

[1] Ibid.

DAY TWO HUNDRED AND TWENTY-SEVEN

Don't Think Like That (2)

Eph.4:18

They are darkened in their understanding, alienated from the life of God because of the ignorance that is in them, due to their hardness of heart.

Yesterday, we learned about putting off, like a stained garment, our old way of thinking, which was futile in its effects and lacked productivity. Paul now introduces another aspect of their old way of thinking – it was in the dark. He writes, "They are darkened in their understanding..." and he is talking about reasoning that has been affected by sin.

The word "darkened" is a translation of the Greek word *eskotōmenoi,* which means 'obscured, hidden, covered by darkness'. To the believers in Rome, Paul wrote in a similar vein: "For although they knew God, they did not honour him as God or give thanks to him, but they became futile in their thinking, and their foolish hearts were darkened." (Rom.1:21) In our text for today, he speaks of the understanding being darkened; in his words to the Roman believers he spoke of their hearts being darkened. Both speak of the inner life. In the inner lives of the unconverted there is a deep darkness.

All this, in the first instance, is the work of the prince of darkness, who blinds the eyes of unbelievers. Paul wrote to the church in Corinth concerning the unconverted saying, "In their case the god of this world has blinded the minds of the unbelievers, to keep them from seeing the light of the gospel of the glory of Christ, who is the image of God." (2.Cor.4:4) I have talked to many about Christ, only to see the darkness in their eyes. They just cannot see it, and it reinforces the truth that evangelism is spiritual warfare, and prayer, therefore, is essential.

The word "understanding" comes from the Greek word *dianoiāi,* which means firstly 'the capacity to think through, the ability to meditate on things'. Harold Hoehner translates it "their reasoning process"[1].

---

[1]   Harold Hoehner, *Ephesians: An Exegetical Commentary,* (Baker Academic, Michigan, 2002), p.584

Here, it speaks of the ability to think clearly. Sin robs us of this capacity or ability, whereas the cleansing and renewing work of the Spirit of truth clears our minds and enables us to think with deep perception.

Secondly, it means the capacity to think at deeper levels. W.E. Vine translates the word *dianoio* as "a thinking through, or over, a meditation, reflecting"[1]. James Strong translates it as "deep thought"[2]. Paul is saying that the unconverted mind thinks at a superficial level, skimming over things, unable to penetrate into the deep purposes of God. The inference is that as believers we have the latent ability to think great thoughts in depth. We also have access to the possibility of disciplined spiritual thinking that takes us to profound places in the vast things of God. We can learn to meditate and muse in the Holy Spirit, and thus become available and receptive to the thoughts of God that are far higher than our own. (Is.55:8,9)

Outside of Christ our thinking is at best limited and darkened. Unenlightened individuals have probed into the meaning of life, but have come up empty. The people of God, however, are recipients of a wisdom and an understanding that is sharp and penetrating and, at times, deeply profound.

Thought

The Spirit of God liberates our capacity to think through the issue of life at deeper levels.

Prayer

Dear Lord, let me think your thoughts after you.

---

[1] W.E. Vine, *Vine's Expository Dictionary of Biblical Words,* (Thomas Nelson, New York, 1985), p.408

[2] *Strong's Hebrew and Greek Dictionaries,* e-sword.net

DAY TWO HUNDRED AND TWENTY-EIGHT

Ignorance Alienates and Hardens

Eph.4:18

They are darkened in their understanding, alienated from the life of God because of the ignorance that is in them, due to their hardness of heart.

One of the strongest messages of the Bible is that God's wisdom and understanding is given, not to the mentally elite, but to the humble and childlike. In Paul's conversation with the church in Ephesus, he is saying that however intelligent people think they are, their thoughts are futile and they are totally in the dark concerning the things of God.

He now goes on to write about the root of their darkened understanding. It is simply their alienation from the life of God. Whereas the body of Christ, both corporately and individually, receives life from the Head that invigorates, empowers and renews, the unbeliever is resourced only from within himself, or from other more sinister sources.

The Wesleyan theologian Adam Clark wrote, "The original design of God was to live in man; and the life of God in the soul of man was that by which God intended to make man happy, and without which true happiness was never found by any human spirit."[1] Only the life of the Spirit of God in us makes us what we were originally designed to be.

The word "alienated" is the Greek word *apēllotriōmenoi,* which means 'to be estranged'. Kenneth Wuest wrote that the word was used of those "who have estranged themselves from God" and also of those who were "shut out from one's fellowship and intimacy"[2]. In other words, these are people who have cut themselves off from God and, as a result, find themselves cut off from God. The former is a deliberate action and the latter is the fruit of that action. Those who alienate themselves find themselves alienated. There is personal responsibility here.

---

[1]   Adam Clark, *Commentary on the Bible,* e-sword.net
[2]   Kenneth Wuest, *Wuest's Word Studies,* Vol.1, 'Ephesians and Colossians', (Eerdmans, Michigan, 1953), p.107

Paul gives two reasons for this alienation. The first is due to "the ignorance that is in them". The word "ignorance" comes from the Greek word *agnoian,* which means 'a want of knowledge or perception'. This, again, is not a want of intellectual capacity but describes a moral and spiritual unawareness. One can be fully aware of events that are happening in the world but totally ignorant of what God is doing in the earth.

The second reason Paul gives is "hardness of heart". The word "hardness" is *pōrōsin* – which means 'a process of hardening, callousing and a making brittle'. This phrase is used often in the Scriptures. The message is that constant resistance to the truth, to the life-giving word of Christ, will inevitably bring about a gradual callousing of the heart. Those who constantly do not want to hear, end up being unable to hear. God spoke through the prophet Zechariah in a similar vein, saying, "They made their hearts diamond-hard lest they should hear the law and the words that the LORD of hosts had sent by his Spirit through the former prophets." (Zech.7:12)

Thought

"A stony heart is a heart not susceptible to impressions."[1]

Prayer

Dear Holy Spirit, soften my heart to receives lasting impressions from heaven.

---

[1]   Keil and Delitzsch, *Commentary on the Old Testament,* e-sword.net

DAY TWO HUNDRED AND TWENTY-NINE

Callous and Greedy

Eph.4:19

They have become callous and have given themselves up to sensuality, greedy to practise every kind of impurity.

Let me recap a little. Futile thinking is a direct result of having a darkened understanding, and that is a result of being alienated from the life of God. A life that is void of God lives in the darkness and is void of spiritually accurate and deep thought. Putting it another way, a hardness of heart leads to spiritual ignorance, alienation from God, darkened understanding and futile thinking. In this passage, John Stott noted a distinct downwards spiral. He wrote, "Hardness of heart leads first to darkness of mind, then to deadness of soul under the judgment of God, and finally to recklessness of life. Having lost all sensitivity, people lose all self-control."[1]

In our text for today, Paul uses the word "callous", employing an exceedingly rare word, found only here in the whole of the New Testament. The word is *apēlgēkotes,* which means 'to cease to feel pain or grief, to become callous, insensible to pain, apathetic to the sufferings of others'. Other translations express this word as meaning "no sense of shame" (NLT); "stifled conscience" (J.B. Phillips); "past feeling" (KJV); "feeling no pain" (MSG). Clinton Arnold writes:

> *The perfect tense suggests that they have reached this point, presumably after a period of rejecting God and his ways, and now there is a hard, impenetrable shell that renders them insensitive to God and describes their ongoing condition.[2]*

Mark Roberts adds another dimension to this by writing, "They have become so used to sin that they do not sense how it wounds their souls and their relationships with others."[3] Sin is basically unbridled selfishness and deeply divisive. People with callous hearts and minds have no idea

---

[1]   John Stott, *The Message of Ephesians,* (IVP, Leicester, 1979), p.177
[2]   Clinton E. Arnold, *Ephesians,* (Zondervan, Michigan, 2010), p.283
[3]   Mark D. Roberts, *Ephesians,* (Zondervan, Michigan, 2016), p.149

of the consequences of what they say or do, and even if they do, they do not care.

Many unconverted people actually love the darkness. The apostle John wrote:

> *And this is the judgment: the light has come into the world, and people loved the darkness rather than the light because their works were evil. For everyone who does wicked things hates the light and does not come to the light, lest his works should be exposed.*

> John 3:17,18

Light exposes the hidden things and therefore, in many instances, there is an animosity against the light and the truth of the gospel.

There is only one way that this kind of heart can be reached, and that is by the Spirit of God speaking and acting through the word of God. The early church fathers often used the word 'compunction' to describe how it happens.[1] It occurs when the heart is pricked or wounded by the sword of the Holy Spirit. The result is a deep remorse, which is the true prerequisite for finding the forgiveness of God. In his letter to the Corinthians, Paul used the phrase "godly grief" which "produces a repentance that leads to salvation without regret" (2.Cor.7:10). Can a calloused heart be touched by God? God says that it can.

Thought

It is vitally important to keep our conscience sensitive to the voice of the Spirit.

Prayer

Lord, see if there be any areas within me that have become insensitive to you and others.

---

[1] I explain it in more detail in *Ephesians: The Church I See,* Vol.1, (Onwards and Upwards, Exeter, 2021), 'Day Eighty-Four', p.192

DAY TWO HUNDRED AND THIRTY

Sensuality

Eph.4:19

They have become callous and have given themselves up to sensuality, greedy to practise every kind of impurity.

Today, we are going to look at a phrase that perfectly sums up the state of an unconverted individual. Such a person has a darkened and hardened heart and mindset. Paul writes that such hardened and unbelieving individuals have "given themselves up to sensuality".

Let's explore the meaning of this word "sensuality". The Concise Oxford dictionary describes 'sensuality' as meaning the "gratification of the senses, or self-indulgence"[1]. My rather large Bloomsbury dictionary says that the word defines "the capacity for enjoying the pleasures of the senses"[2]. Sensuality, then, is anything that arouses and stimulates our basic human desires.

Paul uses the Greek word *aselgeia,* which basically means 'self-indulgence'. Clinton Arnold wrote, "This would include an abandonment of God's design for sexuality and the pursuit of all kinds of sexual pleasures."[3] Robertson called it "unbridled lust"[4]. Kenneth Wuest calls it "wanton lawless insolence"[5]. Wuest also suggests that this is the person "who acknowledges no restraints, who dares whatsoever his caprice and wanton petulance may suggest"[6]. Without any struggle of conscience, they abandon themselves in free and full surrender to whatever pleases them.

When we examine today's societies, self-indulgence and pleasure-seeking are still rampant. We have to remind ourselves that such

---

[1] *The Concise English Dictionary,* 'Sensuality', (Clarendon Press, London, 1990), p.1103
[2] *The Bloomsbury Dictionary,* 'Sensuality', (Bloomsbury Publishing, London, 2004), p.1699
[3] Clinton E. Arnold, *Ephesians,* (Zondervan, Michigan, 2010), p.283
[4] *Robertson's Word Pictures,* e-sword.net
[5] Kenneth Wuest, *Wuest's Word Studies,* Vol.1, 'Ephesians and Colossians', (Eerdmans, Michigan, 1953), p.108
[6] Ibid.

decadence is not a new development of lifestyle. Today we live in a culture where so-called enlightened and liberal thinking minds are free to pursue whatever is to their own personal taste. Such actions are actively encouraged, and anyone who seeks to rein in such behaviour is thought to be antiquated and a hindrance to progress. All this is but a simple recycling of what has always been there in the heart of unregenerate humanity. We may have grown and developed in various technologies but we have remained the same in our sins.

Another term used in the writings of the early church fathers describes this, and it is the word 'concupiscence', which describes a powerful and usually sensual longing. Michael Casey wrote, "Desire is enkindled by the cavalcade of curiosities. This can become so strong that in many cases concupiscence seems already to have crossed the border and have become experience."[1] He also wrote, "The soul is subject to the destructive forces of the concupiscence of the flesh … concupiscence is permanently present in the flesh, and once the soul responds to its incitement or titillation, it freely becomes the slave of sin…"[2]

Thought

Never underestimate the power and the pathway of our basic desires. Sin has an agenda.

Prayer

Dear Lord, help me today to live under the protective and cleansing work of the cross.

---

[1] Michael Casey, *Reading Saint Bernard: The Man, The Medium, The Message,* p.103, *https://doi.org/10.1163/ej.9789004201392.i-406.18*

[2] Michael Casey, *A Thirst for God,* (Cistercian Publications, Kalamazoo, 1988), p.179

DAY TWO HUNDRED AND THIRTY-ONE

Giving Themselves Up

Eph.4:19

They have become callous and have given themselves up to sensuality, greedy to practise every kind of impurity.

I grew up in the Swinging Sixties, that infamous era of free love, LSD and cannabis, rough and authentic blues, Jimi Hendrix and Cream. Wikipedia called it "a youth-driven cultural revolution that took place in the United Kingdom during the mid-to-late 1960s, emphasising modernity and fun-loving hedonism"[1]. It was an era of experimentation and where 'anything goes'.

Two prominent figures stood out in opposition to this rampant and prurient hedonism of the day: Mary Whitehouse and Lord Longford. Even today they are viewed as having been out-of-touch prudes. I think Paul would have called them prophets. Like them, Paul saw the ugly deceptiveness of sensuality, knowing full well that it beckoned and aroused, gave a fleeting experience, and then ensnared people.

He writes that the unconverted Gentiles had "given themselves up to sensuality". The phrase "given themselves up" is *heautous paredōkan,* which literally means 'to give themselves alongside'. Today we would say they have 'sold themselves down the river'. The verb *paradidōmi* means 'to give into the hands of another, to betray, to hand over, give one's self up, present one's self'. It is a wanton, deliberate, lawless insolence that sells itself down the river to unbridled sensuality. It is a stimulating of sexual desire with a smirk of defiance about it.

Now two things happen here. In the first instance, Paul is writing that they have given themselves up to this. This is to do with personal choice, albeit an inadequately informed choice. Seductive temptation will hide the true facts. Listen to the words of Solomon describing the flirtations of a loose woman:

> *With much seductive speech she persuades him; with her smooth talk she compels him. All at once he follows her, as an*

---

[1]   *https://en.wikipedia.org/wiki/Swinging_Sixties*

ox goes to the slaughter, or as a stag is caught fast till an arrow pierces its liver; as a bird rushes into a snare; he does not know that it will cost him his life.

Proverbs 7:21-23

Secondly, Paul writes that it was God who gave them up. He wrote to the church in Rome, living in the midst of a horrendously decadent society, concerning the ungodly, that...

...God gave them up in the lusts of their hearts to impurity, to the dishonouring of their bodies among themselves because they exchanged the truth about God for a lie and worshiped and served the creature rather than the Creator, who is blessed forever! Amen. For this reason God gave them up to dishonourable passions. For their women exchanged natural relations for those that are contrary to nature; and the men likewise gave up natural relations with women and were consumed with passion for one another, men committing shameless acts with men and receiving in themselves the due penalty for their error.

Romans 1:24-27

Clinton Arnold wrote, "This was not a condition thrust upon them involuntarily; they became this way on their own volition. God had allowed them to pursue their own course and immerse themselves into a life of self-indulgence."[1] The hardened fool becomes even more hardened. Their tiptoeing into sin becomes a canter, followed by a running headlong into sin with an unabashed abandonment.

Thought

What we allow becomes either a drift downwards or a movement upwards.

Prayer

Dear Lord, keep my eyes opened that I might not get hoodwinked into a downward drift.

---

[1] Clinton E. Arnold, *Ephesians,* (Zondervan, Michigan, 2010), p.283

DAY TWO HUNDRED AND THIRTY-TWO

Greedy for Impurity

Eph.4:19

They have become callous and have given themselves up to sensuality, greedy to practise every kind of impurity.

Eugene Peterson was passionate about authentic spirituality. He wrote, "Following Jesus means not following your impulses and appetites and whims and dreams, all of which are sufficiently damaged by sin to make them unreliable guides for getting any place worth going." He adds:

> *Grammatically, the negative, our capacity to say No, is one of the most impressive features of our language. The negative is our access to freedom. Only humans can say No. Animals can't say No. Animals do what instinct dictates. No is a freedom word. I don't have to do what either my glands or my culture tells me to do.[1]*

Paul now writes that these unconverted Gentiles are "greedy to practise every kind of impurity". With their conscience calloused and stifled, their self-defiling becomes both deliberate and habitual, descending even further into a greedy pursuit to satisfy every impure lust arising within them. In verse 22, he will go on to use the phrase "deceitful desires". Lust, or inordinate desires, are indeed deceitful. Promising much, they deliver nothing but corruption, bondage and death.

The word "greedy" is from the Greek word *pleonexia,* which, according to Thayer, means the "greedy desire to have more, covetousness, avarice"[2]. Clinton Arnold translates this as "an insatiable desire for more"[3]. The unconverted heart is a bottomless pit that never cries, "Enough!" On the other hand, one of the hallmarks of the mature Christian is contentment. Jesus said, "Take care, and be on your guard against all covetousness, for one's life does not consist in the abundance

---

[1]   Eugene Peterson, *Subversive Spirituality,* (Eerdmans, Michigan, 1997), p.12
[2]   *Thayer's Greek Definitions,* e-sword.net
[3]   Clinton E. Arnold, *Ephesians,* (Zondervan, Michigan, 2010), p.283

of his possessions." (Lk.12:15) For "covetousness" he used the word *pleonexia.*

The word translated in our reading as "practise" is the Greek word *ergasian,* which essentially means 'to a working'. Vincent wrote, "In Acts 19:25, the word is used of a trade. Not precisely in this sense here, yet with a shade of it. They gave themselves up as to the prosecution of a business."[1] This does not describe something that is occasional, but something that is regular, on the brink of becoming a way of life.

The word 'purity' is, next to the word 'holy', one of God's favourite words. He delights in purity, and he is very responsive to those who have and maintain a pure heart. However, the unconverted heart has a penchant and a love for that which is impure. Its motto, like the pig rolling in the mud in the pen, is 'the dirtier the better'. Pigs love the dirt.

This is a prophetic and clear diagnosis of the condition of unredeemed humanity. The fallen children of Adam and Eve are still rolling around in the mud, loving every moment of it. There is no awareness that Jesus came to live in the same dirt, without being stained and corrupted by it, in order to lift us up out of it, bringing forgiveness and deep cleansing. The sin that men and women roll around in is the very stuff for which he went to the cross.

Thought

Learn to hate the sin that led to the awful event of the cross.

Prayer

Father in heaven, thank you that your dear Son lifted me up and out of the miry pit.

---

[1]   *Vincent's Word Studies,* e-sword.net

DAY TWO HUNDRED AND THIRTY-THREE

Learning Christ

Eph.4:20

But that is not the way you learned Christ!

In verse 17, Paul had written, "...you must no longer walk as the Gentiles do..." He then went on to describe their sordid lifestyles fuelled by their darkened hearts and minds. He did this in order to throw into sharp contrast the huge differences between living an ungodly and a godly life. In effect it was as if he was saying to these new converts, "This is the way you once lived, but you need to know that to keep on living like that is totally incongruent with the way of Christ." This is a challenge that we all need to hear. We cannot import into our life with Christ the practices of our old life. Jesus has called us out of all that.

He then throws in this challenge: "But that is not the way you learned Christ!" This is a very unusual expression, used only here in the New Testament. Martyn Lloyd-Jones calls it "a dramatic and almost an abrupt statement"[1]. Mark Roberts calls this an "awkward bluntness", and writes that "it underscores the fact that Christianity is focused in a person. This person teaches us how to live. This person exemplifies what he teaches. This person is someone with whom we have a living relationship."[2]

If this be so, then it is not so much about learning certain lessons, or even the principles of spiritual life; rather, it is about learning to know a person. Harold Hoehner writes, "The implication is that factual learning is insufficient, the goal is to know Christ personally."[3] There is a world of difference when it comes to learning Christ and learning about Christ. Both are of utmost importance but they are different. I learn Christ by sitting at his feet, listening to his word, responding to what he says and speaking to him in prayer. I learn Christ when I recognise his hand and

---

[1] Dr Martyn Lloyd-Jones, *Darkness and Light,* (Banner of Truth, Edinburgh, 1982), p.78

[2] Mark D. Roberts, *Ephesians,* (Zondervan, Michigan, 2016), p.150

[3] Harold Hoehner, *Ephesians: An Exegetical Commentary,* (Baker Academic, Michigan, 2002), p.594

his voice as I walk through the ups and downs of life. I recognise Christ by his presence. No book or Bible course will give me that. This is all about a personal walk with him. This is about time spent with him in face to face encounters.

God has given us two wonderful gifts. The first one is the indwelling presence of the Father, Son and Holy Spirit. Jesus said:

> *If you love me, you will keep my commandments. And I will ask the Father, and he will give you another Helper, to be with you forever, even the Spirit of truth, whom the world cannot receive, because it neither sees him nor knows him. You know him, for he dwells with you and will be in you.*
>
> John 14:15-17

He then went on to say, "If anyone loves me, he will keep my word, and my Father will love him, and we will come to him and make our home with him." (Jn.14:23) We have to learn how to converse and walk with the triune Life within us.

Secondly, he gave us the Scriptures which, when opened to us by the Spirit of God, feed and nurture this relationship. Learning about him through the words of scripture will enrich, inform and deepen our experience of him. If I truly love someone then I want to find out all I can about them. I want to explore every nook and cranny of their lives. I want to understand their world. And it is like that with Jesus. I want to learn from the prophets who spoke of him and from those who have walked with him. I want to 'converse' with Adam, Moses, Abraham, Isaac and Jacob, and with Samuel and David, Isaiah and Jeremiah, the apostles and Paul. My heart's cry will be, "Tell me about him whom my soul loves."

Thought

All the characters in the Bible, although long dead (Jesus excepted), still speak to us.

Prayer

Dear Lord, my heart's desire is to know you, and learn from you for myself.

DAY TWO HUNDRED AND THIRTY-FOUR

Learning of Christ

Eph.4:20,21

But that is not the way you learned Christ! – assuming that
you have heard about him and were taught in him, as the truth
is in Jesus...

An important fact to take into consideration is that although these Ephesian believers had never met Jesus in his human body, they had met him through Paul. Paul's preaching was an event, an occasion of revelation. As he moved among them, speaking of Christ, suddenly they were encountering Jesus for themselves. It was as if he was speaking to them personally through Paul, manifesting himself through Paul's life. True preaching introduces people to the living Christ, bringing them to a personal encounter.

These believers heard the voice of Jesus in the voice of Paul, and then they experienced first-hand the life of Christ. From there, they were taught in him. Having experienced Jesus for themselves, these new believers were enrolled in the school of Christ. The pastors and the teachers deepened their understanding of who he is and what he had done.

The whole context of these two verses is about learning – learning of, from and about Christ. John Stott cited Markus Barth in pointing out that Paul is "invoking the imagery of a school"[1]. Stott wrote, "You learned Christ" (v.20), "you heard about him" (v.21a), "you were taught in Him" (v.21b).[2]

There is much wisdom in the writings of the early church fathers and the Desert Fathers. Sister Benedicta Ward has written two books – *The Sayings of the Desert Fathers* and *The Wisdom of the Desert Fathers.*[3] Both contain a lifetime of valuable readings. There were also other outstanding followers and teachers of the way of Christ throughout the Middle Ages. Thomas à Kempis (1380-1471) was one of them. In the

---

[1]   John Stott, *The Message of Ephesians,* (IVP, Leicester, 1979), p.179
[2]   Ibid.
[3]   *Sister Benedicta Ward,* (Cistercian Publications, Michigan)

preface to a new edition of his book, *The Imitation of Christ,* we find this statement about the man: he was "a teacher and writer whose life was devoted to patterning his life after Jesus Christ"[1]. Eugene Peterson wrote a book called *Take and Read,* a compendium of books that guides thirsty souls into a rich field of Christian writings. He mentions *The Imitation of Christ,* saying:

> *This is not everyone's favourite, but it is on everyone's list. This is the most widely published and read book on spirituality in our tradition. It is amazing how well its medieval monkishness carries over into the modern world.*[2]

Today, we have access to vast numbers of pastors and teachers who themselves have dug deep into the life of Christ and the ways of God. Love learns, and in order to grow in our walk with Jesus, we need to relish sitting at the feet of those who can teach us the way of Jesus both accurately and experientially.

If we are in earnest about this, we need to separate ourselves from the 'instant' culture that we live in. We need to wean ourselves off the 'memes' and 'eye-catching' slogans so prevalent today. We need to embark on the slow but sure journey of learning Christ – first-hand, and also from those who love him.

Thought

Love loves to learn, and learning and reading are disciplines that pay huge dividends.

Prayer

Lord, give me a learning heart that will chase after the wisdom of the Christ-lovers.

---

[1] Thomas à Kempis, *The Imitation of Christ,* translated by Aloysius Croft and Harold Bolton, (Hendrickson Publishers, Massachusetts, 2004)

[2] Eugene Peterson, *Take and Read – Spiritual Reading – an annotated list,* (Eerdmans, Michigan, 1996), p.7

Day Two Hundred and Thirty-Five

The Truth is in Jesus

Eph.4:20,21

But that is not the way you learned Christ! – assuming that you have heard about him and were taught in him, as the truth is in Jesus...

Harold Hoehner pointed out that Jesus is both "the object and the sphere of a believer's learning"[1]. He is the epicentre of our lives, and it is from him that we derive our life. He himself said, "I am the way, and the truth, and the life." (Jn.14:6) All were embodied in him personally. To know the way, we must know him. To know the truth, we must know him. To know the life, we must know him. This is where we start, continue and end our learning of Jesus.

To aid us, Jesus has given pastors and teachers to the church. We need them to help us on our journey of learning. We need the theologians who have dug deeply into the Scriptures for themselves, and have trawled through the writings of others who have seriously and profoundly walked with God. I recommend the likes of Eugene Peterson, Wayne Grudem, Gordon Fee, Tom Wright and Jim Packer for starters.

Jim Packer, in his seminal book *Knowing God,* wrote, "...if we pursue theological knowledge for its own sake, it is bound to go bad on us. It will make us proud and conceited." He then added:

> *Our aim in studying the Godhead must be to know God Himself the better. Our concern must be to enlarge our acquaintance, not simply with the doctrine of God's attributes, but with the living God Whose attributes they are.*[2]

Thirsting for both God himself and for authentic truth, Eugene Peterson read *Calvin's Institutes of the Christian Religion* each year for twelve years. For him, John Calvin was the consummate theologian. He

---

[1] Harold Hoehner, *Ephesians: An Exegetical Commentary,* (Baker Academic, Michigan, 2002), p.595

[2] J. I. Packer, *Knowing God,* (Hodder & Stoughton, London, 1975), pp.18,19

was clear and precise, and his works saved Peterson from woolly and cultural thinking.

In one of his lectures, Eugene Peterson said, "Truth is like a fence. You paint it, and then you have to paint it again, or clean it, the following year."[1] In the same manner, a piece of wood that has been stained several times reveals a depth of colour and texture. Our sitting at the feet of Jesus and the Scriptures, conversing, learning and reading eternal truths, needs to be regular, inspired and fuelled by our love for him. Likewise, our delving into the writings of the lovers and followers of Jesus needs to be consistent, in-depth, disciplined and systematic.

Peterson also said:

> It's very easy to let our ideas take on a life of their own separated from the way we are living. Truth and spirituality must walk hand in hand. Doctrine and life belong together. If we think wrongly, we are going to end up doing and living wrongly. Truth can go wrong without becoming a lie. It does so when you don't live it. The Logos – the Word – must become incarnate.[2]

The truth that is found in Jesus must also be found living and functioning in us. Jesus the truth must become absorbed into the depths of our lives so that when people touch and hear us, they are touching and hearing him too.

Thought

Truth that is disconnected from life is a dangerous sham.

Prayer

Jesus, make my life an accurate and in-depth representation of all that you are.

---

[1] Eugene Peterson, lectures on 'Soulcraft: The Formation of a Mature Life in Christ', Regents College, Vancouver
[2] Ibid.

DAY TWO HUNDRED AND THIRTY-SIX

Putting Off Your Old Self (1)

Eph.4:22

...to put off your old self, which belongs to your former manner of life and is corrupt through deceitful desires...

I guess that under the ministry of Paul and the teachers, the new converts would have learned many things about knowing and walking with Jesus. Here, however, in these next verses, Paul puts into a few words what the essence of the Christian life is all about. It is not just about modifying or changing our behaviour or our language; it goes much deeper than that. It is more about the total changing of who I am as a person. It is about swapping the old me for a new me.

The phrase "your old self" is coined only by Paul, and just three times. You can find it also in Romans 6:6 and Colossians 3:9. It is literally 'the ancient man'. John Eadie, one of the finest commentators of the Greek text of Ephesians, wrote, "The words are, therefore, a bold and vivid personification of the old nature we inherit from Adam, the source and seat of original and actual transgression."[1]

One of the most important lessons we can learn is that the problem of sin lies, not in what I do or say, but in me myself. I sin because I am a sinner – by nature. Clinton Arnold writes that the old self "is more than an old mind-set or lifestyle. It is a way of referring to believers in terms of their solidarity with Adam in his sin."[2] The Bible teaches us that we were born with an Adamic nature. That simply means that Adam passed on to us all a nature that had an inbuilt propensity to sin and rebel. I sometimes teach that no parent has ever had to teach a child how to be naughty. It just kind of eventually emerges – naturally.

John Gill, the Puritan theologian, wrote, "It is called 'old', because it is the poison of the old serpent, with which man was infected by him from the beginning."[3] The word "infected" is an apt one. The poison of

---

[1] John Eadie, *A Commentary on the Greek Text of Ephesians,* (Robert Carter, New York, 1861), p.347

[2] Clinton E. Arnold, *Ephesians,* (Zondervan, Michigan, 2010), p.287

[3] John Gill, *Exposition of the Entire Bible,* e-sword.net

the serpent corrupted us to the core. It is so deep that although our conversion frees us from the guilt and the power of it all, the curse of it and remnants of it remain within us. In many trying circumstances, we find it erupting, and soiling the atmosphere. John Calvin lamented that "so long as we dwell in the prison of the body, we must constantly struggle with the vices of our corrupt nature, and so with our natural disposition"[1].

Paul is saying here that the saints were to lay aside this corrupted old self, with its inbuilt natural proclivity for, or inclination towards, sin. The phrase "put off" is from the Greek word *apothesthai,* which means 'to put off or aside or away'. In other words, don't be reluctant about this. The old self is doing us no good at all. We must become almost brutal in our war against our old self.

In another passage he toughened the language by writing, "We know that our old self was crucified with him in order that the body of sin might be brought to nothing, so that we would no longer be enslaved to sin." (Rom.6:6) Although the wording is in the past tense here, the sentiment is the same. We need to take this ancient Adamic nature to the cross, putting it to death, again and again.

Thought

Our sin took Jesus to the cross. Therefore, learn to loathe it, and give it no room.

Prayer

Lord, help me to see that the natural me is corrupted, and needs drastic treatment.

---

[1] John Calvin, *Institutes of the Christian Religion,* (Hendrickson Publishers, Massachusetts, 2008), p.399

DAY TWO HUNDRED AND THIRTY-SEVEN

Putting Off Your Old Self (2)

Eph.4:22

...to put off your old self, which belongs to your former manner of life and is corrupt through deceitful desires...

Jesus knew the absolutely devastating effect of sin. He had observed its effects on the first couple, and then in their descendants. It was like the opening of a Pandora's box, spilling its poisonous and corrupting influence down through the ages. He carried no misconceptions about its origins and power.

We, on the other hand, seem not only to downplay its cruel effects, but even at times to deny its presence! Much modern psychology relegates sin to the after-effects of our upbringing, putting the cause to external circumstances. Nothing can be further from the truth. Sin resides firmly within the human soul.

This same Jesus, when issuing a challenge for men and women to follow him, said, "If anyone would come after me, let him deny himself and take up his cross and follow me. For whoever would save his life will lose it, but whoever loses his life for my sake will find it." (Matt.16:24,25) He insisted that they do three things:

The first was to "deny himself". The Greek word is *aparnēsasthō,* which basically means saying to oneself, "I want no more to do with you. I disown you; I want to forget you; I want to lose sight of you and all that you have been up to." This is biblical self-denial. To help us with this, let us think about the true meaning of baptism. According to Paul, "we were buried with him in baptism into death" (Rom.6:4). Then he wrote, "We know that our old self was crucified with him." It is as if I am saying to the old me, "You have done nothing but mess up my life, and today, in baptism, I renounce you. I will no longer allow you to influence me in any way whatsoever." Experience, however, tells us that we will have to say that again and again throughout the rest of our lives here on the earth.

The second is to "take up his cross". This follows hard on the trail of the first. To take up our cross means two things: firstly to accept the suffering and the scandal of being associated with him, whatever that may cost; and secondly to put to death, on a daily basis, that which is natural and ungodly in us.

True Christianity is not a weekend hobby that soothes our troubled hearts each Sunday. It is a way of life that costs us everything. The paradox is that although Jesus paid the ultimate price for us to be forgiven, to walk with him requires that we pick up our own cross. A.W. Tozer wrote, "We want to be saved, but we insist that Christ does all the dying."[1] Charles Spurgeon wrote, "There are no crown-wearers in heaven who were not cross-bearers here below."[2] The true gospel is defined as, "Come, die and then live!"

The third is "follow me". Christ has taken up residence in us by his Holy Spirit. Whereas beforehand, I called all the shots in decision-making, now I find another voice within me calling me to another way. At first, this new way cuts across my normal inclinations/reactions to life, and I find that I have different choices to make. I can either do it my way or his. He calls us to journey with him, in his direction, not ours. He calls us to walk at his pace, not ours.

Thought

Don't pussyfoot around the old self. Show him the door.

Prayer

Lord, help me to disown who I was in order that I may embrace who you made me to be.

---

[1] A.W. Tozer, *The Root of the Righteous,* (Christian Publications, Harrisburg, 1955), p.66

[2] Charles Spurgeon, *Gleanings Among the Sheaves,* (Facsimile Publisher, 2015)

DAY TWO HUNDRED AND THIRTY-EIGHT

Renewal in the Spirit of the Mind (1)

Eph.4:23

...and to be renewed in the spirit of your minds...

There are many spiritual gurus who will tell us to be true to our inner 'self'. My question is: what 'self' is that? If it is my old 'self', then I want nothing to do with him. No more self-assertion or self-seeking! I found that my unconverted 'self' led me astray. If, however, it is the new 'self', then I want all of him.

Paul now uses an interesting turn of words. He says to the Ephesian believers, "...be renewed in the spirit of your minds..." In the previous verses, he had outlined both the futility and the darkness of the natural mind. Here, he says that this is the very area that God, by the Spirit, wants to work on. The way we think determines how we live. Their wrong thinking had led them further and further into the behaviour of the darkness. God now wants to show them another way of thinking.

He uses, firstly, the word "renewed". The Greek word is *ananeousthai*, which means "to be renewed, to be renovated by inward reformation"[1]. Mark Roberts points out here that the verb is in the passive voice, "indicating that we do not renew ourselves. Rather the agent of our renewal is God."[2] He goes on to say that "the verb is also a present indicative, which suggests an ongoing process"[3]. The work that the Spirit starts in us will continue right up to our entrance into heaven and, I believe, beyond.

Secondly, Paul tells them where the renewing will take place. It will be not simply in the mind, but in the *spirit* of the mind. John Eadie (1810-1876) was a professor of biblical literature and hermeneutics. In his time, he was one of the finest expositors of the New Testament. His perceptions are thorough, thought-provoking and well worth pondering over. On this text he wrote:

---

[1] Kenneth Wuest, *Wuest's Word Studies,* Vol.1, 'Ephesians and Colossians', (Eerdmans, Michigan, 1953), p.110

[2] Mark D. Roberts, *Ephesians,* (Zondervan, Michigan, 2016), p.152

[3] Ibid.

The mind remains as before, both in its intellectual and emotional structure – in its memory and judgment, imagination and perception. These powers do not in themselves need renewal, and regeneration brings no new faculties. The organism of the mind survives as it was, but the spirit, its highest part, the possession of which distinguishes man from the inferior animals, and fits him for receiving the Spirit of God, is being renovated. The memory, for example, still exercises its former functions, but on a very different class of subjects; the judgment still discharging its old office, is occupied among a new set of themes and ideas; and love, retaining all its ardour, attaches itself to objects quite in contrast with those of its earlier preference and pursuit.[1]

He then went on to write:

The change is not in mind psychologically, either in its essence or in its operation; and neither is it in the mind as if it were a superficial change of opinion either on points of doctrine or practice: but it is in the spirit of the mind; in that which gives mind both its bent and its materials of thought. It is not simply in the spirit as if it lay there in dim and mystic quietude; but it is in the spirit of the mind; in the power which, when changed itself, radically alters the entire sphere and business of the inner mechanism.[2]

Thought

God the Holy Spirit gives us life-changing and life-giving fuel for thought.

Prayer

Dear Lord, please renew the way I think and also inspire the contents of my mind.

---

[1] John Eadie, *A Commentary on the Greek Text of Ephesians,* (Robert Carter, New York, 1861), p.351
[2] Ibid, pp.351,352

DAY TWO HUNDRED AND THIRTY-NINE

Renewal in the Spirit of the Mind (2)

Eph.4:23

...and to be renewed in the spirit of your minds...

I remember years ago being at a concert where the Christian rock band 'Second Chapter of Acts' were playing. The MC and speaker that night was Barry Maguire, famous for his song in the sixties, 'Eve of Destruction'. His opening statement was this: "Many say that we Christians are brainwashed. Too right! My brains were filthy!" Our minds need to be washed clean, and our thought life needs to be constantly renewed by the Holy Spirit and regular exposure to the word of God.

The Greek word *ananeousthai,* which has been translated "renewed", is used only here in the New Testament. This is yet another case of Paul lifting out words from the Greek Old Testament and secular usage, and inserting them into his writings.

Paul is writing about something much deeper and far more powerful than natural thought processes. He is writing about "the spirit of the mind". The human spirit is that faculty within us that, when touched and made alive by the Holy Spirit, enables us to be conscious of God. The Holy Spirit then pours new ways of thinking and brand-new thoughts into our spirits, which then rise to inspire and instruct our own minds. Bishop Westcott, in his commentary on the Greek text of Ephesians, wrote, "The spirit, by which man holds communion with God, has a place in his higher reason. The spirit when quickened furnishes new principles to the νοὸς [Greek for 'mind' – pronounced 'noos']."[1] Very basically, the Holy Spirit gives us holy fuel for thought. He comes to us and says, "Think about these things," and, "Let me give you something to think about."

Paul wrote to the church in Rome, "...be transformed by the renewal of your mind..." (Rom.12:2) He wrote to the believers in Philippi, "Finally, brothers, whatever is true, whatever is honorable, whatever is

---

[1] B.F. Westcott, *St Paul's Epistle to the Ephesians,* (Macmillan & Co, London, 1906), p.68

just, whatever is pure, whatever is lovely, whatever is commendable, if there is any excellence, if there is anything worthy of praise, think about these things." (Phil.4:8) He also wrote to the saints in Colossae, "Set your minds on things that are above, not on things that are on earth." (Col.3:2)

The change comes from within. It is both revelatory and revolutionary truth, gained in prayerful study of the Scriptures under the tutelage of the Spirit.

Using an agricultural term, it is helpful to imagine that our mind has been like a field that has been seriously neglected for years. It is full of potholes, stones, brambles and weeds. The ownership of the field has changed hands, and the new owner wants to sow good seed in it. But before that can happen, the holes must be filled in, the stones removed and the brambles and weeds uprooted. The holes speak of gaps in our thinking, the stones speak of hardened thinking, the brambles and weeds speak of thinking that stifles and prevents the growth of good thoughts and concepts. Such it was with our minds that were full of things and thoughts unworthy and unfruitful. The terrain of our mind needs cleansing before it can be ploughed and new things sown. God the Holy Spirit will do this, and we will start thinking differently. New concepts and principles will be birthed in us.

Thought

Allow the Holy Spirit to challenge and change the way we think, giving us new thoughts.

Prayer

Dear Holy Spirit, make the meditations of my heart refreshingly pure and beautiful.

DAY TWO HUNDRED AND FORTY

Putting on Your New Self (1)

Eph.4:24

...put on the new self, created after the likeness of God in true righteousness and holiness.

Paul has been saying that these new Ephesian converts need to lay aside their old way of doing life. There were practices and thought patterns that needed to be discarded and left behind them. They were then to allow the Holy Spirit to drop into their spirits new and different ways of walking. William Hendriksen put it this way: "This renewal is basically an act of God's Spirit powerfully influencing man's spirit ... with respect to God and spiritual realities."[1] They were to be taught brand-new and much higher thoughts and concepts.

Around 740 years before Christ, God spoke through Isaiah the prophet, saying, "...my thoughts are not your thoughts, neither are your ways my ways, declares the LORD. For as the heavens are higher than the earth, so are my ways higher than your ways and my thoughts than your thoughts." (Is.55:8,9)

At the same time all this is taking place, Paul writes that they are to put on "the new self". He also wrote to the believers in Colossae about the need to put on "the new self, which is being renewed in knowledge after the image of its creator" (Col.3:10). In his letter to the church in Rome, he put it this way: "...put on the Lord Jesus Christ, and make no provision for the flesh, to gratify its desires." (Rom.13:14)

Kenneth Wuest writes, "Since the old man refers to the unsaved person dominated by the totally depraved nature, the 'new man' refers to the saved person dominated by the Divine nature."[2]

Harold Hoehner makes this insightful comment: "Worthy of note is that the old person does not remain with the new person. Dualism is not suggested or implied. One cannot be a Christian and a non-Christian at

---

[1]   William Hendriksen, *Ephesians,* (Banner of Truth, Edinburgh, 1976), p.215
[2]   Kenneth Wuest, *Wuest's Word Studies,* Vol.1, 'Ephesians and Colossians', (Eerdmans, Michigan, 1953), p.111

the same time."[1] To walk into the new, we must leave behind the old. We must not carry past behavioural and thoughts patterns with us into the kingdom of heaven. Our new life will not blend with the old one.

To reinforce this concept, let me tell a story. A wealthy landowner came to visit one of his tenants who lived in a ramshackle farm cottage. He informed him that he wanted to build him a new house, and of course the tenant was delighted! The next morning, the tenant awoke to the sound of a heavy engine. As he peered out of his window, he saw a huge bulldozer that was approaching and aiming towards demolishing the cottage. He rushed out and remonstrated with the driver, who also happened to be the landowner. The tenant informed the landowner that he couldn't demolish the cottage with all its memories. The landowner replied that he had to in order to be able build the new house for the tenant. The old cottage could not fit into the new house, and the new house was not going to incorporate it.

The new self was the life of Jesus, and the new life that we now have in Christ is not just the 'housing' of Christ within us by the Spirit, but the 'manifesting' of Christ by his Spirit.

Thought

When we seek to blend the old life with the new, we end up with a seriously diluted faith.

Prayer

Lord, help to let go of the old life completely, that I might fully step into the new life fully.

---

[1] Harold Hoehner, *Ephesians: An Exegetical Commentary,* (Baker Academic, Michigan, 2002), p.610

DAY TWO HUNDRED AND FORTY-ONE

Putting on Your New Self (2)

Eph.4:24

...put on the new self, created after the likeness of God in true righteousness and holiness.

In Christ we have been given a new identity and a new location. We are his and we are in him. Clinton Arnold, writing of this new identity, says:

> *This new self is a new identity that these believers have already acquired at the time of their conversion when they were sealed with the Holy Spirit and were joined to Christ in his death, resurrection and ascension. The new self is who believers now are in terms of their solidarity with Christ.[1]*

They are in his family, and they are to take on the family likeness. Arnold continues by saying:

> *Nevertheless, Paul calls them to put on this new identity. This amounts to a growing recognition of the truth of who they are now in Christ Jesus. It also involves an actualization of this identity through a transformed way of thinking and bringing their lives into conformity with the defining characteristics of this new identity – righteousness and holiness.[2]*

This new identity is the new self. In the beginning, God created man and woman in his own image and likeness. The fall of Adam, however, left us with much of his image but robbed us of his likeness. We became shaped instead into the likeness of the prince of darkness. But now we have been born again – a new creation – and we are being restored to the likeness of God. The phrase "after the likeness of God" in the Greek language is *kata Theon* – 'according to God, after God'. It is according to and consistent with who and what God is in himself. It is the clear message of the New Testament that upon our conversion we begin to

---

[1]   Clinton E. Arnold, *Ephesians,* (Zondervan, Michigan, 2010), pp.289,290
[2]   Ibid, p.290

start to take on being re-established and reshaped into the likeness of God.

Paul goes on to write that this is manifested "in true righteousness and holiness". A better reading of this text is *ktisthenta en dikaiosunē kai hosiotēti tēs alētheias,* literally, 'fabricated in righteousness and holiness stemming from truth'. The Greek word *tēs* indicates genitive of source. The NASB has it, "...created in righteousness and holiness of the truth." Kenneth Wuest's literal translation has it, "...created in righteousness and holiness of truth."[1]

Truth will inspire and motivate righteous and holy living. Therefore, giving serious attention to, and soaking our hearts and minds in, the word of God will fill us with deep desires to walk a pure life before God. Truth will cleanse and refresh us whereas lies will pollute and contaminate us. Paul wrote to both Timothy and Titus about "truth that accords with godliness" (1.Tim.6:3 / Tit.1:1). His message there was that truth is synonymous and congruent with godly living. Truth seeks to outwork itself into the way we live before God and each other. We become a true representation of what God is like.

Eugene Peterson put it like this in the Message. He translates this text as speaking of "an entirely new way of life – a God-fashioned life, a life renewed from the inside and working itself into your conduct as God accurately reproduces his character in you"[2].

Thought

Taking on God's character and likeness is a powerful witness to the world around us.

Prayer

Dear God, wherever I am today, may I reflect you accurately in my speech and actions.

---

[1]   Kenneth Wuest, *The New Testament, An Expanded Translation,* (Eerdmans, Michigan, 2004), p.454

[2]   Eugene Peterson, *The Message,* (NavPress, Colorado, 2002), p.2131

DAY TWO HUNDRED AND FORTY-TWO

Putting on Your New Self (3)

Eph.4:24

...put on the new self, created after the likeness of God in true righteousness and holiness.

The unknown writer to the Hebrews had a very high view of who Jesus is. In the opening verses of his letter he wrote that Jesus was "the exact imprint of his nature" (Heb.1:3). Kenneth Wuest translates that as "the exact reproduction of His essence"[1]. The words "imprint" and "reproduction" are translations of the Greek word *charaktēr*. Our high calling is to become Christlike, who is himself exactly like his Father. The character and likeness of God is to be deeply imprinted into our lives.

The character of God is marked, according to Paul, by two things. The first thing that he mentions is the word "righteousness". The Greek word is *dikaiosunē,* and the technical meaning is, according to W.E. Vine, "the character or quality of being right or just; it was formerly spelled 'rightwiseness', which clearly expresses the meaning"[2]. It is thinking rightly, speaking rightly and acting rightly. I would also say the emotional meaning of this word is the warm, welcoming, clean and truthful nature of God.

This righteousness of God is not only given as a garment, it is the character of God *inworked*. God not only imputes righteousness, he imparts it and works it into us. Grace fully and deeply restores what sin has ruined. We learn to take on board all that he is into our daily living. It creates an attractive beauty to our lives.

The second thing that Paul mentions is "holiness". This is the character of God *outworked*. The sphere of the holy is where God delights to live. He is holy and he is at home where there is holiness. Authentic holiness has an intrinsic beauty about it. 'Holiness' is a comely

---

[1] Kenneth Wuest, *The New Testament, An Expanded Translation,* (Eerdmans, Michigan, 2004), p.515

[2] W.E. Vine, *Vine's Expository Dictionary of Biblical Words,* (Thomas Nelson, New York, 1985), p.535

word. The more I have read the Scriptures, the more I have come to understand and feel that 'holy' is one of God's favourite words. He desires that we walk in holiness too.

Some time ago I was reading in Isaiah, and I saw two words that connected with each other. The prophet in prayer to God said, "Look down from heaven and see, from your holy and beautiful habitation..." (Is.63:15) and he also spoke of "our holy and beautiful house where our fathers praised you" (Is.64:11). In these two verses, the word "holy" – qôdesh – was linked with the word "beautiful". The Hebrew word he used for "beautiful" was tiph'ârâh which means 'beauty, comeliness'. These two words were being brought together here. These two concepts are married; they belong together. My main thought throughout this is that holiness is beautiful, holiness is attractive, holiness is comely. The beauty is on the outside and holiness is on the inside, and yet the work of the Holy Spirit is to create, shape and form holiness inside us in such a way that it becomes visible – beautifully so.

These two aspects of God are rooted and flow from truth. Marvin Vincent wrote, "Righteousness and holiness are attributes of truth."[1] Truth is the opposite of deception, and truth has a sanctifying, cleansing and inspiring effect, encouraging us to be positively like Jesus and his Father in all respects.

Thought

The dedicated ministry of the Trinity is to reproduce the Life in you.

Prayer

Father, submerge me in your truth that I may rise soaked in your Life.

---

[1] *Vincent's Word Studies,* e-sword.net

DAY TWO HUNDRED AND FORTY-THREE

Stop Telling Lies but Speak the Truth

Eph.4:25

Therefore, having put away falsehood, let each one of you speak the truth with his neighbour, for we are members one of another.

Truth plays a huge part in the Christian life. The word is so important that it is found nearly 90 times in the New Testament. Upon our conversion we find ourselves relating to the One who is the truth, the life and the way. His influence begins to challenge the lies that lie deep within, and which used to come out of our mouths. Truth is profoundly relational.

Paul now moves on to another section where he mentions a number of areas that all deal with interpersonal relationships. He reinforces the fact that what we believe must translate into relational behaviour, especially in the company of others. It is simply not enough to work hard on our relationship with the Lord whilst not caring about our relationship with his children, and also with those outside the church. Our walk with the Lord must spill out into our walk with those around us. The one should affect the other. Put another way, how we treat our brothers and sisters in the faith is an accurate indicator of our actual relationship with the Lord.

Firstly, Paul mentions lying. He says that falsehood was a part of their old way of life, which now must be left behind. The word that he uses is *pseudos,* and it means "a lie, a conscious and intentional falsehood; in a broad sense, whatever is not what it seems to be"[1]. It is more literally 'the lie'.

Jesus, speaking of Satan, said, "He was a murderer from the beginning, and does not stand in the truth, because there is no truth in him. When he lies, he speaks out of his own character, for he is a liar and the father of lies." (Jn.8:44) Lies are part of the old life and are used to deceive, protect, divert attention or cover up. Lies are satanic in origin. Peterson said that "the best lies are 98% truth. The devil uses the truth

---

[1] *Thayer's Greek Definitions,* e-sword.net

251

like a needle. He pushes it into us, and then starts to thread his lies into us, and starts to weave them into our lives."[1] Truth, however, is healthy, and releases the flow of the Spirit through the body.

Paul creates a contrast, and he will do this often in these next few verses. He is saying in effect that these new Christians should stop the destructive lying that came from their past, and they should start telling the truth that will give shape and form to their new lives. The Greek wording – *laleite alēthieian* – is constructed in such a way (the present tense with the imperative) that it "stresses that truthful speech should be an ongoing and characteristic pattern of the way believers talk"[2].

Paul says that the reason we speak the truth to each other is because "we are members of one another". Lies are destructive to relationships. Truth, on the other hand, is completely constructive, building bridges and strengthening and encouraging trustful relationships. Lies destroy; truth constructs.

Thought

Lies unravel things, but truth enhances that which God is seeking to build.

Prayer

Lord, help me to see my mouth as an instrument for constructing beauty in people's lives.

---

[1] Eugene Peterson, lectures on 'Soulcraft: The Formation of a Mature Life in Christ', Regents College, Vancouver

[2] Clinton E. Arnold, *Ephesians,* (Zondervan, Michigan, 2010), p.300

DAY TWO HUNDRED AND FORTY-FOUR

Disciplined Anger (1)

Eph.4:26,27

Be angry and do not sin; do not let the sun go down on your anger, and give no opportunity to the devil.

One does not have to go far in order to notice the destructive power of anger. People talk of the 'red mist' that appears and is often a prelude to a ferocious act of anger that explodes and rips apart relationships. The book of Proverbs has many injunctions about its negative force. For example: "Whoever is slow to anger has great understanding, but he who has a hasty temper exalts folly;" (14:29) "A hot-tempered man stirs up strife, but he who is slow to anger quiets contention;" (15:18) "A man of wrath stirs up strife, and one given to anger causes much transgression." (29:22)

Yet here, Paul writes, "Be angry," but then adds a rider: "…and do not sin." In part, Paul is quoting Psalm 4:4 – "Be angry, and do not sin…" The balance is found in the personal discipline of self-control. Often in the Scriptures, the term "slow to anger" is found. God is said to be "slow to anger", and men and women should be the same. Anger is to be felt, but it must be managed well. A man called Will Rogers once wrote, "People who fly into a rage always make a bad landing."[1]

Anger in itself is not a sin. It is, in fact, a God-given emotion, but like all other emotions, anger must be kept on a tight leash. God gets angry, but he is perfectly in control of his emotions, and he uses them purposefully. This is opposed to the wild destructive force of anger that many of us know about.

There are two kinds of anger – righteous and unrighteous – and there are also three Greek words for anger. The first one is *orgizesthe* – 'an abiding and settled habit of the mind aroused under certain circumstances'. This is also found in the first part our text for today; it is an anger that is guided by reason. This is the righteous anger of God which brings a deserved judgment.

---

[1] *https://www.brainyquote.com/quotes/will_rogers_378677*

The second one is *parorgismō,* which is 'an anger that is accompanied by irritations, exasperation and bitterness'. This is the one found in our text today. William Hendriksen translates it, "Let not the sun go down on that angry mood of yours..."[1] Francis Foulkes wrote, "It is more strictly 'provocation', the personal resentment that righteous anger can become when harboured and brooded over in the heart."[2] This sort is forbidden.

The third one is *thumos,* which is 'a turbulent commotion, a boiling agitation of feelings and passions – a boiling up and soon subsiding'. It is frequently used in the seeking of revenge. Later, Paul will go on to say that this sort of anger is strictly forbidden. (Eph.4:31)

Paul is saying that we must not let our anger take us into sin. Anger is always wrong when it becomes a propellant towards destruction. Anger, unchecked and out of control, will bring about much damage. I remember visiting a home where the husband had a serious problem with anger, mainly verbal, against his wife and children, and I told him that I felt that the walls of his home were "covered with blood".

Paul then adds to his argument by saying, "...give no opportunity to the devil." Uncontrolled anger opens the door for Satan to introduce pain, bitterness and deep resentments that begin to fester and cripple relationships. It is better translated, "Stop giving the Devil a place, an opportunity, power or occasions for acting." Squeeze him out of your relationships! Give him nowhere to stand, let alone enter.

Thought

Anger is always a choice. We need to take personal responsibility for our anger.

Prayer

Lord, teach me the balance between a right and a wrong anger.

---

[1]   William Hendriksen, *Ephesians,* (Banner of Truth, Edinburgh, 1976), p.207
[2]   Francis Foulkes, *Ephesians,* (IVP, Leicester, 1999), p.141

DAY TWO HUNDRED AND FORTY-FIVE

Disciplined Anger (2)

Eph.4:26,27

Be angry and do not sin; do not let the sun go down on your anger, and give no opportunity to the devil.

Before we move on, I think it is important that we have a second look at this whole issue of anger. Yesterday we noticed that anger is a God-given emotion. We also noticed, however, that anger, unchecked and unmanaged, will quickly lead to sin. Anger, like its counterpart love, is a powerful emotion that needs careful administration and plenty of personal discipline.

I love reading naval and military historical novels. In the beginning of the eighteenth century, many frigates and ships of the line (think HMS Victory) would carry 32-pounder cannons. A ball from one of these cannons could punch a hole through two feet of solid oak at a distance of two miles. If you managed to manoeuvre your ship round the stern end of your enemy's ship, a broadside from these cannons would totally demolish each deck, cutting through the masts, and killing most of the crew along the full length of the ship. They were powerful and terrible weapons. When in use, and also when not in use, they were held with ropes to restrain them. In a conflict or in a storm, a 'loose cannon' would wreak havoc. In a similar manner, the emotion of anger is like one of those 32 pounders, incredibly effective, yet must be roped down by personal discipline.

Throughout the biblical record, we can see clear evidence of the anger of God. It was manifested in the narrative of the Great Flood, where everything living, except for Noah and his immediate family, was destroyed. (Gen.7:22,23) It was also manifested in the fire from heaven that took out Sodom and Gomorrah. (Gen.19:24,25) God's anger was just, it was powerful and it was measured. Lawrence Richards has written:

One of the first facts to establish is that God's anger is no capricious thing, nor is it expressed in temper tantrums. God's anger is provoked: it is his righteous response to specific human failures and sin ... God's anger is a measured response to sin – a response about which his OT people were thoroughly warned.[1]

In the New Testament we see evidences of the anger of Christ. Probably the most notable is found in the scenario where he made a whip and overturned the tables in the temple. (Matt.12:12) That he was indignant and angry about how his Father's house was being treated is implied, but it was controlled. Nobody got hurt. There was another occasion when he was in a synagogue, faced with a man with a withered arm and also a group of religious officials who were watching him "to see whether he would heal him on the Sabbath, so that they might accuse him" (Mk.3:2). Mark records that Jesus "looked around at them with anger, grieved at their hardness of heart, and said to the man, 'Stretch out your hand.' He stretched it out, and his hand was restored." (Mk.3:5) Here, the anger was mixed and carefully balanced with grief and compassion.

Anger, when felt, must be specifically directed. There are always injustices and neglect that must affect and move our hearts with anger, but then it must be brought to bear carefully. To withhold anger when it is due is moral abdication. To let it run riot is moral insubordination.

Thought

God's anger is manifest in the right way at the right time in the right way.

Prayer

Dear Lord, help me to handle wisely and compassionately your anger towards injustice.

---

[1] Lawrence O. Richards, *Expository Dictionary of Bible Words,* (Marshall Pickering, Basingstoke, 1988), p.48

Day Two Hundred and Forty-Six

Stop Stealing; Work Instead

Eph.4:28

Let the thief no longer steal, but rather let him labour, doing honest work with his own hands, so that he may have something to share with anyone in need.

Paul continues with his contrasts. He now speaks to another aspect of where their old way of living needed to be replaced by another. Here he is actually saying to them that they need to "bear fruit in keeping with repentance" (Matt.3:8). The NLT puts it this way: "Prove by the way you live that you have repented of your sins and turned to God." What we have here is that the thief who was shirking is now encouraged to be working. Instead of taking he needed to start giving, demonstrating that a major shift had taken place in his life.

Stealing has many facets. It can range from breaking into people's houses to petty pilfering from the workplace. When I first became a Christian, I was working in an engineering factory, sharing a shop floor with over two hundred other men. Over me was a Mr Thomas, the foreman, a likeable rogue whose bonus was determined by the bonus earned by all those under his charge. My task was to set up and operate a very large capstan lathe. When the set-up was complete, I would then call for the timekeeper to watch me make the first components. But before he came, I would gear down my machine to make it work somewhat slower. As he watched me working at this lower gear, he would eventually give me a time for each piece. When he left, I would then change the gearing so that the lathe would produce at a faster pace, and my bonus was effortlessly increased. Then Jesus began to work in my heart, and I was swiftly convicted of theft. When I made this moral adjustment, thus decreasing my levels of bonus, I found that I also quickly incurred the wrath of Mr Thomas! The cost of following Jesus in doing the right thing began to bite.

The Greek word for "steal" in our text for today is *kleptetō,* which means 'to commit a theft, to take away by stealth'. A kleptomaniac is "someone with an obsessive urge to steal, especially when there is no economic necessity"[1]. Such activity was rampant in the pagan society of the Near East.

Paul would write to Titus, teaching that "bondservants are to be submissive to their own masters in everything; they are to be well-pleasing, not argumentative, not pilfering, but showing all good faith" (Ti.2:9,10). We can translate that from 'bondservants and masters' to 'employees and employers'. The same principles apply. The word "pilfering" in this particular text is the Greek word *nosphizomenous*. It means 'to set apart or separate for one's self, to purloin, embezzle, withdraw covertly and appropriate to one's own use'.

Stealing takes little effort, whereas working requires much. When Paul writes "let him labour", he uses the Greek word *kopiatō,* meaning 'to grow weary, tired, exhausted, to labour with wearisome effort'. It is a good thing to be fatigued by hard work. Harold Hoehner wrote that work provides in three ways: for one's own material needs, something useful and good for society, and an opportunity to help others.[2]

Thought

We need to move from taking to earning, then from gaining to giving.

Prayer

Father, teach me afresh the dignity of hard work.

---

[1] *Bloomsbury English Dictionary,* (Bloomsbury Publishing Plc, London, 2004), p.1034

[2] Harold Hoehner, *Ephesians: An Exegetical Commentary,* (Baker Academic, Michigan, 2002), p.628

DAY TWO HUNDRED AND FORTY-SEVEN

Stop Bad-Mouthing; Build Church Instead

Eph.4:29

Let no corrupting talk come out of your mouths, but only such as is good for building up, as fits the occasion, that it may give grace to those who hear.

On many occasions I have found myself in conversations where someone has been bad-mouthing. The effect has always been that I have eventually left with my soul stained, my heart depressed and, if I wasn't careful, my opinions of others tainted.

Paul now moves on to the contrast between bad speech and good speech. He says, in the first instance, "Let no corrupting talk come out of your mouths..." The word "corrupting" is a translation of the Greek word *sapros,* which means 'rotten, putrid'. Some time ago, my wife and I were sitting down at our dining table eating a meal. She turned to me and said, "I can smell vinegar!" It wasn't the sort of meal that would require vinegar, and so we were puzzled. The next day, reaching for an apple from the fruit bowl on the table, she saw that it was completely rotten. It was this smell that was permeating the room, and so we quickly had to remove it, wash all the other pieces of fruit, and wash the bowl also. That's what corrupting talk does. It permeates the atmosphere, giving off an unpleasant odour, and wants to infect those in close proximity.

Clinton Arnold points out that the word *sapros* was used to describe "rotted wood, diseased lungs, rancid fish, withered flowers and rotten fruit"[1]. All these were unreliable, unusable, off-putting and unattractive. This is a good description of those out whose mouth come "corrupting talk". Westcott cited a Hebraism: "Let every corrupt speech, if it is suggested in thought, be refused utterance."[2]

Paul also writes that they should use speech that is "good for building up". Instead of their words being destructive, they should be con-

---

1   Clinton E. Arnold, *Ephesians,* (Zondervan, Michigan, 2010), p.305
2   B.F. Westcott, *St Paul's Epistle to the Ephesians,* (Macmillan & Co, London, 1906), p.74

structive. The Greek phrase *pros oikodomēn tēs chreias* is interesting. It is is literally 'for the building up of the need'. Harold Hoehner translates it as "the building up of that which is lacking"[1]. Commenting on this, Clinton Arnold writes, "The expression suggests that believers should be attentive to the emotional needs and concerns facing their brothers and sisters and then focus comments on encouraging and affirming them."[2]

Paul also writes that they should use speech that "fits the occasion". This phrase is actually a slight interpolation upon the Greek text, which reads more literally 'if any is good'. In other words, where a need was seen or felt, they should search for words that were helpful in the meeting of those needs. This would require some compassionate forethought. We need to engage our heart as well as our mind before we start speaking.

Lastly, he writes that they should use speech that will "give grace to those who hear". The very essence of grace is giving. It begs the question: what are we bringing and giving into our conversations?

Thought

Words that are filled with grace impart strength and beauty to the listeners.

Prayer

Dear Lord, fill my mouth with building and empowering words today.

---

[1] Harold Hoehner, *Ephesians: An Exegetical Commentary,* (Baker Academic, Michigan, 2002), p.628

[2] Clinton E. Arnold, *Ephesians,* (Zondervan, Michigan, 2010), p.305

DAY TWO HUNDRED AND FORTY-EIGHT

Building a Culture of Graceful Speech

Eph.4:29

Let no corrupting talk come out of your mouths, but only such as is good for building up, as fits the occasion, that it may give grace to those who hear.

Let me take another pause here because this whole issue of speech is so important. Paul would go on to write later in the letter, "Let there be no filthiness nor foolish talk nor crude joking which are out of place, but instead let there be thanksgiving." (Eph.5:4) There is speech that is definitely *out of place*, and there is speech that is *perfectly in place*.

There is a powerful little proverb found in the Bible. It is that "a word fitly spoken is like apples of gold in a setting of silver" (Prov.25:11). The next verse says, "Like a gold ring or an ornament of gold is a wise reprover to a listening ear." (Prov.25:12) Eugene Peterson put the two together in his own poetic style: "The right word at the right time is like a custom-made piece of jewellery, and a wise friend's timely reprimand is like a gold ring slipped on your finger."[1] It all fits together beautifully!

Gold and silver together look very beautiful. Solomon no doubt was thinking of a very beautiful piece of jewellery, one that caught the eye. But it was not the flash of a diamond, because that is momentary; it was the constancy of silver and gold being skilfully crafted together. The whole thrust of this little phrase is that it fits together beautifully. There is *a right word* and *the right setting*.

The phrase "fitly spoken" literally means 'words running on their wheels'. They run smoothly on a course, taking people somewhere on a journey. They add to the conversation, sometimes lifting it to new levels, sometimes bringing a sense of revelation that stills and awes. There are other words that bring conversations to a grinding halt – they are like sticks in the spokes. There are others that are like sword thrusts. They cut into conversations and even into people's hearts, and they prevent

---

[1] Eugene Peterson, *The Message,* (NavPress, Colorado, 2002), p.1146

progress. A Proverb talks of one "whose rash words are like sword thrusts" (Prov.12:18).

The issue is one of personal agenda. A listening mouth will hear the drift of the conversation; a seeing mouth will watch for the direction of the conversation; a caring mouth will want to give something that will encourage the depth and tone of the conversation. Defensive talk and selfish talk both distract and seize up conversations. Getting over our personal point of view can be counterproductive at times. There is a time to speak, and there is a time to keep silent. What we do need to do is to be involved in the creating of something that is beautiful in its own time. A conversation that is well contributed into can take us to some wonderful places. A right word into a troubled heart can bring a soothing wave of healing. It starts with a deep-seated concern for others.

For those of us in ministry, our craft is a word craft. And even if we are not in ministry as such, our lives revolve around spoken and written words. Shepherds of the flock are to be skilful with people, and also skilful with words. And the skill is not only in the choice of words, but also in the timing of words, as well as the spirit in which they are communicated.

Thought

Let your next conversation be with a gentle heart, seeking to contribute and enhance things.

Prayer

Dear Holy Spirit, teach me your language and the way you speak to the saints.

DAY TWO HUNDRED AND FORTY-NINE

Treating the Holy Spirit Gently (1)

Eph.4:30

And do not grieve the Holy Spirit of God, by whom you were sealed for the day of redemption.

Dr R.T. Kendall once told a story of a British couple sent to be missionaries in Israel. They were given a home in Jerusalem. After they had moved into their new home, they noticed that a dove had come to live in the eaves of the roof. They were thrilled with the presence of the dove and received it as a sign from the Lord of his favour on their ministry in Israel. But they noticed that every time they slammed a door, the dove would fly away. If they raised their voices in argument, the dove would fly away.

One day, the husband asked his wife, "Have you noticed the dove flying away when we slam doors or argue?" "Yes," she replied, "I am so afraid the dove will fly off and never return." He nodded and spoke words that would forever change their lives: "Either the dove adjusts to us, or we adjust to the dove."[1]

Paul now inserts another comment about the Holy Spirit being the One who seals us in Christ. He did this earlier in the letter, writing, "In him you also, when you heard the word of truth, the gospel of your salvation, and believed in him, were sealed with the promised Holy Spirit, who is the guarantee of our inheritance until we acquire possession of it..." (Eph.1:13,14) This time, however, it is different, and it begs our attention. Paul adds, as a preface, an injunction that these new believers should not grieve the Holy Spirit. The word he uses is *lupeite*, which can be translated 'to cause pain, grief, distress or sorrow'. Eugene Peterson wrote that the word "grieve" is "a personal, relational verb"[2]. Only a person can be grieved, and such the Holy Spirit is.

The word "grieve" is also found in the writings of the prophet Isaiah where he wrote, "But they rebelled and grieved his Holy Spirit..."

---

[1] *http://www.charismamag.com/spirit/spiritual-growth/33417*
[2] Eugene Peterson, *Practise Resurrection,* (Hodder & Stoughton, London, 2010), p.201

(Is.63:10) The Hebrew word used there is *'âtsab,* which means, in its primitive sense, 'to cut'. Think of 'being cut to the quick' by someone's words or action. Think of 'cutting words', and we are getting near to it. We can cut and wound the Holy Spirit, making him suffer.

The verse preceding this verse gives us a clue. It is all about how these early Christians spoke to each other. Clinton Arnold wrote that "rotten talk is not only harmful to the health of the Christian community; it grieves the Spirit of God"[1] .When we hurt God's people with our words, we hurt also the Holy Spirit, who lives in them. When we let a critical spirit bring divisions, we wound and cause distress to the Holy Spirit who is at work deeply within us to bring us together. Mark Roberts wrote, "Since the Spirit forms the community of God's people, and since the unity of the Spirit is central to God's cosmic purposes, anything we do that divides this community distresses the Spirit."[2]

Jesus also gave us a clue by saying that the way we treat even the least of our brethren, we do it to him. (Matt.25:40) The manner in which we speak to the children of God is noticed and felt by heaven.

Thought

The way we treat each other has an immediate effect on the Holy Spirit.

Prayer

Dear Holy Spirit, help me to see you, and be aware of you, in my brothers and sisters.

---

[1] Clinton E. Arnold, *Ephesians,* (Zondervan, Michigan, 2010), pp.305,306
[2] Mark D. Roberts, *Ephesians,* (Zondervan, Michigan, 2016), pp.155,156

DAY TWO HUNDRED AND FIFTY

Treating the Holy Spirit Gently (2)

Eph.4:30

And do not grieve the Holy Spirit of God, by whom you were sealed for the day of redemption.

There is a very good reason why the Holy Spirit is often referred as being like a dove. Christian artists have usually portrayed the Spirit as a dove. Marvin Vincent wrote, "The dove was an ancient symbol of purity and innocence, adopted by our Lord in Matthew 10:16. ['innocent as doves'] It was the only bird allowed to be offered in sacrifice by the Levitical law."[1] There is an innocence about a dove.

In Genesis, we read of Noah sending a dove out from the ark. It came back because, as the scripture records, "the dove found no place to set her foot" (Gen.8:9). Noah sent the dove out a week later, and it returned and "behold, in her mouth was a freshly plucked olive leaf" (Gen.3:11). A week later, she did not return at all. Albert Barnes wrote, "From this event, the olive branch became the symbol of peace, and the dove the emblem of the Comforter, the messenger of peace."[2] The dove is peaceful.

In the Song of Solomon, the Bridegroom calls the bride "my dove". He says, "O my dove, in the clefts of the rock, in the crannies of the cliff, let me see your face, let me hear your voice, for your voice is sweet, and your face is lovely," (Song.2:14) and again, "Open to me, my sister, my love, my dove, my perfect one..." (Song.5:2) The picture here is of a faithful, tender, innocent, inoffensive and gracious spirit. A lover of purity and quietness. The bride of Christ is endued with the same spirit, and therefore should be manifesting all these qualities.

We often talk of the mighty power of the Holy Spirit, and we are right to do so. Yet there is something tender about his power. It is neither brutal nor forceful. Eugene Peterson wrote, "What we must realise in all of this is that the Holy Spirit is above all courteous. There is no coercion,

---

[1] *Vincent's Word Studies,* e-sword.net
[2] Albert Barnes, *Notes on the Bible,* e-sword.net

no manipulation, no forcing. The Holy Spirit treats us with dignity, respects our freedom."[1]

Rick Renner is the senior pastor of the Good News Church in Moscow. In one of his books he describes his research into the word "grieve". He discovered that the word *lupeite* is from the word *lupē,* "which denotes a pain or a grief that can only be experienced between two people who deeply love each other"[2].

Gordon Fee saw "the Holy Spirit as person, the person of God Himself; the Holy Spirit as God's personal presence; and the Holy Spirit as God's empowering presence"[3]. What we learn here is that God – the Father, the Son and the Holy Spirit – is deeply in love with us, with you. He is the One deeply within you, closer than your best friend, closer even than your spouse. He is the lover of your soul, and therefore we need to treat him as such. We also need to see afresh that he is also deeply within each of our brothers and sisters around us, being their closest friend and lover, and is fiercely jealous over them.

Thought

Those who harm God's children by word or deed find themselves wounding God.

Prayer

Lord, help me to love your children like you do.

---

[1] Eugene Peterson, *Practise Resurrection,* (Hodder & Stoughton, London, 2010), p.202

[2] Rick Renner, *Sparkling Gems from the Greek,* (Harrison House Publishers, Tulsa, 2003), p.9

[3] Gordon Fee, *God's Empowering Presence,* (Baker Academic, Michigan, 1994), p.5

DAY TWO HUNDRED AND FIFTY-ONE

Stuff to Put Away from You

Eph.4:31

Let all bitterness and wrath and anger and clamour and slander be put away from you, along with all malice.

Eugene Peterson cites a scholarly friend, Professor Dale Bruner, as calling the Holy Spirit "the shy member of the Trinity"[1]. Peterson continued by writing:

That seems right to me. The Spirit is a quiet but powerful nurturing presence ... The adjective 'shy' in this Trinitarian context has nothing to do with timidity or hesitancy, but is a well-placed caution against expecting flamboyance as evidence of the Spirit.[2]

Now Paul returns to behavioural traits, and again they are all relational words, albeit in the negative. They are, without exception, in direct contradistinction to the life and demeanour of the Holy Spirit. Look at the list: bitterness, wrath, anger, clamour, slander and malice. None of these six things are anything to do with the Holy Spirit. In fact, I believe he walks away from them.

Firstly, there is "bitterness", called by Aristotle that "embittered and resentful spirit that refuses to be reconciled"[3]. The next two words are similar – "wrath and anger". John Stott wrote, "...the former denoting a passionate rage and the latter a more settled and sullen hostility."[4] The fourth word is "clamour", and the Greek word that Paul uses is *kraugē,* an old word literally meaning 'an outcry'. This is when 'a slanging match' commences where people start shouting, screaming and yelling at each other. It is a violent outburst. Again, all this is utterly devoid of the Holy Spirit.

---

[1] Eugene Peterson, *Practise Resurrection,* (Hodder & Stoughton, London, 2010), p.200

[2] Ibid, pp.200,201

[3] John Stott, *The Message of Ephesians,* (IVP, Leicester, 1979), p.190

[4] Ibid.

The next word, "slander", is a translation of the Greek word *blasphēmia,* which is literally 'a speaking against someone in order to defame them'. Stott felt that is was usually "behind their backs"[1]. Be aware that although the one spoken against may not be conscious of what is being spoken of them, the Holy Spirit certainly is, and when we secretly belittle or slander of one of God's children, heaven is very much on the alert.

The last word that Paul uses is "malice". Francis Foulkes cites C.L. Mitton as saying that this is an inclusive word that gathers "up all that has been specified and anything else of a similar kind not precisely mentioned"[2]. We could also use the word 'malicious' to describe the evil atmosphere of the heart that brings all these other things to bear.

All these things we are to put away. Paul uses the word *arthētō,* which literally means 'to pick up and carry away, to make a clean sweep'. I imagine walking with the Holy Spirit into my heart – the house he now lives in – and going with him into every room, picking up the rubbish that has been so relationally destructive, putting it in a black bin liner and taking it outside to be collected as garbage.

Thought

An integral part of the walk is learning to see the rubbish in our hearts and getting rid of it.

Prayer

Lord, search my heart, and see if there be any wicked way within me. (Ps.139:23,24)

---

[1] Ibid.
[2] Francis Foulkes, *Ephesians,* (IVP, Leicester, 1999), p.145

DAY TWO HUNDRED AND FIFTY-TWO

How to Be With Each Other

Eph.4:32

Be kind to one another, tenderhearted, forgiving one another, as God in Christ forgave you.

Here, at the end of this chapter, we come to a trilogy of Christlikeness. In the previous verse, Paul has mentioned behavioural traits that were totally incongruent with the life of Christ. Now he mentions three behavioural traits that sum up the life of Christ.

The first trait is kindness. Kindness is something that is only expressed in relationships. One can be kind to oneself, but if you are the only one that you are kind to, that is pretty self-centred. So, Paul specifically says, "Be kind to one another..."

The word he uses is the Greek word *chrestos,* and it means 'to be useful, to be employed, to be serviceable'. The KJV translates the word as "gentleness". Albert Barnes says that the word means "to be good-natured, gentle, tender, affectionate. It is opposed to a harsh, crabby, crooked temper. It is a mildness of temper, a calmness of spirit, an unruffled disposition."[1] There is a gentle tenderness that is present in this word.

William Barclay noted that old wine was called *chrestos,* in that it is mellow.[2] Kenneth Wuest says that *chrestos* is that "quality that should pervade and penetrate the whole nature mellowing in it all that is harsh and austere"[3]. When Jesus said, "My yoke is easy," (Matt.11:30) he used the word *chrestos* – in that it does not chafe or bruise us. Kind people are not bruising to others.

The second trait is tender-hearted, and this is a translation of the Greek word *eusplagchnoi,* which means 'well compassioned'. This

[1] Albert Barnes, *Notes on the Bible,* e-sword.net
[2] William Barclay, 'Galatians and Ephesians', *The Daily Study Bible,* (St Andrew Press, Edinburgh, 1985), p.51
[3] Kenneth Wuest, *Wuest's Word Studies,* Vol.1, 'Galatians', (Eerdmans, Michigan, 1953), p.160

describes one who is always manifesting an impressionable heart towards others as opposed to a hard heart. It is talking about a heart that is allowing itself to be affected by the plights of those around. This is so much like Jesus, who was 'moved with compassion' when he saw the lost, lonely and leaderless people around him. Tender-hearted people allow their heart to be bruised by the misfortunes of others.

The third trait is forgiveness. Here, Paul uses the Greek word *charizomenoi*. The word means 'to grant favour'. Kenneth Wuest translates it as "to forgive in the sense of treating the offending party graciously". Again, this trait has all the hallmarks of the life of heaven, of Christ, of God. Christ was bruised for our iniquities. True forgiveness costs.

This last one has God as the prime example of forgiveness. Paul writes, "...as God in Christ forgave you." He wrote to the church in Colossae that they should be "bearing with one another and, if one has a complaint against another, forgiving each other; as the Lord has forgiven you, so you also must forgive" (Col.3:13). Forgiveness is not deserved, but it is freely given. It does not cost the offender, but it does cost the one who is expressing forgiveness. This is the principle that God has set in place, and he asks us to run with it. Like him, we should be magnificent and generous in forgiveness.

Thought

If there is one thing that God would ask of us, it is this: that we become like him.

Prayer

Dear Father, help me in my daily living to express all that you are to those around me.

Bibliography

Books and Commentaries

Clinton E. Arnold, *Ephesians,* (Zondervan, Michigan, 2010

David Atkinson, *The Message of Genesis 1-11,* (IVP, Leicester, 1990)

Kenneth Bailey, *Jesus through Middle Eastern Eyes,* (SPCK, London, 2008)

Hans Urs Von Balthasar, *Prayer,* (Geoffrey Chapman, London, 1961)

William Barclay, *Galatians and Ephesians,* The Daily Study Bible, (St Andrew Press, Edinburgh, 1985)

William Barclay, *The Revelation of John,* The Daily Study Bible, (St Andrew Press, Edinburgh, 1983)

William Barclay, *The Plain Man looks at the Beatitudes,* (Collins, London, 1963)

Bede, *A History of the English Church and People,* (The Folio Society, London, 2010)

Andrew Bonar, *The Life of Robert Murray M'Cheyne,* (Banner of Truth, Edinburgh, 1972)

Charles Bridges, *The Christian Ministry,* (Banner of Truth, Edinburgh, 1976)

Charles Bridges, *Proverbs,* (Banner of Truth, Edinburgh, 1977)

F.F. Bruce, Paul, *Apostle of the Free Spirit,* (Paternoster Press, Exeter, 1977)

F.F. Bruce, *The Epistle to the Ephesians,* (Pickering Paperbacks, Glasgow, 1983)

F.F. Bruce, *The Epistles to the Colossians, to Philemon, and to the Ephesians,* (Eerdmans, Michigan, 1984)

F.F. Bruce, *Romans,* (IVP, Michigan, 1983)

Walter Brueggemann, *The Message of the Psalms,* (Augsburg, Minneapolis, 1984)

John Calvin, *Genesis,* (Banner of Truth, Edinburgh, 1965)

John Calvin, *Institutes of the Christian Religion,* (Hendrickson Publishers, Massachusetts, 2008)

John Calvin, *Sermons on Ephesians,* (Banner of Truth, Edinburgh, 1979)

Michael Casey, *A Thirst for God,* (Cistercian Publications, Kalamazoo, 1988)

Michael Casey OCSO, *Strangers to the City,* (Paraclete Press, Massachusetts, 2005)

Michael Casey OCSO, *Sacred Reading,* (Liguori/Triumph, Missouri, 1996)

Michael Casey OCSO, *Toward God,* (Triumph Book, Missouri, 1996)

Ian Cowley, *The Contemplative Minister,* (The Bible Reading Fellowship, Abingdon, 2015)

Robert Culver, *Systematic Theology, Biblical and Historical,* (Mentor, Ross-shire, 2005)

R.W. Dale, *The Epistle to the Ephesians,* (Hodder and Stoughton, London, 1897)

William Henry Davies, 'Leisure', *Oxford Book of Victorian Verse* (Oxford University Press, 1971)

Anthony C. Deane, *St Paul and His Letters,* (Hodder & Stoughton, London, 1942)

James D.G. Dunn, *The Christ and The Spirit,* Vol.2, (Eerdmans, Cambridge, 1998)

James D.G. Dunn, *The Theology of Paul the Apostle,* (T&T Clark, London, 1998)

John Eadie, *A Commentary on the Greek Text of Ephesians,* (Robert Carter, New York, 1861)

Theodore Epp, *Living Abundantly – Studies in Ephesians,* (Back to the Bible, Nebraska, 1973)

Gordon Fee, *God's Empowering Presence,* (Baker Academic, Michigan, 1994)

Gordon Fee, *The First Epistle to the Corinthians,* (Eerdmans, Michigan, 1987)

Gordon Fee, *Revelation,* (Cascade Books, Oregon, 2011)

Everett Ferguson, *Backgrounds of Early Christianity,* (Eerdmans, Michigan, 1987)

G.G. Findley, *The Epistle to the Ephesians, Expositor's Bible,* (Hodder & Stoughton, London, 1892)

Richard Foster, *Celebration of Discipline,* (Hodder & Stoughton, London, 1989)

Richard Foster, *Prayer,* (Hodder & Stoughton, London, 1992)

Francis Foulkes, *Ephesians,* (IVP, Leicester, 1999)

F.W. Grosheide, *Commentary on the First Epistle to the Corinthians,* (Eerdmans, Michigan, 1980)

Norman Grubb, *After C.T. Studd,* (Lutterworth Press, London, 1940)

Wayne Grudem, *Systematic Theology,* (IVP, Leicester, 1994)

Donald Guthrie, *Galatians,* (Thomas Nelson and Sons, London, 1969)

Robert Haldane, *The Epistle to the Romans,* (Banner of Truth Trust, London, 1958)

George E. Harpur, *Ephesians,* Zondervan Bible Commentary, (Zondervan, Michigan, 2008)

William Hendriksen, *Ephesians,* (Banner of Truth, Edinburgh, 1976)

William Hendriksen, *Galatians,* (Banner of Truth, Edinburgh, 1968)

Harold Hoehner, *Ephesians: An Exegetical Commentary,* (Baker Academic, Michigan, 2002)

Philip E. Hughes, *The Second Epistle to the Corinthians,* (Eerdmans, Michigan, 1977)

Brian Keenan, *Four Quarters of Light: An Alaskan Journey,* (Transworld Publishers, London, 2004)

Thomas à Kempis, *The Imitation of Christ,* translated by George F. Maine, (Collins, London, 1971)

Thomas à Kempis, *The Imitation of Christ,* translated by Croft and Bolton, (Hendrickson, Massachusetts, 2004)

Thomas à Kempis, *Meditations on the Life of Christ,* (Baker Books House, Michigan, 1978)

R.T. Kendall, *The Sermon on the Mount,* (Chosen, Minnesota, 2011)

Derek Kidner, *Genesis,* (IVP, Leicester, 1990)

Derek Kidner, *Proverbs,* (IVP, London, 1974)

A.F. Kirkpatrick, *The Book of Psalms,* (Cambridge, Cambridge University Press, 1957), xcviii

Catherine LaCugna, *God for Us: The Trinity and Christian Life,* (Harper, San Francisco, 1973)

Kenneth Leech, *Soul Friend – a Study of Spirituality,* (Sheldon Press, London, 1980)

H.G. Leupold, *Exposition of the Psalms,* (Evangelical Press, London, 1972)

C.S. Lewis, *The Lion, the Witch and the Wardrobe,* (HarperCollins, London, 2000)

Jack London, *The Call of the Wild,* (Global Classics, 2014)

Jeff Lucas, *You've Got Mail,* (Spring Harvest, Uckfield, 2002)

Martyn Lloyd-Jones, *God's Way of Reconciliation,* (Evangelical Press, London, 1972)

Martyn Lloyd-Jones, *God's Ultimate Purpose,* (Banner of Truth, Edinburgh, 1978)

Martyn Lloyd-Jones, *The Unsearchable Riches of Christ,* (Banner of Truth, Edinburgh, 1979)

Dr Martyn Lloyd Jones, *Christian Unity,* (Banner of Truth, Edinburgh, 1980)

Dr Martyn Lloyd-Jones, *Darkness and Light,* (Banner of Truth, Edinburgh, 1982)

Gordon MacDonald, *Forging a Real World Faith,* (Highland Books, East Sussex, 1990)

Ralph P. Martin, *The Epistle of Paul to the Philippians,* (Tyndale Press, London, 1963)

Alister E. McGrath, *Christian Theology,* (Blackwell Publishing, Oxford, 2010)

Thomas Merton, *Merton on St Bernard,* (Michigan, Cistercian Publications, 1980)

Alec Motyer, *The Message of Philippians,* (IVP, Leicester, 1984)

Watchman Nee, *The Ministry of God's Word,* (Christian Fellowship Publishers, New York, 1971)

Watchman Nee, *The Spiritual Man,* (Christian Fellowship Publishers, New York, 1977)

Watchman Nee, *The Release of the Spirit,* (New Wine Press, Chichester, 2007)

Watchman Nee, *Sit, Walk, Stand,* (Victory Press, London, 1977)

J.I. Packer, *Knowing God,* (Hodder & Stoughton, London, 1975)

J.I. Packer, *God has Spoken,* (Hodder & Stoughton, London, 2016)

A.T. Pierson, *George Müller of Bristol,* (Pantianos Classics, 1899)

Eugene Peterson, *The Message,* (NavPress, Colorado, 2002)

Eugene Peterson, *Working the Angles,* (Eerdmans, Michigan,1987)

Eugene Peterson, *Travelling Light,* (Helmers & Howard, Colorado Springs, 1988)

Eugene Peterson, *Eat This Book,* (Hodder & Stoughton, London, 2006)

Eugene Peterson, *Practise Resurrection,* (Hodder & Stoughton, London, 2010)

Eugene Peterson, *A Long Obedience in the Same Direction,* (IVP, Illinois, 2000)

Eugene Peterson, *Christ Plays in Ten Thousand Places,* (Hodder & Stoughton, London, 2005)

Eugene Peterson, *The Contemplative Pastor,* (Eerdmans, Michigan, 1989)

Eugene Peterson, *The Jesus Way,* (Hodder & Stoughton, London, 2007)

Lawrence O. Richards, *Expository Dictionary of Bible Words,* (Marshall Pickering, Basingstoke, 1988)

Mark D. Roberts, *Ephesians,* (Zondervan, Michigan, 2016)

Richard Rohr, *The Divine Dance,* SPCK, London, 2016)

Thomas Schreiner, *Paul, Apostle of God's Glory in Christ,* (IVP, Leicester, 2001)

W. Graham Scroggie, *The Unfolding Drama of Redemption,* Vol.3, (Pickering & Inglis, London, 1970)

Charles H. Spurgeon, *Treasury of David,* 6 volumes, (Marshall Brothers, London)

John Stott, *The Message of Ephesians,* (IVP, Leicester, 1979)

Merrill C. Tenney, *New Testament Survey,* (IVP, London, 1961)

Anthony Thiselton, *New Testament Interpretation,* (Paternoster Press, Cumbria, 1992)

A.W. Tozer, *The Divine Conquest,* (Oliphants, London, 1965)

A.W. Tozer, *The Root of the Righteous,* (Christian Publications, Harrisburg, 1955)

W.E. Vine, *Vine's Expository Dictionary of Biblical Words,* (Thomas Nelson, New York, 1985)

B.F. Westcott, *St Paul's Epistle to the Ephesians,* (Macmillan & Co, London, 1906)

Stephen Westerholm, *Perspectives Old and New on Paul,* (Eerdmans, Michigan, 2004)

Dallas Willard, *The Spirit of The Disciplines* (Harper & Row, San Francisco, 1988)

J. Rodman Williams, *Renewal Theology,* 3 volumes, (Zondervan, Michigan, 1996)

Tom Wright, *Paul – A Biography,* (SPCK, London, 2018)

Kenneth Wuest, *Wuest's Word Studies,* Vol.1, 'Ephesians and Colossians', (Eerdmans, Michigan, 1953)

Kenneth Wuest, *Wuest's Word Studies,* Vol.1, 'Galatians', (Eerdmans, Michigan, 1953)

Kenneth Wuest, *The New Testament, An Expanded Translation,* (Eerdmans, Michigan, 2004)

Philip Yancey, *What's So Amazing About Grace?* (Zondervan, Michigan, 1997)

Articles

E.M.B Green, article on 'Ephesus', *New Bible Dictionary,* (IVP, London, 1970)

S.S. Smalley, article on 'Mystery', *The New Bible Dictionary,* (IVP, London, 1970)

D.H. Wheaton, article on 'Diana', *New Bible Dictionary,* (IVP, London, 1970)

Lecture Notes

Gordon Fee, lectures on 'The Revelation', Regent College, Vancouver, 2009

Eugene Peterson, lectures on 'Soulcraft; The Formation of a Mature Life in Christ', Regents College, Vancouver

Eugene Peterson, lectures on the 'Beatitudes', lecture 5, Regents College, Vancouver

Gordon Fee, lectures on 'The Revelation', Regent College, Vancouver, 2009

Electronic Sources

www.expositors.org/blog/select-resources-for-preaching-ephesians
www.dailychristianquote.com/tag/mystery

E-SWORD.NET

Baker's New Testament Commentary, e-sword.net

Albert Barnes, *Notes on the Bible,* e-sword.net

Adam Clark, *Commentary on the Bible,* e-sword.net

Keil and Delitzsch, *Commentary on the Old Testament,* e-sword.net

Expositor's Bible Commentary, e-sword.net

Jamieson, Fausset and Brown commentary, e-sword.net

John Gill, *Exposition of the Whole Bible,* e-sword.net

Matthew Henry's Commentary on the Whole Bible, e-sword.net

Thayer's Greek Definitions, e-sword.net

A.T. Robertson's Word Pictures, e-sword.net

Strong's Hebrew and Greek Dictionaries, e-sword.net

The Preacher's Commentary, e-sword.net

M.R. Vincent, *Vincent's Word Studies,* e-sword.net

Other Books by Alan Hoare

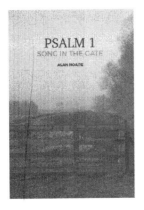

Psalm 1: Song in the Gate
ISBN: 978-1-78815-548-9

"Here is where we cut our teeth in praying, as we take upon our lips the prayers of others. As we make our way through the psalms – praying, singing, weeping – we will become more and more aware of the God who inspired them in the first place. They will bring us to both an intimacy with, and a deep, holy respect for, the Father, the Son and the Holy Spirit."

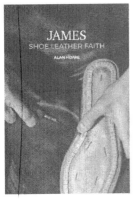

James: Shoe Leather Faith
ISBN: 978-1-78815-547-2

"The Scriptures must at times challenge what we believe and feel. The words of God not only heal and restore us, but they at times cut right into the core of our being, into the revealing of our hidden motives."

Alan Hoare's infectious enthusiasm for digging deeper into God's word is evident throughout this powerful 64-day devotional study of the letter of James.

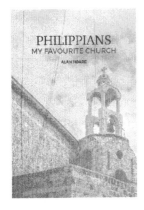

Philippians: My Favourite Church
ISBN: 978-1-78815-693-6

Through 100 daily readings, in-depth study and practical application, Alan Hoare takes us through Paul's letter to his "favourite church" – the church in Philippi. As he demonstrates how to systematically read and apply scripture, you will find yourself eager to start digging out the incredible riches and treasures found in the Word of God, not only on the surface, but also just underneath.

Available now from all good bookshops.